WES MONTGOMERY

Wes Montgomery's autograph (courtesy of Robert Yelin)

WES MONTGOMERY

BY
ADRIAN INGRAM

COPYRIGHT 2008

ASHLEY MARK PUBLISHING COMPANY
Blaydon on Tyne NE21 5NH, United Kingdom.

www.FretsOnly.com

WES MONTGOMERY by Adrian Ingram
Second Edition © 2008.

All rights reserved. No part of this book may be used or reproduced in any manner whatsoever without written permission, except in the case of brief quotations embodied in critical articles and reviews.

For information write to Ashley Mark Publishing Company, 1 & 2 Vance Court, Trans Britannia Enterprise Park, Blaydon on Tyne, NE21 5NH, United Kingdom. www.FretsOnly.com.

First edition - JUNE 1985.

Second Edition - JULY 2008.

Typeset and printed in the United Kingdom.

Designed by Maurice J. Summerfield

ISBN 978-1-872639-68-0

FRONT COVER PHOTO
COURTESY: DUNCAN SCHIEDT
BACK COVER PHOTO
COURTESY: RIVERSIDE RECORDS

WES MONTGOMERY

CONTENTS

CHAPTERS

1	Beginnings	11
2	The Riverside Years	21
3	Commercial Success	33
4	Guitaristically Speaking	45
5	Impressions	59

APPENDICES

1	Recordings	71
2	Film Footage	111
3	Transcriptions & Methods	115
4	Compositions	123
5	Chord Shapes	127
6	The Octave Technique	131
	Bibliography	135

'UEM DI DILIGUNT
ADULESCENS MORITUR'.

'He whom the Gods favour
dies young'. – PLAUTUS, BC 254-184
           (Bacchides IV. 816)

FOREWORD

Dear Adrian,

I'm honoured that you would ask me to write something for your book about Wes. First let me say that Wes was an honest, natural jazz musician and my favourite player – not only because of his unique octave style, but because everything he played was improvised, it swung and was jazz all the way.

He put himself totally into his music, to me he was the best of the jazz guitar players.

Joe Pass

Special Thanks to:

Serene Montgomery Woods, June Ingram, Ervena Floyd, Dr Leo and Mrs Rita Harper, Jimmy and Delores Coe, Donald West of The Indiana Historical Society Library, Karen Cohen of Indianapolis Public Library, Gilbert Taylor of Indianapolis Children's Museum, Pete Pipkin, Robert Yelin, Maurice J. Summerfield, William Bay, David Baker, Duncan Schiedt, Steve Khan, Larry Coryell, Barney Kessel, Barbara McQueen, Alan Noble, W. H. Whitehouse, Guitar Player Magazine, Pete Welding, Joe Wicker, Ivor Mairants, Kevin Eubanks, Richard Cobby, Stan Dawson, Alonzo Pookie Johnson, Richard Cottance, Lloyd De Wester Jnr., Dil Shaw, Ike Isaacs, Herb Ellis, Wander Indiana Tourism Board, Tommy Tedesco, Crescendo Magazine, Terri Hinte, Fantasy-Prestige-Milestone-Stax records, Jazz Journal International, The Indianapolis News, Joe Pass, Martin Taylor, Cedric West, Orrin Keepnews, The Record Centre (Birmingham), Jazz Gems, Mole Jazz, Emily Remler, The Indianapolis Star, Dave Barcock of The Guitar Record Centre, `downbeat' magazine, Ian Wroe.

BEGINNINGS

Wes Montgomery and trombonist David Baker 1959.

BEGINNINGS

"When I started I bought the whole works. I got a box of picks because I felt sure there'd be the right one in there for me. I refused to play unamplified, so I'm sitting in my house playing, you know – happy, but when I used my brand new amplifier I guess I didn't think about the neighbours. Soon they started complaining pretty heavy. But I was enjoying myself because it wasn't noise to me, it was music."
Wes Montgomery[1]

Wes was born John Leslie Montgomery in Indianapolis on 6 March 1923 into a large and relatively poor family. His mother and father separated quite early and consequently, Wes, Monk (who later became famous for pioneering the Fender bass) and an older brother who died early went to live with their father in Columbus, Ohio.

Whilst in Columbus Wes attended Champion High School, but although he was always very interested in music he never received any formal tuition. It was Wes' brother Monk two years his senior, who kindled the fire. Monk left school aged fourteen to work as a 'coal and ice boy', selling whatever the season demanded, aware of Wes' increasing enthusiasm for music, he saved up $13 to buy him a four string (tenor) guitar from a local pawnshop. At that time, 1935, the year of the great depression, thirteen dollars was a lot of money and Wes spent a great deal of time with his new instrument hoping to justify his brother's purchase.

Monk, who later became instrumental in the formation of the Mastersounds and the Montgomery Brothers, acting as a catalyst for the musical family, reported that Wes was:

"Doing a good job on guitar by the time he was twelve or thirteen."[2]

Wes, however, later disagreed with Monk's statement:

"I used to play tenor guitar, but it wasn't really playing. I've really gone into business since I got the six string, which was like starting all over."[3]

As Wes did not acquire his 'six-string' until six or seven years later it is likely that he had underestimated the importance of this early start. Even though the fingerboard and the tuning of a six-string guitar would present new and different problems Wes would certainly have developed some basic techniques (co-ordination, touch, etc.) from the time he had spent working with the tenor guitar.

When he was seventeen the brothers moved back to Indianapolis and began gigging fairly regularly. Wes

Wes Montgomery 1959.

PHOTO: DUNCAN P. SCHIEDT

began an apprenticeship as an arc welder and a year later, 1943, married Serene. They met at a local dance Serene recalled:

"He said I had the most prettiest eyes he had ever seen," and added "When he would get mad at me, I'd ask him 'Now what happened to my pretty eyes?'"[4]

They'd both laugh and the argument would be over.

It was during one such visit to the local dance that Wes first heard a Charlie Christian record.[5] He was amazed with Christian's new hornlike approach to electric guitar playing, so much so that the following morning he went downtown and spent $350, he could ill afford, on a new six-string guitar and amplifier. Frustrated that he didn't sound like Christian right away, Wes spent every spare moment of the next eight months trying to master the instrument. Serene remembers those days well and recalls:

"Wes and Monk played those instruments all the time, often times right through the night."

Although Wes became obsessed with his new toy and Charlie Christian's music in particular, his main aim was to justify recklessly spending such a large amount of money.

> "I didn't want to be a musician, but there was all that guitar looking at me."[6]

He did justify his purchase and in a surprisingly short time; by the time he reached his twentieth birthday he was playing Charlie Christian solos regularly at the 440 Club.

Besides his regular night gigs, Wes worked a variety of day jobs often losing them for taking short spells out to go on the road. The first brief experiences of life on the road came from short stints with the Brownskin Models and Snookum Russell.

> "Well, I got pretty good and went on the road with a group. We starved. At that time I didn't realise that you'd work one gig in Kansas City, the next in Florida, and the next would be in Louisville. You know, a thousand miles a night. That was really tough, man."[7]

At that time the Montgomery's resided at 1217 Cornell (now a major highway) and a growing family meant that Wes had to earn regular money. The first day job that he held down for any length of time was with Pope's Milk Company, Serene recalls:

> "Early on Wes worked at Pope's, the milk plant, he didn't bring home much money, but we sure drank a lot of milk!"

Wes supplemented his daytime income from Pope's with his earnings from playing gigs in Indianapolis. The Keys Supper Club, The 19th Hole, Club 440, The Ritz, The Cactus Club and the 500 Club were some of the places where Wes played regularly at that time.

His first real break came in 1948 when bandleader Lionel Hampton came through and hired him. The local Indianapolis musicians had heard that Hamp., was about to pass through the mid-west and was hiring fresh musicians along the way. Serene remembers Wes being apprehensive about auditioning but he decided to go anyway figuring that he had nothing to lose. Hamp., was impressed with the young guitarist's ability to play Charlie Christian type lines and hired him on the spot, despite the fact that he could neither read musical notation, nor chord symbols.

Wes auditioned for Hamp., on or around 15 May 1948 and to everyone's surprise left Indianapolis that same day. Serene remembered:

> "I came home and passed Wes as he was leaving the house carrying a suitcase. 'Where are you going?' I asked. Wes replied 'Oh I'm going on tour, I've just joined Lionel Hampton's Band'."

Wes stayed with Hamp. for two years but found life on the road away from his family for considerable lengths of time unpalatable and quit the band in 1950. Serene remembers:

> "Wes hated being away from home. Whenever he arrived at a gig the first thing he would do was phone home, we always knew where he was and how we could contact him if we needed to."

Wes had a mortal fear of flying, in fact he avoided doing so until his European tour of 1965. This meant that, whilst the rest of Hampton's band often arrived between gigs quickly and in relative comfort, Wes always chose to drive between gigs irrespective of the distances involved. Musicians used to relate incredible stories about his stamina, driving between gigs as far apart as New York and San Fransisco, Detroit and Miami. This gruelling schedule must have contributed to Wes' distaste for life on the road. Sadly Wes did not get the break or the exposure that he needed with Hamp., but he did gain valuable experience playing alongside such seasoned professionals as bassist Charlie Mingus, trumpeter Fats Navarro, keyboard player Milt Bruckner and of course Lionel Hampton himself.

Wes made several recordings while he was with the Hampton band which confirm how heavily he relied on what he had learnt from listening to Charlie Christian records.*

Disappointed, but wiser for the experience, Wes returned home to Indianapolis to a series of non-musical day jobs, his wife and family.

Slowly Wes began to gig again, firstly with the Eddie Higgins Trio, Higgins – piano, Walter Perkins – drums and Bobby Cranshaw – bass, and then with the Roger Jones Quintet, Jones – trumpet, Willie Baker – reeds, Leroy Vinegar – bass and Willis Kirk – drums. He also did a lot of playing with the Montgomery/Johnson Quintet; Monk Montgomery – bass, Buddy Montgomery – piano and vibes, Alonzo Pookie Johnson – reeds and Sonny Johnson – drums. This, by all accounts, very promising group, auditioned for Arthur Godfrey and made several excellent recordings under the direction of Quincey Jones. Unfortunately these recordings cannot be traced today. David Baker, jazz educator and long time associate of the Montgomery family remembers:

> "Those recordings were particularly good, the group modelled themselves on the groups of George Shearing which were of course very popular at that time.
> Wes and his brothers were perfectionists, particularly Wes. We had free use of Chuck Bailey's Indianapolis rehearsal studio during the 50s, providing that Chuck was allowed to keep the tapes rolling while we rehearsed. Wes was always in there rehearsing some band or another. I remember some big band sessions

---

*Montgomery's recordings with the Hampton band have been re-issued on Lionel Hampton – Jay Bird – Black Lion Star Power series – intercord INT 27.032 (1977).

Left to right: Billy Williams, Unknown vocalist, Jaz Wormick, Lionel Hampton, A.C. Grey, Gene Morris, Lester Bass, Johnny Sparrow.

Wes Montgomery with Lionel Hampton Band 1949.

PHOTO: DUNCAN P. SCHIEDT.

PHOTO: DUNCAN P. SCHIEDT

Wes Montgomery Trio at the '500 Room' Essex House Hotel, Indianapolis 1959. Sonny Johnson - drums, Melvin Rhyne - organ.

he did for me and I remember him rehearsing with Mel (Rhyne) for his first solo record. No one knows what happened to any of those recordings, but Wes was really playing."

Unfortunately nothing came of either the Montgomery/Johnson quintet's audition for Arthur Godfrey or the recording session with Quincy Jones but the group did find itself regular work. In 1955 the quintet took over from Roger Jones at the Tropics Club on 10th Street where the group played their 'Shearingesque' music mainly for dancers. This residency lasted until 1957 when Buddy and Monk along with Richard Crabtree (piano) and Benny Barth (drums) decided to try their luck on the West Coast.

The new Montgomery group, minus Wes, called themselves the Mastersounds and were lucky enough to land a contract with Pacific Jazz Records shortly after their arrival on the coast. Wes was reluctant to leave Indianapolis with his brothers, particularly after his experience on the road with the Lionel Hampton band, but he did spend some time with them in San Francisco for a short-term residency at the Jazz Workshop.

Wes' connection with the Mastersounds gave him an 'in' with a record company and it wasn't long before Dick Bock of Pacific Jazz invited him to join his brothers in a recording session. The resulting session took place in Indianapolis on 30 December 1957 and included a young Freddie Hubbard (trumpet), Waymon Atkinson and 'Pookie' Johnson (saxophones), Buddy Montgomery (vibes), Joe Bradley (piano), Monk Montgomery (bass), Paul Parker (drums) and Wes. The session produced seven tunes: 'Sound Carrier', 'Lois Ann', 'Bud's Beaux Arts', 'Bock to Bock', 'All the Things You Are', 'Billie's Bounce' and 'Finger Pickin'.

The first six were released on The Montgomery Brothers and Five Others (PJ 1240), while Finger Pickin', a quartet feature for Wes, was released as part of the collection, Have Blues Will Travel (Vogue LAE 12156), and as a single.

Although the Montgomery Brothers and Five Others was an important jazz album, introducing for the first time on record the combined talents of Wes Montgomery and Freddie Hubbard, it was not particularly successful. Wes' recording debut (discounting his unrepresentative Lionel Hampton sides) enhanced his growing reputation, particularly amongst jazz guitarists, but the LP was not really the success it should have been. Wes continued to play his usual circuit of gigs in Indianapolis, whilst the Mastersounds resumed their work on the West Coast.

The brothers had hoped that the record, if successful, would have enabled them to tour as a unit. Monk and Buddy missed Wes and would dearly have loved him to become a permanent member of the group at that time, but they were under contract as the Mastersounds, whilst Wes had decided not to leave Indianapolis. Wes however occasionally compromised by travelling to the coast to play with them and they in turn used him whenever possible as a guest soloist on their albums. As a result he joined his brothers as a featured soloist on two more Pacific Jazz albums, 'The Montgomery/Land Quintet' (Pacific Jazz PJ 5) and 'Kismet' (Pacific Jazz WP 1243) both of which were recorded in Los Angeles. 'Kismet' was recorded in April 1958 and released later the same year. The Montgomeryland album was recorded in two separate sessions, April 1958 and October 1959, each with different personnel. Wes, Monk and Buddy were joined by Pony Poindexter (alto saxophone) and Louis Hayes (drums) for the 1958 session to record 'Monk's Shop', 'Summertime', 'Falling in Love with Love' and 'Renie', a tune written for Wes' sister Ervena.

A year later the brothers were joined by Harold Land (tenor saxophone) and Tony Bazely (drums) for the session which produced: 'Far Wes', 'Old Folks', 'Wes' Tune', 'Hymn for Carl', 'Montgomeryland Funk' and 'Stompin' at the Savoy', the last three were not included on the Montgomeryland album but used on compilation albums at a later date.

'Montgomeryland' was an excellent jazz album containing some classic Wes Montgomery, particularly his solo in 'Falling in Love with Love', which was certainly one of the solos which helped to establish him as an important 'new' guitarist:

> "Above all keep an ear on the guitar; Wes' solo on 'Falling in Love with Love', a moving example of his ability to transform a ballad into a blues, has all the properties of a jazz classic" Dick Hadock[8]

> "On another of my favourite tracks 'Falling in Love with Love', he lays down a milestone in jazz with one of the most beautiful solos ever played on the guitar. Phrasing, timing, ideas and sound are out of this world. On this track in particular, one can appreciate the strange, beautiful sounds he gets with his thumb." Cedric West[9]

Although 'Montgomeryland' was an excellent showcase for Wes' talent, both as a performer and a composer (he composed four tunes out of the eight on the album) it was not of any immediate advantage to him, as its release date was delayed until 1960, by which time he had already begun to make waves with his first album as a leader for Riverside Records.

'Kismet' on the other hand was, largely due to the subject matter, condemned by the critics as light cocktail music with little depth or emotion and as a result was not taken seriously by the jazz-record buying public. 'Kismet' did not have the same 'down-home' quality as 'The Montgomery Brothers and Five Others' or 'Montgomeryland'. It was unquestionably 'Polite' jazz but despite this it did contain some fine music. Wes' playing was particularly good on 'Baubles, Bangles and Beads', a track which has since been re-issued on several compilation albums.[10] Neither 'Kismet' nor 'The Montgomery Brothers and Five Others' brought Wes any immediate widespread recognition, he remained permanently based in Indianapolis and continued to play with his brothers whenever the opportunity arose. It was not until almost three years later (January 1960) that he was able to team-up with his brothers on a regular basis once more, though he did manage one more session with them for Pacific Jazz, when he appeared as a guest on the Jon Hendricks album 'A Good Git-Together' (World Pacific Records WP 1283).

Despite this surge in playing and recording activity Wes remained in his home town doing more or less what he had always done, unaffected by any critical acclaim, or otherwise, which came his way.

Slowly but surely he was acquiring a solid reputation. Musicians visited Indianapolis especially to hear him play and at one stage it was rumoured that the Modern Jazz Quartet wanted him to join them.

One thing is certain, Wes more than paid his dues in Indianapolis. Although he developed his style in relative obscurity, he did not, as many critics would have us believe, develop in a vacuum. There were several excellent guitar players situated in and around Indianapolis during the fifties and there were certainly a lot more places to play jazz then than there are now. Wes knew and respected these guitarists, catching their gigs when he could. David Baker remembers that Wes enjoyed the guitar playing of Carol De Camp, John Blanchard, Specs Maynard, Bill Jennings, Henry Gootch and Paul Wheaton. Pookie Johnson remembers also that he and Wes would sometimes drive across to Detroit to hear a young guitarist called Kenny Burrell.

Coincidentally Les Spann the guitarist/flautist who plays with techniques similar to those employed by Wes (thumb and octaves) was stationed for a period at nearby Fort Harrison and was active for a time on the local jazz scene.

Wes could not readily recall many of these names by the mid-sixties, not altogether surprising when one considers that his musical preferences had gravitated from guitarists to horn players and he was more likely to be found listening to Wayne Shorter (tenor saxophone), John Coltrane (tenor and soprano saxophone) or Miles Davis (trumpet). Wes did remember though that he once tried to get some guitar lessons from Indianapolis guitarist Alex Stevens (without success) and that a be-bop guitarist from Chicago called George Henry made a lasting impression on him. Clearly Wes learnt his trade from a full gig book, he always expected the highest standards from himself and in almost 20 years of steadily paying his dues these standards were beginning to place him in the national arena.

BEGINNINGS
1. Wes Montgomery talks to Valerie Wilmer, *Jazz Monthly*, May 1965.
2. Sleevenotes from the album Movin' by Maggie Hawthorn – Milestone M47040.
3. Wes Montgomery 1925-1968. A rare unpublished interview with Ralph J. Gleason, *Guitar Player*, July/August 1973.
4. *Indianapolis News*, 1 June 1977. Powers/Serene Montgomery inverview.
5. Solo Flight, Charlie Christian with the Benny Goodman Orchestra, New York, 4 March 1941.
6. *National Observer* (USA), 24/6/68.
7. Wes Montgomery a previously unpublished article with Ralph J. Gleason – *Jazz and Blues,* October 1973.
8. Sleevenotes from the album Montgomeryland by Dick Hadock – Pacific Jazz PJ5 (1959).
9. The Man Who Does the Impossible, Cedric West – *Crescendo Magazine,* May 1963.
10. The Montgomery Brothers – Pacific Jazz 17. Beginnings – Blue Note BN LA 531 H2. The Montgomery Story – Fontana 688 113 2L. Easy Groove Pacific Jazz 17.

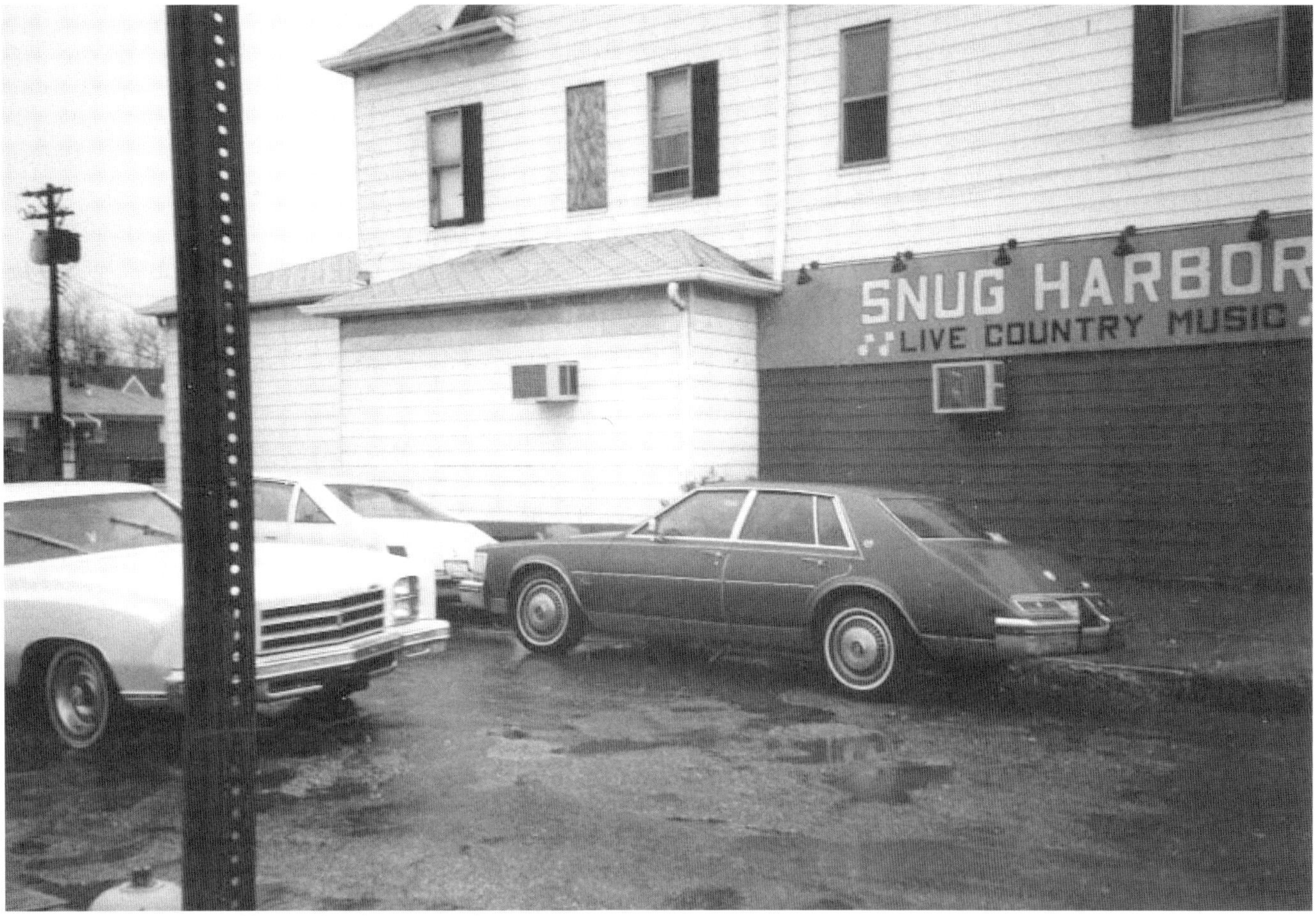

PHOTO: JUNE INGRAM

Snug Harbour Club (formerly The Tropics).

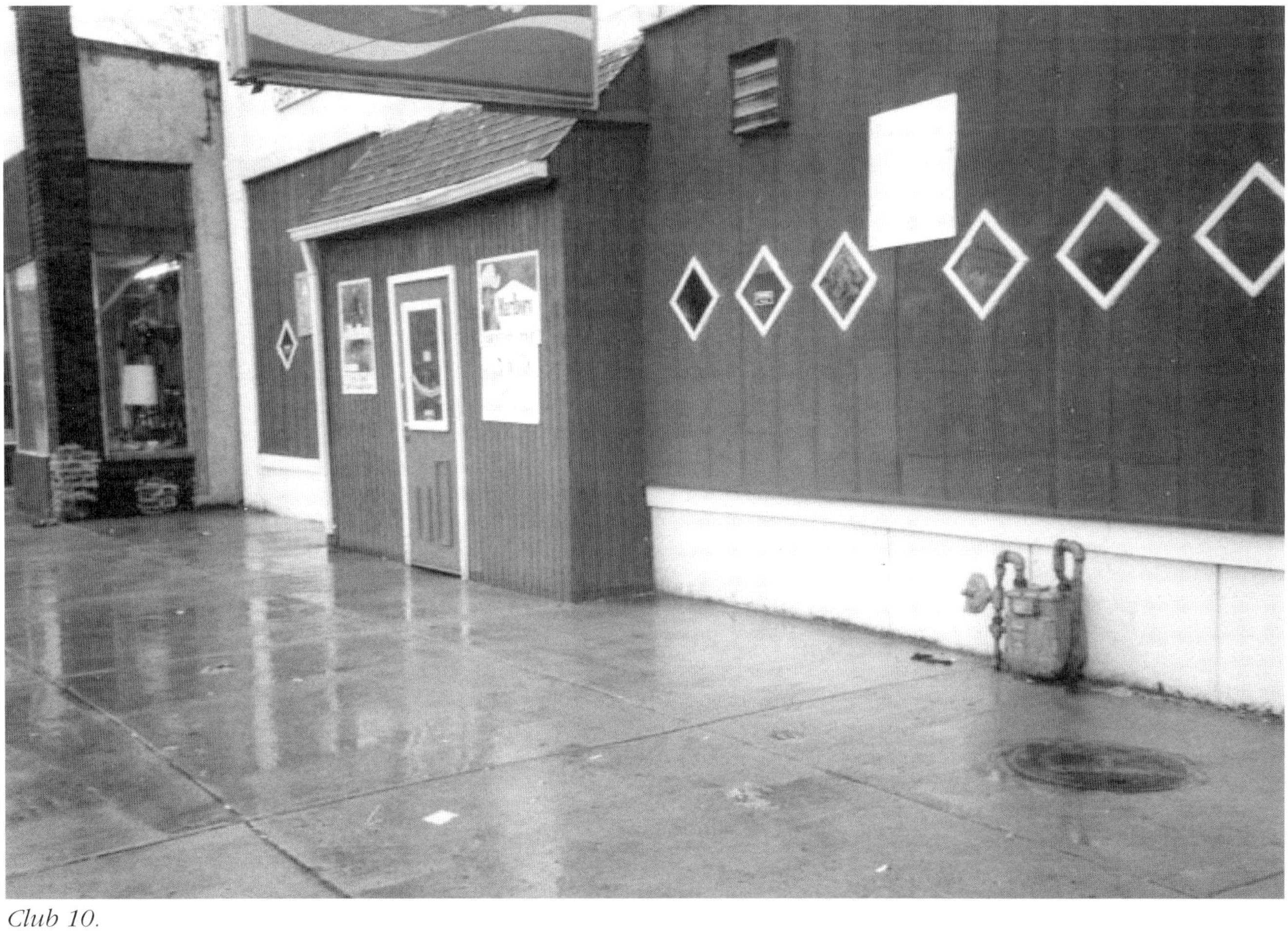

PHOTO: JUNE INGRAM

Club 10.

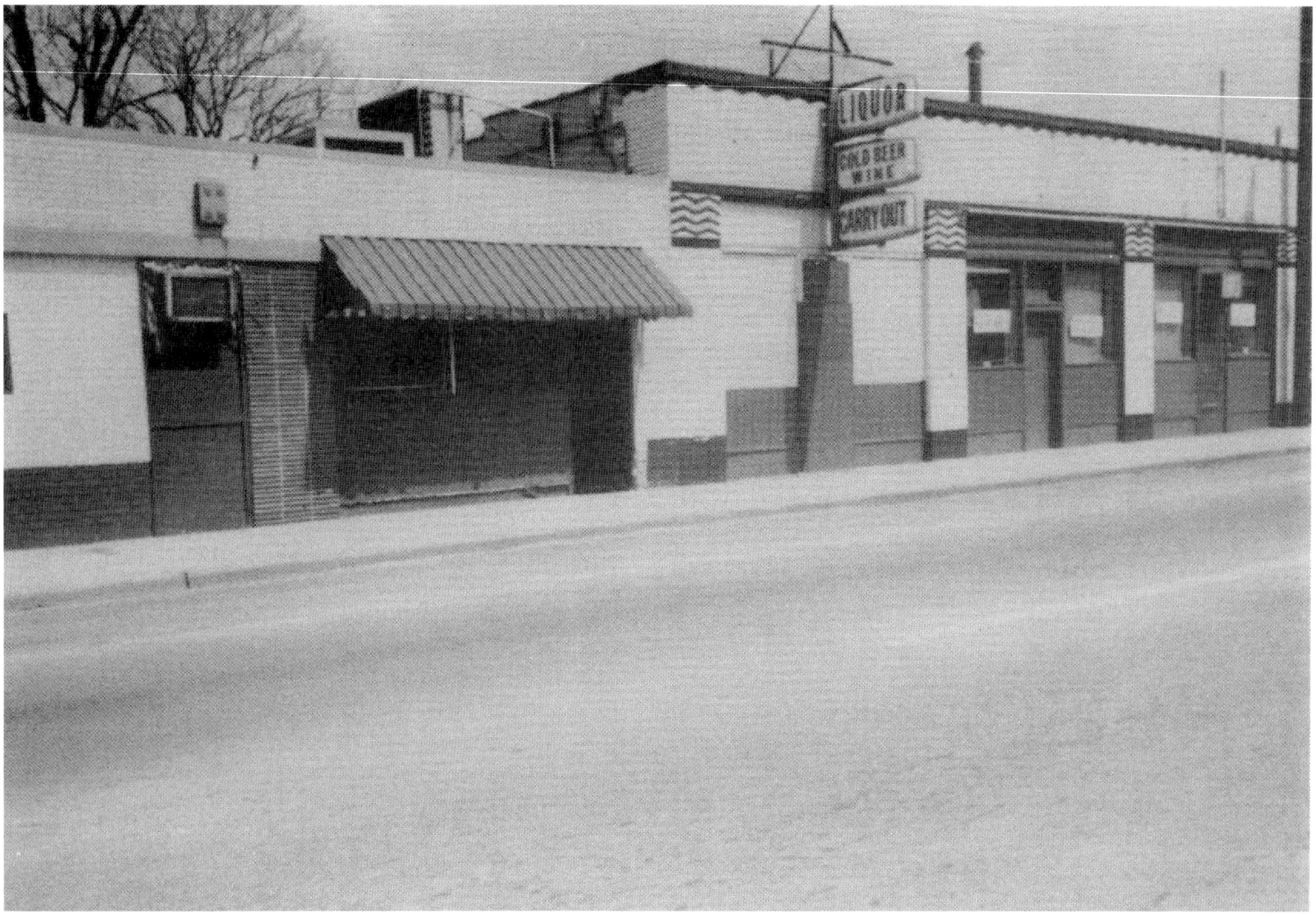

PHOTO: JUNE INGRAM

The Hub Hub Club.

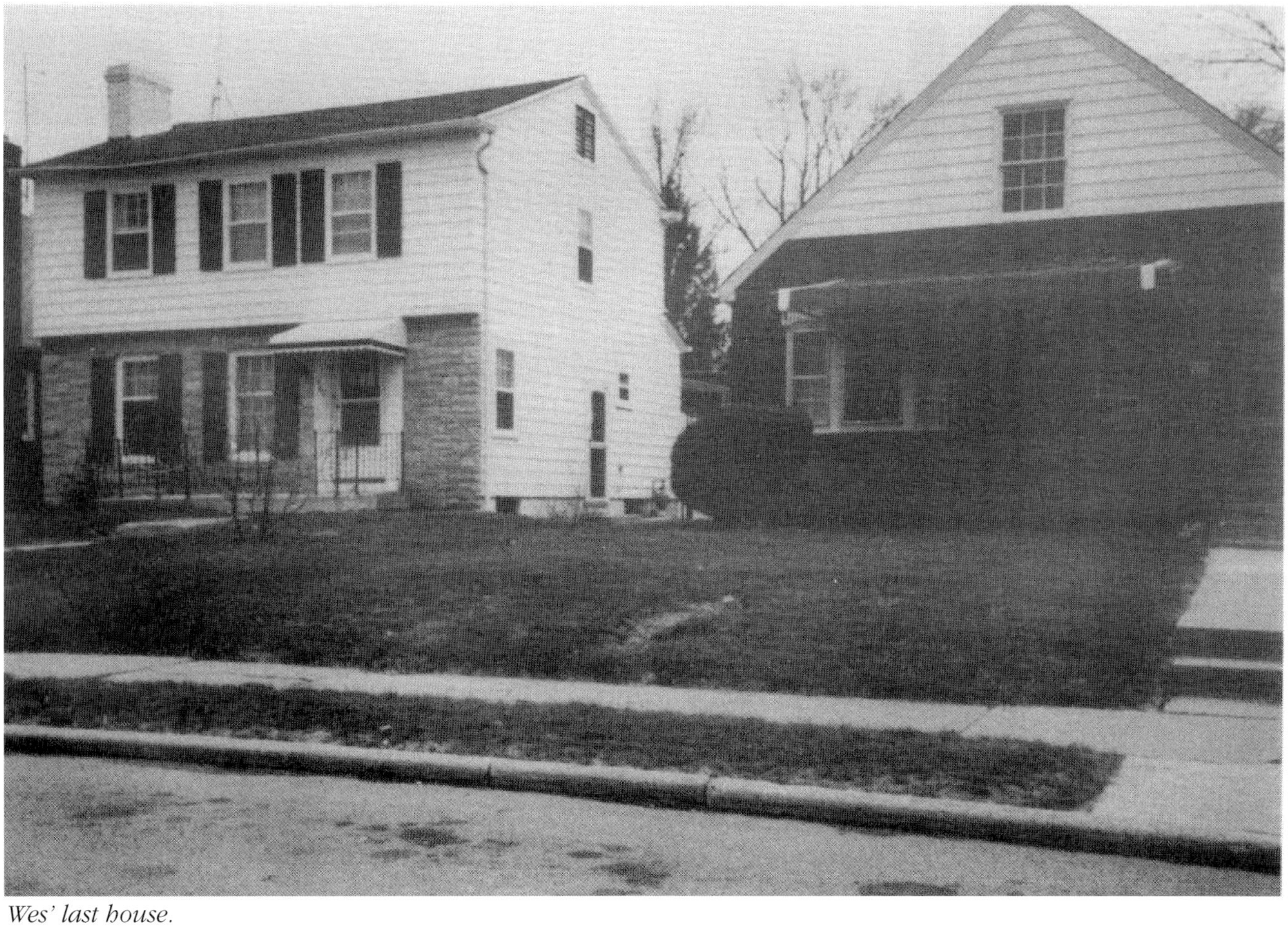

PHOTO: JUNE INGRAM

Wes' last house.

THE RIVERSIDE YEARS

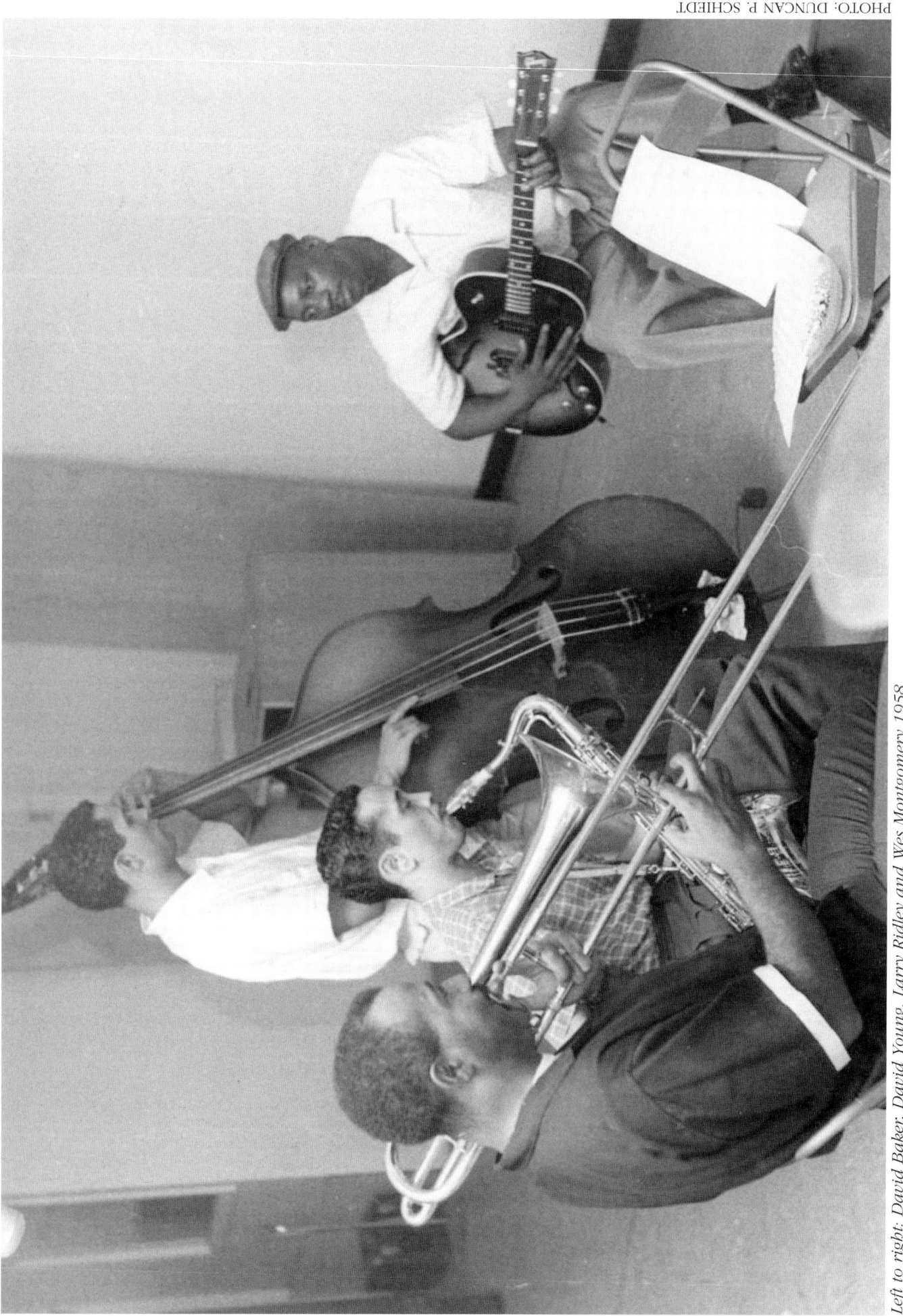

PHOTO: DUNCAN P. SCHIEDT.

Left to right: David Baker, David Young, Larry Ridley and Wes Montgomery 1958.

THE RIVERSIDE YEARS

"As far as I'm concerned, Cannonball Adderley opened the door for me. He called Riverside Records once, when he was in Indianapolis, and just raved about me to Bill Grauer and Orrin Keepnews. He had never heard me, but on the strength of Cannonball's recommendation he guaranteed me a record date."
Wes Montgomery[1]

Between 1959 and 1964 when he was signed to Riverside Records, Wes established and consolidated a position for himself as a major jazz performer. He won the *Down Beat* readers' and critics' polls in 1961 and 1962 and the 'talent deserving wider recognition' in 1960.

Wes did not play any differently during this period, but he did make records and in retrospect it was these records that helped establish him. He was surprised by the public response to these albums and astonished with his *Down Beat* Poll wins, particularly as he felt that his playing was better during the early 50's.

"I was surprised to win the *Down Beat* thing. I think I was playing more in 1952 than I ever have."[2]

Wes might have played with more youth and vigour in 1952 it's true, but the real hallmark of his style was taste and maturity. He may not have realised, but his playing *had* improved with several years of steady gigs behind him. He had learnt how to pace a solo, how to climax and which notes to leave out. In short, Wes had matured, developing through the years an instinctive and uncanny ability to put the right notes in the right places, both melodically and rhythmically.

Gunther Schuller, the jazz critic and author, was one of the first people to write about Montgomery in the national press. In May 1958, after attending a concert by the Wes Montgomery Trio (Wes Montgomery – guitar, Melvyn Rhyne – organ, Paul Parker – drums); Schuller wrote the article 'Indiana Renaissance' for the magazine *Jazz Review*. The following extract gives an impression of the quality of Wes' playing at that time.

"Superlatives come much too easily in writing about Wes Montgomery. Yet all the well-chosen superlatives in the world – even an accurate description of his playing, could tell us only *what* he plays and very little about its intrinsic *quality*. This has to be heard. Knowing this, I nevertheless feel obligated to write about Wes, because even a second-hand, inadequate report about a man of his calibre is better than none, and in a way almost has to be written, however inadequately.

Left to right: David Young, Larry Ridley and Wes Montgomery.

The thing that is most easy to say about Wes Montgomery is that he is an extraordinarily spectacular guitarist. Listening to his solos is like teetering continually at the edge of a brink. His playing at its peak becomes unbearably exciting, to the point where one feels unable to muster sufficient physical endurance to outlast it. In its totality it is playing that combines the perfect choice of notes – i.e. purity of creative ideas – with a technical prowess that the jazz of yesteryear, the jazz of the jam sessions and cutting contests had, but that, I'm afraid, the jazz of today has almost completely lost.

Montgomery casts his solos in a formal pattern which he seemingly never varies, and perhaps never should, since it has an unfailing dramatic effectiveness and since, in any case, the content of his solos more than compensates for any limitations of form. This formal design consists of a single line, primarily melodic ideas at a moderate dynamic; the second part is conceived entirely in 'impossible to play' octaves; while the third section continues on yet another level in even 'impossibler' block chords, bringing the solo dynamically and in terms of rhythmic density to its ultimate climax – at which point I guarantee the listener will be limp. (I should add at this point for the benefit of any perplexed guitarists that Wes plays sans pick.) In the 'octave' and 'block chord' sections of his solos, Wes employs a highly personal, unorthodox technique. (he is, as one might suspect, self-taught on the instrument.)

This approach, of course, owes much of its sure-fire success to the psychological frame of mind it produces in the listener. By setting up a priori an almost impossible target, Wes keeps the listener constantly on the edge of his seat as he steadily pursues this target over a period of six to ten choruses, eliminating one musical obstacle after another until the ultimate goal has been reached. The physical side of this is as fascinating as the musical. Towards the climax of his solos, guitar and man become entirely one, and both seem no longer earth-bound."[3]

Although the magic of a live Wes Montgomery performance was rarely to be caught on disc, his early recordings contained enough elements of his unique style and ability to quickly earn him a widespread audience. His increasing popularity amongst 'hard-core' jazz fans can only be attributed to the exposure he gained from these Riverside recordings. How Wes came to sign with Riverside is a story often told, but worth repeating.

By 1959 Wes was the proud father of six children. His day-job at P. R. Mallory's, where he was employed as a welder working on batteries and heavy-duty radios, hardly paid enough for the management of such a large family. Once more Wes was forced to supplement his income with whatever playing gigs he could find. As a result he committed himself to an unbelievably gruelling schedule; he worked at Mallory's factory from 7 am to 3 pm, played a gig at the Turf Bar from 9 pm to 2 am, and then rushed across Indianapolis to the after-hours Missile Room to play another gig from 2.30 to 5 am!

Wes was not as young as he was and the toll of working at least two jobs almost continually since 1943 was beginning to show. Pookie Johnson recalls that he had several blackouts during this period. This tough schedule, along with his long-standing habit of chain-smoking may well have initiated an early heart condition. However, despite the obvious toll on his health, Wes really enjoyed these gigs, especially the Missile Room, where he was free to play as he wished and where he was eventually 'spotted' and 'signed' for Riverside Records.

On 7 September 1959 Cannonball Adderley, George Shearing and Lennie Tristano played at the Indiana Theatre during a nationwide tour. Wes, a long-standing fan of both Shearing and Adderley, attended the concert and invited the musicians to visit the Missile Room after the show to hear his trio. That same evening Cannonball Adderley, George Shearing, who had already heard a lot about Wes, and Lennie Tristano went over to the Missile Room especially to catch the gig. Duncan Schiedt, an organiser of the Indianapolis Jazz Club, recalls the evening.

> On 7 September 1959, the Indiana Theatre in Indianapolis, Indiana, hosted a touring package show called the 'Newport Jazz Festival'. Several established groups comprised the bill, among them the George Shearing and Lennie Tristano groups (which included Warne Marsh and Lee Konitz), as well as Cannonball Adderley and his combo. I was present with my camera, and took some stage shots of the performances, then went backstage for a while to mingle with the musicians. During the intermission, Wes Montgomery appeared in the wings, and talked with the musicians, inviting them to come over to the Missile Lounge, where his trio was currently appearing, after the show. The Missile Lounge, on West Street, was close to downtown, and situated in the lower floor of one of a group of old buildings near a street corner. It was patronized mainly by the local black population, and was known to be an 'after-hours' spot, that is, operating until much after the official closing time for such places. My recollection is that the authorities largely ignored this violation, but occasionally there would be a police action to keep things 'orderly'. It would be closed on time for a while, then slip back into its usual pattern.
>
> After the stage show ended, I drove over to the Missile Lounge, and got a seat in the music area, near the little stage where Wes' trio performed. Wes was there, adjusting his amplifier, but things were quiet. In due time there was a slight traffic at the entrance, and in walked Adderley, and the two blind pianists Shearing and Tristano, with accompanying people. They all repaired to a dark corner of the area, after being greeted by Wes. Eventually Sonny Johnson, the drummer, arrived, and last, Melvin Rhyne, the organist. After a moment, Wes said to Rhyne, "Do you know who's here tonight?" Rhyne glanced around the room, and said, "No – who?" Wes said, "Well, over in the corner there are Lennie Tristano, George Shearing and Cannonball Adderley." At this Melvin's mouth dropped open, and it was obvious that he was shocked by being in the same room with such illustrious musicians, and about to perform for them.
>
> The set began, and before the first number was halfway through, Cannonball moved to a table directly in front of Montgomery, who was already showing his marvellous, unique technique. The next memory I have is that Cannonball leaned way back in his chair, kind of slumped, and rolled his eyes to the ceiling as if 'knocked out' – which he evidently was. He stayed rooted to this table all the time I was there.
>
> The next time I heard anything was when news came to our Indianapolis Jazz Club programme people that Wes would not be able to fulfil a booking he had with us in a couple of weeks hence. He had been scheduled to play as co-leader with trombonist Dave Baker's group, which included among others, Larry Ridley on bass and David Young on tenor. Wes had, on the recommendation of Adderley when he returned to New York City, been approached by Riverside Records to make a series of recordings for their label and he lost no time in accepting.[4]

Orrin Keepnews of Riverside Records told the story in the sleevenotes of Wes' first LP for the company[5] of how Cannonball Adderley started the ball rolling for Wes;

> "It started when Cannonball Adderley, just back in New York after a tour on which he spent one day in

Montgomery's home town of Indianapolis, charged into Riverside Office and announced, in a monologue that went something like this 'There's this guitarist in Indianapolis ... you've got to get him for the label ... here's his phone number'.

Cannonball, I have come to know, is one of the sounder and least-easily-flipped judges of jazz talent around. His excitement would have been quite enough for me. But, as it happened, in the issue of *Jazz Review* that I picked up the same day, there was composer-musician-critic Gunther Schuller, normally an objective and calmly analytical writer, describing the same Wes Montgomery in superlatives usually used only by the writers of album notes: 'extra-ordinarily spectacular ... unbearably exciting ... purity of creative ideas ... unfailing dramatic effectiveness'.

Five days later, I was in Indianapolis, spending some eight hours at the Turf Bar and the Missile Room. Long before the night was over I knew that Adderley and Schuller had not been guilty of exaggeration."[6]

Cannonball's enthusiasm was just the break that Wes needed and this time he was ready for it. Having recently suffered several black outs he realised that he could no longer continue his hectic schedule without risking serious damage to his health. The record deal with Riverside was all that was needed to convince him that the time was right to make another go of it as a professional.

Wes left Indianapolis for New York on 4 October taking with him his regular trio Melvin Rhyne, organ and Paul Parker, drums. Keepnews had booked them into Reeves Sound Studios for two full days (5th and 6th). After twenty years as a guitarist Wes was finally to cut his first album as a leader!

The material that Wes chose for the album was typical of the trio's repertoire at that time, the medium tempo jazz classics, 'Round Midnight', 'Whisper Not' and 'Satin Doll', were contrasted with 'hard-bop' treatments of Ecorah (Horace Silver) and Wes' own 'Missile Blues'. The album was an excellent showcase, ranging from a spellbinding treatment of 'Round Midnight' to the technically astonishing 'Missile Blues'. Besides his magnificent technique and unfailing good taste Wes had a fine sense of humour and was never afraid to show it in his music. In Jerome Kern's 'Yesterdays', he introduced lots of chromatic octaves, toying with the final resolution of the tune, whilst in his own 'Missile Blues' he quoted Charlie Christain's 'Air Mail Special' riff in the second chorus of his solo.

The finished LP 'A Dynamic New Sound, The Wes Montgomery Trio' (Riverside RLP 1156) had mixed reviews but was well received amongst musicians and guitarists; more importantly it enabled Wes, now a professional, to obtain regular work playing the kind of music he had always wanted to play.

He kept the trio together for almost four months playing jazz clubs and concerts mainly in the mid-western States. The trio finally split, on amicable terms, in January 1960 when rumours that the Mastersounds had disbanded were confirmed and Wes once again had an opportunity to join his brothers on a permanent basis. In early February *Downbeat* magazine reported:

> "San Francisco jazz fans were shocked. The Mastersounds, recent winners in the New Star Award in the Combo division in the Downbeat International Jazz Critic's Poll, were breaking up.
>
> 'Was it true?' the street buzzed! Yes, it was true. At the end of their engagement at the Jazz-Workshop, where the group got its start a couple of years ago, the Mastersounds would disband. As of February 1, they were no more.
>
> The Montgomery Brothers, Monk (Fender bass) and Buddy (vibes), are joining forces with the third Montgomery brother, Wes (guitar), to form a new group known, not surprisingly, as The Montgomery Brothers. At press time, saxophonist Harold Land and drummer Lawrence Marable were expected to round out the group. Buddy Montgomery will double on vibes and piano.
>
> The new group, which is not yet under contract to anyone, is rumoured to be negotiating with Columbia Records ..."[7]

Land was unable to join the group on a permanent basis, but drummer Marable did. The record deal was not with Columbia but with Fantasy, a subsidary of Riverside Records. Wes, however, did not join his brothers immediately, he went first to New York where he spent four prolific days at Reeves recording studios. On 26 and 28 January he recorded what many consider to be his finest album, 'The Incredible Jazz Guitar of Wes Montgomery' (Riverside RLP 12-329), and on the 25th and 27th he recorded as a sideman on cornetist Nat Adderley's LP 'The Work Song' (Riverside 12-318).

The 'Incredible Jazz Guitar Of' sessions found Wes in the company of Tommy Flanagan (piano), Percy Heath (bass) and Al Heath (drums), all highly accomplished musicians whose work he knew and respected. This sympathetic unit was exactly what was needed to bring out the best in him and, with the recent birth of his seventh child, daughter Toni, and the promise of playing with his brothers, Wes was on peak form.

The eight tracks on the album, 'Airegin', 'Polka Dots and Moonbeams', 'In Your Own Sweet Way', 'Gone With the Wind' and Wes' own 'West Coast Blues', 'D-Natural Blues', 'Four on Six' and 'Mr Walker', were all of an exceptionally high standard. 'West Coast Blues', a classic example of Wes' three-tier improvisational approach,* must rank alongside

---

*See page 47 of guitaristically Speaking.

Django Reinhardt's 'Nuages' or Charlie Christian's 'Solo Flight' as a milestone in jazz guitar playing.

It would be difficult to pick out any one tune for special consideration, but mention must be made of the excellent, 'Gone With the Wind'; John Duarte, guitar critic and composer, called this

> "Six and a quarter miraculous minutes of non-stop guitar. The flow of invention never stops, the taste is impeccable and, when all is done, the technical command takes your breath away."[8]

Apart from the specific timing of six and a quarter minutes, Duarte could easily have been talking about any track on the record and for once an album was aptly titled. Not surprisingly it rated a five star review (the highest possible) in *Downbeat* magazine and was selected as a *Downbeat* subscription gift.

By comparison, the Nat Adderley record was rather low-key. The number of 'front-line' soloists; Nat Adderley (cornet), Bobby Timmons (piano), Sam Jones, Keter Betts (cello) and Wes meant that the solo space was at a premium. Nevertheless, Wes contributed some fine guitar playing particularly on the two tracks where the sextet was slimmed down to a trio (Adderley, Jones and Montgomery), 'Violets for Furs' and 'I've Got a Crush on You'. Of the two albums it was 'The Incredible Jazz Guitar of Wes Montgomery' which earned him both an international reputation and respect from the critics. The latter resulted in Wes winning the 1960 Downbeat Critic's New Star award.

In early February, after a short break in Indianapolis, Wes left both his hometown and his family to join his brothers on the West Coast, where the group was preparing to begin a residency at the Hungry I Club in San Francisco. It was early days and the group, still improving, did not yet feel ready to commit themselves to record. In fact Wes was to go on and cut three more albums before recording again with his brothers, one as a leader 'Moving Along' (Riverside RLP 342), 11 and 12 October and two as a sideman, 'West Coast Blues' (Riverside RLP 920), 17 and 18 May, with tenor saxophonist Harold Land and the topical 'Pollwinners' album (Riverside RLP 355), 21 May and 5 June, led by the musician largely responsible for Wes' recording contract, alto saxophonist Cannonball Adderley.

1960 was a good year for Wes, to add to his *Downbeat* critic's award he accrued a second place in *Metronome* readers poll and was voted 'Most promising jazz instrumentalist of the year' in *Billboard* (by jazz disc jockeys and A+R men).

To add to this impressive list, the Montgomery Brothers were signed by Fantasy Records and were booked to play at the prestigious Monterey Jazz Festival, where the group were an unqualified success.

> "The Montgomery Brothers quartet opened the Sunday night concert at 7.25 pm. With Wes on guitar, Buddy on piano, Monk on string bass and Lawrence Marable on drums, the group started in a happy and healthily swinging vein. The outstanding soloist was brother Wes, who brought to the stage a talent that had not even begun to be heard..."[9]

The happily swinging vein was captured in their first LP which was recorded in San Francisco shortly after their Monterey appearance.

The group's first album, 'The Montgomery Brothers' (Fantasy 8052) included two standards; 'Lover Man', 'June in January', and three original compositions, 'Bud's Tune', 'Jingles' and 'Monterey Blues' (D-natural Blues) two of which ('Jingles' and 'D-natural Blues') were penned by Wes. The album was highly acclaimed and although Wes was not, strictly speaking, the leader most listeners bought the record for his playing. Barney Kessel called 'June in January' a guitar playing masterpiece and still feels today that this track contains some of Wes's best playing.

Their next album 'Grooveyard' (Riverside RLP 362) was recorded in New York on 3 January (1961) for Riverside to coincide with their schedule of gigs on the East Coast.

'Grooveyard' was favourably received and once again the focus of attention was on Wes' guitar playing; a point well-illustrated in the following *Jazz Journal* record review:

> "This is a thoroughly unpretentious, very musical album. The brothers attempt nothing at all way-out, or ultra clever and the result is a record that makes good listening without strain. The whole thing of course revolves around brother Wes, a guitarist of enormous technique, with an ability to swing. He plays heaps of chords and his approach sometimes verges on the classical style, but he is also a strong single string player with an inventive turn of phrase."[10]

Wes did not record again until August when he fronted a group which included Hank Jones (piano), Ron Carter (bass), Les Humphries (drums) and Ray Barretto (congas), the cream of East Coast musicians.

The album 'So Much Guitar' (Riverside RLP 9382) included an unaccompanied guitar solo in a chordal style, the ballad 'While We're Young'. This was the first time that Wes had played this way on record and it came as an eye-opener to those who thought he was mainly an 'octaves' man. Following the success of his composition 'West Coast Blues', which was rapidly being adopted by other jazz musicians and had been recorded by Cannonball Adderley on the LP 'African Waltz' (Riverside RLP

WEST COAST BLUES

'West Coast Blues', Wes' most popular composition was adopted by The Mastersounds, René Thomas, Sonny Rollins, Cannonball Adderley and Montgomery himself.

377), Wes contributed two more compositions, 'Something Like Bags' and 'Twisted Blues'.

Like the 'Incredible Jazz Guitar of Wes Montgomery', 'So Much Guitar' demonstrated the versatility of his playing, ranging from the lyrical beauty of 'While We're Young', to the down-home earthy rendering of 'One for My Baby'. After the recording sessions in New York Wes returned to San Francisco to rejoin his brothers at the Jazz Workshop. When they had finished the Jazz Workshop gig he went home to his family in Indianapolis but unfortunately, as he hated being away from home, was unable to stay for very long. A studio had been booked in LA and plans had been made for the Montgomery Brothers to record an all-star album with the prominent pianist George Shearing. The album 'Love Walked In' (Jazzland 55) was recorded on 9 and 10 October and would have, without question, given the Brothers valuable exposure, especially after Shearing's commercial success had given him almost superstar status (for a jazz musician). In jazz terms the record was disappointing the tracks were concise (the shortest being 2.10 and the longest 4.47) and the improvisation seemed cautious and tame. The Brothers seemed altogether too polite and subdued, recalling their earlier attempts at chamber or cocktail jazz ('Kismet' – World Pacific WP 1243). Whether this was the concept of the album, or whether the brothers were holding back on purpose to accommodate Shearing is unclear, but the album did neither party justice.

Meanwhile the Jazz Workshop, where the Montgomery Brothers were regular peformers, had booked the controversial John Coltrane group which included: Coltrane (tenor and soprano saxophone), Eric Dolphy (alto saxophone, bass clarinet and flute), McCoy Tyner (piano), Reggie Workman (bass) and Elvin Jones (drums). The group, which had also been booked for the 1961 Monterey Jazz Festival, invited Wes to join them, an offer which he, being an ardent Coltrane fan, lost no time in accepting. He played with the group at the Workshop and the Festival but declined an offer to join them on a permanent basis. It was later revealed that Wes did not think he was good enough to join the Coltrane Group! Common consensus of opinion was that Wes in fact outshone the rest of the group as the following review of the Monterey Festival reveals:

> "Besides his regular rhythm section, made up of pianist McCoy Tyner, bassist Reggie Workman and drummer Elvin Jones, Coltrane had guitarist Wes Montgomery and reed man Eric Dolphy with him. The six men had been working together at San Francisco's Jazz Workshop for a few days previous to the festival. The Group played only three tunes, though it was on stage for almost an hour.
>
> Montgomery stood out amongst the soloists, his choruses marked by his wonderful rhythmic flair. His solos were notable for diversity of approach. On 'My Favourite Things', he used call and response devices within his solo, with periodic returns to the melody and linear improvisatory passages as counter balances. On 'Naima', a ballad, Montgomery employed octaves, the total effect being an extension of the melody. Montgomery's most exciting work – he seemed as if he would swing off the stand – was on the third tune 'So What?'
>
> Coltrane and Dolphy had intonation trouble throughout the set, but both overcame the problem to a certain extent and played some exciting solos, though neither was as moving or as consistant as Montgomery."[11]

Wes was, without question, one of the successes of the festival and would, had he chosen to accept the invitation, have made a valuable contribution to the Coltrane group. However, he enjoyed working with his brothers who were about to embark on a Canadian Tour.

In the previous year things had gone very well for the Montgomery Brothers; they had recorded two albums under their own name and one with pianist George Shearing. They had scored a moderate success at the 1960 Monterey Festival and had managed to work fairly regularly.

1961 did not seem quite so promising as it was gradually becoming harder for the group to find work, a consequence of the widespread decline in jazz venues caused by the rapid growth in pop music. Finance-conscious club owners began to employ smaller units in order to save money. Had Wes been the leader of a smaller group, perhaps an organ trio, he would have found work easily.

The group struggled for a time finding work where they could, but after the Canadian Tour the situation became critical and they were forced to disband. During the period between his appearance at the Monterey Fesitival (Autumn 1961) and the demise of the group (Spring 1962), Wes cut another two records, one with his brothers 'The Montgomery Brothers in Canada' (Fantasy 8066) and one with vibes player Milt Jackson 'Bags Meets Wes' (Riverside RLP 407).

The record 'Bags Meets Wes' with its impressive personnel: Montgomery, Jackson, Wynton Kelly (piano), Sam Jones (bass) and Philly Joe Jones (drums), had promised to be as good as the superlative 'Incredible Jazz Guitar of Wes Montgomery' but, as often happens with 'all-star' albums, the results were disappointing, as none of the players appeared to be at their best. As one might have expected, Wes turned out some excellent guitar playing, particularly on the ballad 'Stairway to the Stars', he also contributed two compositions: 'Blue Roz' and 'Jingles'. 'Bags Meets Wes' was a relaxed affair lacking the urgency, humour and compulsion of Wes' best work.

'The Montgomery Brothers in Canada', was however somewhat better, probably because it was recorded live and Wes was less inhibited (he disliked recording studios). A highlight of the album was Wes' sensitive treatment of the Dennis/Brent tune 'Angel Eyes' which began with a lush unaccompanied chordal treatment of the tune and developed into a sensuous flow of single-line improvisation. When reviewing the album *Downbeat* once again singled-out Wes as the outstanding member of the group:

> "Playing before an audience in Canada The Montgomery Brothers are loose, relaxed and swinging in these pieces.
> Wes is the main focus of interest, particularly when building a strong, slow treatment of 'Eyes' ..."[12]

Both albums rated only three stars in *Downbeat* reviews, but were better received by the readership who were, without question, on Wes' side, having voted him number one jazz guitarist in the 1961 annual readers' poll.

Saddened by the demise of the Montgomery Brothers, Wes returned home to his family in Indianapolis, where he rejoined his friends organist Melvin Rhyne and drummer George Brown for a series of local gigs. He settled easily into his former routine of anonymous local Club work and did little nationally for almost ten months.

That June to fulfil the terms of his recording contract Wes drove out to Berkeley, California to play a few gigs with his brothers and to cut a live album at Tsubo's Coffee House, a location chosen for its relaxed atmosphere and excellent acoustics. Wes had always wanted to record a live album with the personnel of his choice, so when he found out that the Miles Davis group were in California and that they had a few free days between gigs he took the opportunity of using what was considered to be the finest rhythm section of the day: Wynton Kelly (piano), Paul Chambers (bass) and Jimmy Cobb (drums). The group was completed by tenor saxophonist Johnny Griffin who recalled:

> "The first time I worked with Wes (apart from jamming) was for a recording session at the Tsubo Club on San Francisco Bay. At that time in San Francisco apart from Wes and his brothers and me (I was working at the Jazz Workshop) the Miles Davis Sextet with his fantastic rhythm section; Wynton Kelly on piano, Paul Chambers on bass, and Jimmy Cobb on drums were at the Blackhawk. Orrin Keepnews wanted us to make an album in a club with a live audience. On 25 June 1962 (our day off for me and Miles' Sextet), we all turned up at the Tsubo. We played, just like we'd play in a club, with an audience, like crazy, with no other idea than to take off musically."[13]

The resulting album 'Full House' (Riverside RLP 434) contained three Montgomery compositions, 'Full House', 'Cariba' and 'SOS'. It also contained a wonderful chordal treatment of the Lerner and Loewe ballad 'I've Grown Accustomed to her Face'. 'Full House' is generally acknowledged as one of Wes' best albums for Riverside ranking alongside the earlier 'Incredible Jazz Guitar of Wes Montgomery'.

The album was very well received and Wes once again topped the annual *Downbeat* Readers' and Critics' Polls, despite his lack of national activity. He did not record again in 1962, but continued to gig in and around Indianapolis where he chose to revive his 1958/9 organ trio.

> "I had a feeling about the instrumentation, that it could be a *sound*. That's why I worked on it, to try to get it in that direction, because I think it's a little different. A lot of places we go, when they see the organ coming in, they're expecting rock and roll, but after they hear us play they like it."[14]

Wes worked the trio in and around Indianapolis until April while he prepared to record his first album with strings ('Fusion' – Riverside RLP 472). Because he could not read music, the arrangements for this album were pre-recorded. Wes was extremely self-conscious about recording with musicians who were such good readers and didn't want them to be waiting around while he learnt his parts. The album was completed in New York on 18 and 19 April, when, to give the album more spontaneity and to avoid the sterile situation of Wes playing to a pair of headphones, a small string section was brought in to overdub some parts. Wes recalled the difficulties involved:

> "With me not reading music, I can have trouble with the violin players. Everybody else on the date had music all over the place; I'm sitting there with the guitar. All they know is they've been called in for the job; they see they've got ten tunes and they just play it down from the music.
>
> On this album, I gave the arranger, – it was Jimmy Jones – the titles of the tunes. Then I sat down and played them to give him the keys. I just wanted each tune to be in a different key; you find you have more contrast that way.
>
> I was still working in Indianapolis at that time, and I had to go back with my trio. When he'd got the tunes and the keys from me, he had three weeks to write all the arrangements. Then I would come in and we'd take two days to record ... I go in, and Jimmy Jones is giving me the outline on the piano. Except that he can't *play* the whole section. I'm still in trouble. I said to him 'Look, I'll tell you what you should do. Just give me the places – like, if I have to play the intro, or the ending, of if you've got a special opening I'm supposed to do, that's all I want to know. Because these are all

the number one string players, and for them to be waiting around till I got it – that's out.'

We got through six tunes in a two-and-a-half-hour session. People said it sounded relaxed, but it had my head kinda tight. I have a complex to know I'm sitting here and like, playing a guessing game, in a sense."[15]

It is astonishing that Wes played so poetically in a situation which was totally different to anything he had previously encountered. His improvising developed logically and coherently from Jones' skilful arrangements as if by great deliberation. Wes felt that 'Fusion' was his best record to date and was saddened by its poor press. Pete Welding awarded it 2½ stars (a bit better than poor) in his *Downbeat* review and wrote:

> "As attractive, uninvolved background music, the disc succeeds but attempt's nothing ambitious. One wishes only that Montgomery, Jones and producer Keepnews had set their sights on loftier heights."[16]

Wes was back in the studio again on the 27th, this time with his trio (Jimmy Cobb replaced George Brown on drums) for the session which produced 'Boss Guitar' (Riverside RLP 459). 'Boss Guitar' contained six standard tunes: 'Besame Mucho', 'Dearly Beloved', 'Days of Wine and Roses', 'Canadian Sunset', 'The Breeze and I', 'For Heavens Sake' and two tunes by Wes: 'The Trick Bag' with its complex be-bop head, and 'Fried Pies', a blues. Fortunately this album received a better *Downbeat* review.

> "Nobody who digs Montgomery will be disappointed by the guitarist's contributions here. From the gently chording of Wine to the cooking, horizontally stretched blues of Pies, everything is achieved with taste, skill, excitement when it is required, relaxation when it is called for."[17]

Following the release of this album Wes took the trio with his regular drummer George Brown to the East Coast for a promotional tour which included venues in Washington DC (The Showboat Lounge), Boston (The Jazz Workshop) and New York. The group received a mixed reception, mainly because of the organ which was not after all an instrument with universal appeal. Melvin Rhyne however was one of the least obtrusive players, whose gentle touch was a perfect foil for Wes, particularly while sustaining chords on ballads like 'Round Midnight' and 'Dreamsville'. Wes said of him "He doesn't hog it, his conception is like a piano players – a piano players' touch."[18]

The trio remained together for eighteen months, but it was ironically the organ, a major transport problem, which eventually forced them to disband.

> "Organ's too heavy to make two weeks here and two weeks there. I figured I must be jinxed, because take Jimmy Smith or Jack McDuff or Jimmy McGriff – all those cats. They never have any trouble. The minute they get in a town about twenty or thirty cats just *happen* to be standing about, so two or three of them give 'em a hand and bam – they got it! But anytime I get in a town, I don't care what time of day it is – no-one's in sight! So it's a jinx really!"[19]

The trio went into the studios twice before they disbanded for, what turned out to be their last recording sessions together and Wes' last for the Riverside company. They were in fact amongst the last sessions done by any jazz musician for that label, which was to change hands and cease its jazz recording activities by 1964, before the material from the trio's final sessions was released.

As a result both producer Orrin Keepnews and Wes lost their control over the finished product and two albums 'Guitar On the Go' (Riverside 494) and 'A Portrait of Wes' (Riverside 492) were released without their approval.

Keepnews had prepared two acetates of the best takes from the first session (10 October 1963) and sent one to Wes, who expressed unhappiness about the results. Consequently the trio returned to the studios on 27 November to re-record the initial takes and some new tunes.

In the final few months of the companies existence neither Montgomery nor Keepnews were able to assemble a satisfactory master tape.

Following the sudden death from a heart attack of Riverside's president Bill Grauer the master tapes passed out of Keepnews' control and the new owners decided to compile the two albums.

By the time they were released Wes had changed both his record company and his direction. Creed Taylor his new producer, had decided to record him in a more commercial setting, favouring highly arranged big bands in place of the loose small group 'blowing sessions' characteristic of the small specialist company, Riverside.

From a 'purists' point of view the Riverside years were without question Wes' most prolific. He recorded no less than nineteen albums, two of which were immediately accepted as 'jazz classics'. If he had recorded these albums alone he would have warranted a place amongst the finest guitar players of the century. His change of record company heralded a change of music and his subsequent recordings for labels other than Riverside, grew progressively more commercial with each release.

THE RIVERSIDE YEARS
1. The Thumb's Up or What the View is Like From the Top – Bill Quinn, *Downbeat* Annual Guitar Issue, 27 June 1968.
2. Wes Montgomery by Ralph Gleason– *Jazz and Blues*, October 1973.
3. Indiana Renaissance – Gunther Schuller, *Jazz Review*, September 1959.

4. Duncan Schiedt interview with the author, Indianapolis, April 1984.
5. + 6. The Dynamic New Sound of The Wes Montgomery Trio – Riverside RLP 1156.
7. End of the Mastersounds – *Downbeat*, February 1960.
8. Wes Montgomery by Jack Duarte – *BMG Magazine*, September 1962.
9. J. Tynam reporting on the 1960 Monterey Jazz Fesitival – *Downbeat*, November 1960.
10. Review of The Montgomery Brothers album 'Grooveyard' (Riverside RLP 362) – *Jazz Journal*, April 1962.
11. Monterey Jazz Festival 1961, a report of Wes Montgomery with the John Coltrane Group – D. Demichael, *Downbeat*, November 1961.
12. Review of 'The Montgomery Brothers in Canada' (Fantasy 3323) – *Downbeat*, March 1962.
13. Johnny Griffin/M. Cullaz – *Jazz, Hot,* February 1969.
14. Wes Montgomery, Organ-ic Problems and Satisfactions by Ira Gitler – *Downbeat, 6 July 1964.*
15. The Last Words of a Great Jazzman – Wes Montgomery/Les Tomkins, *Crescendo,* July 1968.
16. Pete Welding's review of the album 'Fusion' (Riverside RLP 472) – *Downbeat,* June 1964.
17. Review of 'Boss Guitar' (Riverside 459) – *Downbeat,* September 1963.
18. Organ-ic Problems and Satisfaction (see Note 14).
19. Wes Montgomery Talks to Valerie Wilmer – Musicians Talking – *Jazz Monthly,* May 1965.

Standel Custom Amplifier - identical to the one used by Wes Montgomery.

PHOTO: DAVE BARCOCK

Promotional advert used by Gibson Guitars 1964.

COMMERCIAL SUCCESS

Wes Montgomery.

COMMERCIAL SUCCESS

"I decided that if people were going to hear Wes Montgomery, I would have to record him in a culturally acceptable context. Now I wasn't particularly enamoured of the idea of surrounding Wes with strings, but if that was a way of getting him known to more people, that is the way it had to be."
Creed Taylor[1]

It is indeed rare for any jazz musician to receive popular acclaim and even more so when that musician is first and foremost an instrumentalist. Ironically most of the jazz musicians who have achieved a measure of commercial success have, with the exception of the big band leaders, achieved it not for their undoubted instrumental expertise but for their singing! Most people know, or have heard of, jazz musicians like Louis Armstrong, Nat King Cole and George Benson, but how many, besides a minority audience of jazz enthusiasts, know about major figures in jazz? Bix Beiderbecke, Coleman Hawkins, Lester Young, Clifford Brown, Charlie Parker, Ornette Coleman and John Coltrane, just a few from the role call of brilliant jazz musicians who remain in almost total obscurity to the general public.

A jazz musician must have an immediate appeal to receive anything like the popular and critical acclaim that Wes did, for seldom does a jazz instrumentalist attain such a privileged status. Wes was something of an enigma, most of his music appealed not only to the general public but also the discerning jazz fan and it was this very duality that placed him amongst an exclusive handful of jazz musicians which included the likes of George Shearing, Errol Garner and Stephane Grapelli.

Bill Quinn, one of the few jazz critics who remained sympathetic to Wes' music during his commercial period, wrote in a perceptive *Downbeat* article:

> "When the Unit (Wes' Group) kicks off into any of the two dozen or so numbers with which the audience is familiar, and the chorus of approbation goes up. 'Yeah', be advised that one of Jazz's greatest public relations men is at work – he is talking to both square ears and round!"[2]

Very few critics tolerated Wes' commercial success particularly his three albums for the A + M label.[3]

Bill Quinn's assessment provided, in retrospect, a highly perceptive evaluation of the man's music. Dan Morgenstern's posthumous review of a Wes Montgomery LP (Greatest Hits), a compilation of the A + M Material), painted a similar picture:

> "Maybe I'm rating these collections of commercial successes from a great musician's legacy too highly, for these *are* commercial, and sometimes the arrangements become intrusive or restricting. But how he could make his instrument sing! Regardless of setting, he never played a metricious note, and though it would have been better if he had not been forced to prove it so often, he could transform tap water to vintage wine."[4]

These reviews, however, were an exception to the rule for after he gained the Grammy award for the best instrumental jazz performance in 1967 ('Goin' Out of My Head') Wes received consistently poor press of which the following examples were typical.

> "His latest albums were very fine as such things go, but to those of us who had heard him swing, they were tantamount to hearing Horowitz play 'Chopsticks'."
> Chris Albertson[5]

> "The music is the epitome of successful commercial formula jazz, sleek and purring like a champion cat. That it is occasionally more shadow than substance is to be expected ..."
> Pete Welding[6]

> "The fact that one may wish to discount much of Wes Montgomery's later work (it was aimed at a different market) as the tone gradually lost it's sparkle and the phrasing became more flaccid, cannot detract from the quality and value of his early recordings."
> Alexis Korner[7]

> "Still we must regret that Montgomery's gifts were turned so completely towards the radio industry's idea of what a good record was, for that idea allowed little room for large areas of his talent."
> J R Taylor[8]

> "Now that Montgomery has attained some measure of commercial success, I wonder if he'll ever make another good album, ... maybe he'll record serious music again under a pseudonym."
> Harvey Pekar[9]

> "There is a tremendous democratic pull in America to simplify everything, iron out all the wrinkles, reduce it to it's lowest denominator, pasteurise, homogenise; and somehow Wes Montgomery went down that disassembly line."
> James Sallis[10]

> "Ironically, the salient feature of this present album (The Small Group Recordings) is that all the material stands in strong contrast to that which earned Wes Montgomery his wide popularity. That material crossed through the borders of pop and came dangerously close to entering the middle-of-the-road territory inhabited by Muzak: Lush arrangements

> featuring a veritable 'Who's Who' of top studio musicians, but leaving very little room for Wes to do more than play pretty for the people."
> Chris Albertson[11]

Commercial success began for Wes in 1965 shortly after he changed record labels from Riverside to Verve. Creed Taylor who had started producing for Verve in 1962, when Norman Granz sold the label to MGM, approached Wes with a copy of a Little Anthony and the Imperials tune 'Goin' Out of My Head', with the suggestion that he might include it on his next album.

Although Wes was at first reluctant to record the tune, he was eventually persuaded to do so. The results amazed them both, for the resulting album, 'Going Out of My Head', won a Grammy award and transformed Wes' entire career, allowing him the luxury of spending the last years of his tragically short life in financial security.

Taylor who is, even now, particularly proud of his short yet fruitful association with Wes, recalls the circumstances leading up to the recording:

> "Once I got over the hump of giving Wes that Anthony and the Imperials record, he was a joy to work with. Oliver Nelson helped persuade Wes to record the number. From that point on things went very smoothly. I worked with the arranger, he would put a piano sketch on tape and send it to Wes wherever he happened to be on the road. He'd rehearse between jobs and then come into the studio to record. He didn't read at all and was very self-conscious about it — but he was a natural musician.
>
> I think his recordings for Riverside had been, to say the least, loosely produced. The producer would call the artist, the artist would put a rhythm section together and then they would play for a while. But there comes a point with those jamming albums, with interminable solos, when you have to acknowledge that they are not reaching many people, and they would never get the artists played on radio stations, which is mandatory for record sales in the United States.
>
> I decided that if people were going to hear Wes Montgomery, I would have to record him in a culturally acceptable context. Now I wasn't particularly enamoured of the idea of surrounding Wes with strings, but if that was a way of getting him known to more people, then that was the way it had to be"[12]

'Goin' Out of My Head' was actually Wes' fourth recording for Verve, the previous three, 'Movin' Wes' (Nov 64), 'Bumpin' ' (May 65) and 'Smokin' ' at the Half Note (June/Sept 65) were recorded in rapid succession and the two albums were on general release at the time of 'Goin' Out of My Head' sessions. 'Movin' Wes' and 'Bumpin' ' had already been, by jazz sales standards, significant successes.

Creed Taylor took great care and deliberation to place Wes in commercial yet tasteful settings. It is surely inconceivable that a producer should hire sidemen the calibre of Phil Woods, Ernie Royal, Herbie Hancock and Donald Byrd; arrangers Oliver Nelson and Don Sebesky, to produce records specifically for monetary returns. Yes it's true that Taylor compromised his playing, he openly admits it, but the question is, did this compromise nurture Wes' talent, or restrict it?

Montgomery certainly felt that he learnt from having to adapt:

> "Sure I've had to adapt myself to making these kinds of records. You learn more by adapting. When somebody has to adapt *you*, you're not learning anything; *they're* learning it. But when you're doing the adapting you find out more ways to do things."

Gone were the casual Riverside sessions where Wes had a free reign to stretch out and play exactly as he wished. What Taylor did was to produce a new foil for Wes, constricting him to fewer bars of improvisation, yet at the same time heightening the intensity of his playing. Anyone who is doubtful about Wes' output after he changed record labels need only listen to his blistering solos on Caravan ('Movin' Wes') and Naptown Blues ('Goin' Out of My Head') to hear just how effective at it's best Taylor's concept was. Unfortunately Creed Taylor's formula for commercial packaging was not consistant and it seemed that with each consecutive album release the constriction grew until finally Wes was given little more than the opportunity to state a melody in octaves.

'Goin' Out of My Head' was recorded on the 7, 8 and 22 December 1965 at the Rudy Van Gelder Studios, Englewood, New Jersey. The arranger and conductor for these sessions was the talented Oliver Nelson who had at his disposal: five trombones three trumpets, five doubling reeds and a rhythm section which was augmented by Candido (congas) and an extra piano. The musicians chosen by Taylor and Nelson to complete this force were world-class, including amongst them, Phil Woods, Herbie Hancock, Donald Byrd, Joe Newman, Jimmy Cleveland, Quentin Jackson, Grady Tate and George Duvivier.

The finished product, however, was not unanimously received, particularly with the 'hard-core' jazz press, the fact that the record sold in extremely large quantities was, of course, further damnation.

As Wes' success grew so did his alienation from the 'jazz elite', after all one couldn't be a jazz musician and financially successful at the same time! Arguments have raged for many years now about the extent to which commerciality undermines a musician's artistic integrity and whether or not a jazz musician has the right to compromise his art by placing financial security before artistic expression. Most of the jazz critics complained that Wes had compromised his art in no uncertain terms.

Joe Pass, a fellow jazz guitarist, however, felt that Wes did not sacrifice his artistic integrity, despite the enormity of his success:

> "Wes Montgomery became a big seller, and he played much more sophisticated guitar than you'd normally hear on the radio. (Tenor Saxist) Stan Getz became very big without playing any differently, maybe songs that weren't as long or not as intricate, but I don't think either of these artists sacrificed their integrity. They played what they felt. I think a lot of it was packaged around them afterwards. They sold because somebody said 'Let's do it!' "[13]

The critic's hostility towards Wes was of course, nothing new, after all Nat King Cole, Louis Armstrong and Charlie Parker (after recording an album with strings) received similar receptions when their records began to sell.

Fortunately Wes was a wise man, as much the philosopher as the musician, his long apprenticeship of 'dues-paying' and the time spent in day-jobs had furnished him with a wisdom that not only enabled him to rationalise the situation but also endeared him to everyone he met. Wes' philosophical perception of his new-found success helped him to accept the harsh and sometimes negative criticism he was receiving at that time.

> "I want to tell people – this is those who write about it as well as the public – not to worry about what it's called; worry about whether it pleases people. That's what it's all about anyway, people are the final judges...
>
> "Those who criticise me for playing jazz too simply and such are missing the point. When I first came up big on the Billboard Charts they couldn't decide whether to call me a jazz or a pop artist. There is a different direction on my records these days; there is a jazz concept to what I'm doing, but I'm playing popular music and it should be regarded as such.
>
> "In the first place, people are not listening as well as they think they are, in all cases. I have changed my playing just as many others have, to fit with the times...
>
> "When you start to make it slightly, everyone talks like you're a millionaire. But let's not forget that this isn't the Beatles or somebody – nobody ever makes it *that* big in jazz."[14]

Wes' dichotomy was however never really problematic, for he fully understood his schrizophrenic situation. On his gigs Wes continued, as always, to play good swinging jazz, whilst on disc he played popular music comparable in depth and quality to the classic records that Sinatra made with Nelson Riddle Orchestra. Clearly, Wes compromised his art only on disc, and the fact that he occasionally showed signs of displeasure was to be expected for he knew that he could never reach as wide an audience as he would have liked to with specialist jazz records like those he had made for Riverside.

> "It doesn't matter how much artistry one has: it's how it's presented that counts ... I have seen what happend to people like Tatum and Coltrane. Though Coltrane died before his thing had been completely resolved Tatum died at a time when he should have enjoyed all the benefits of being the greatest piano player in existence."[15]

James Sallis made the following observations about the public and jazz the art form in his book 'The Guitar Players':

> "Until recently, straight jazz had little currency among general listeners and thrived primarily as a ghetto art with a small audience of hardcore fans, intellectuals and other artists. What *is* surprising is that Wes Montgomery, this innovative soft-spoken pure jazz guitarist, became popular at all."[16]

Whilst guitarist Joe Pass described the financial difficulties confronting jazz musicians more than a decade after Montgomery's death:

> "It's hard to make a living in jazz. I've been playing, actual gigs, for more than 30 years, and it's only within the last few years I've been able to say, survive by playing jazz solely, make a living at it."[17]

The sixties were lean years for the jazz musician, jazz guitarists in particular suffered from the unprecedented growth in pop music. Wes' immense talent enabled him to cross barriers, which were all too prevalent at that time, with playing that was at once both timeless and universally appealing, a combination of qualities seldom found in a jazz guitarist. Wes had a special magic, an indefinable warmth, a sound and a style which brought him a success that was unique for the period. Those who criticise him for playing commercially and consequently taking the easy way out, should remember that many of the most gifted players of the era: Barney Kessel, Howard Roberts, Herb Ellis, Jim Hall, Jimmy Raney, Kenny Burrell, Sal Salvador, Johnny Smith, Dennis Budimir and many more, opted for the relative security of sessions, Broadway pit orchestras and television.

Given such a social environment, Wes must be admired for managing to provide for his wife and children without lowering his standards, he may not have played as much jazz on disc as the critics would have liked him to, but this shouldn't really detract from the value of what he did play.

Ironically much of the criticism levelled in the mid 60s was for what he didn't play rather than what he did!

Although Wes was a creative artist and an individualist, unlike many, he could never put himself or his music before his family commitment. Few guitarists would have given up a promising career with the Lionel Hampton Big Band at the height of it's popularity to devote more time to their wife and children. His love for life and fellow human beings 'I don't know any strangers' he once said, helped keep his music vital and fresh, music which communicated his contagious enthusiasm for life.

James Stewart had this to say of Wes after collaborating with him on the Wes Montgomery Guitar Method:

> "Wes was a marvellous man. He was developed in other areas than music. His spiritual being was developed, he was warm, and loved to give his music."

Tenor saxophonist Johnny Griffin a long time friend and associate spoke affectionately of his qualities:

> "Wes was a marvellous person. He didn't drink, and was very difficult about what he ate. He only ate things that his mother taught him to eat. He had seven kids. He was the perfect father. He spoke slowly, thinking about what he was going to say, never letting out a word he did not want, and all with great humour. Wes was a serious type, no drugs, no drink, only rarely jamming in the clubs, no women. He was always well dressed, but was a bit fat like a sausage. When he buttoned his jacket, well ... but he always had that smile ... His sense of rhythm and tempo, his melodic and harmonic intuition were phenomenal. And what's more extraordinary is that he was self-taught. He had a fantastic creative force. Everything in life he did was rounded out, definitive. No waste of energy or emotions."[18]

When Wes reached the summit of his career in 1968 he told reviewer Bill Quinn:

> "Everything relates to life. Some musicians might feel so personal about their contribution that they cut off the rest of the world to concentrate exclusively on their thing. I don't indulge in music to that extent that it destroys my interest in other things, with me, music is still a hobby."

This unpretentious attitude towards his own music played a major part in it's success. No matter how much the critics argued and debated, the qualities of late period Wes Montgomery, there was no escaping the fact that it communicated with and gave pleasure to an extremely large and varied audience.

The classical guitar composer/critic John Duarte wrote in the BMG magazine article 'Wes Montgomery – Natural Genius':

> "Talent of this order will impress itself on those with perception, no matter what boundaries it has to cross."[19]

Approaching music as a hobby helped Wes to retain his innocence and enthusiasm, each new playing experience was met with an excitement that comes only from the joy of discovery. Wes was happiest when he was learning, he really enjoyed for instance recording with a baroque style accompaniment ('The Road Song'). His enthusiasm for a challenge, for trying out new things and for stretching his ability to it's full potential did not however enjoy a corresponding enthusiasm from the critics. Wes could never understand why the critics should dislike music that had obviously proved such a challenge, music that he had responded to and learnt from. Wes' first album to border on commerciality was 'Fusion' (Riverside 472) an album recorded in 1963 with a full string orchestra. Wes was puzzled by the critics' response to the record, he said in a *Crescendo* magazine article:

> "The first time I recorded with strings I was very disappointed with the critical comments I got. I don't know what's wrong with these people, man – unless they feel like music is nothing but hard sounds all the time. I mean, beauty comes in a lot of ways. To me, that was the finest thing I'd done up to that time."[20]

Wes enjoyed the discipline of adapting to different musicians and different situations, he wanted to create music of lasting beauty. Playing good swinging jazz came easy, it was so natural to him, and after all he had already flexed his improvising muscle on several excellent Riverside albums. However, playing simple, yet at the same time meaningful, music with depth of emotion and lasting aesthetic beauty was different that *was* a challenge, a challenge that could not inhibit such a creative talent.

Whatever Wes played he made his own, regardless of musical setting. Gary Giddens, in the chapter 'Jazz Musicians Consider Wes Montgomery' from the excellent book *Riding on a Blue Note,* wrote:

> "With each (A + M) release Montgomery became more encumbered by pretentious arrangements. It is the highest possible tribute to the man's genius that he managed to inject so much feeling, such unmistakable soul into situations that clearly displeased him.

The most depressing part about Wes' success was that he gradually became a victim of his own popularity and the situation which displeased him the most was not ironically his commercial recordings, but the reluctance of his audience to let him play anything other than the tunes from his best selling LPs. Barney Kessel recalls:

> "I remember talking with Wes Montgomery when he was playing in a packed club. He wasn't bitter, just realistic. He said "See those people out there? They didn't come to hear me, they came to see me play one, two or three of my hit records, because when I decide to do a tune of mine or Coltrane's 'Giant Steps' instead of 'Goin' Out of My Head', they get bored and start talking. In fact they get very insulted, because they drove 60 miles to hear 'Tequila' so they can sing this one part and show their friends they know what's happening. They're not here to see if I'm better this year than last, they're here to hear me perform like it was a record hop'."[21]

Though Wes remained fairly optimistic about this dilemma, his guitarist friends complained bitterly:

> "You know, he really was a heck of a jazz player, but you wouldn't know it from the last two or three years

of his career. You would think that all he could play was the melody and octaves, and I saw him when he was performing in jazz clubs. I'd drop off and have a drink with him and he would complain that every time he really tried to play anything they would get up and walk out if he didn't play 'Goin' Out of My Head'. The audience was very mad if he didn't play it the way he played it on record. Here is a very creative guitar player who should have been heard, but wasn't."
Howard Roberts[22]

This extract from a Howard Robert's *Guitar Player* interview aptly illustrates the difficulties that confronted Wes, difficulties of which he was acutely aware. It seemed that as the years passed by it grew inevitable that he could never please everyone no matter how hard he tried or what he did, for sadly, he was caught between critics and jazz fans demanding pure jazz on one side, and the general public demanding perfect renditions of his hit records on the other.

George Benson, a guitarist who found himself in similar circumstances to Wes during the 1970s once remarked:

"People who love jazz musicians, love us when we play what we want to play, and we're starving. But as soon as you commercialise your sound, as Wes did, the jazz fans and critics are down on you! Wes told me about this a week before he died. He was very unhappy and disturbed by this attitude."[23]

Wes had good reason for being unhappy and disturbed, it was impossible for him to live and support his family on the earnings made from playing straight jazz, but on the other hand, when he played music of a more commercial nature, music that gave him a respectable, thought not decadent, living (which he was surely entitled to after 25 years apprenticeship) he was accused of 'selling out'.

In retrospect it is hardly surprising that he chose the more lucrative commercial avenue, with his character and understanding of the needs of others he could do little else. Wes may not have had quite so much fun with his music towards the end of his life as he had had in the early years but he was amply compensated in the knowledge that he was providing a hitherto unthinkable security for his wife and family whilst at the same time giving pleasure to literally thousands of people.

It would have been impossible for Wes to put himself and his desire to play pure jazz before such important considerations, his family came first and he was always fully conscious of his responsibilities towards them. As a result he continued to make records which adhered strictly to the Creed Taylor middle-of-the-road formula, monopolising on the huge and unprecedented success of 'Goin' Out of My Head'. It was inevitable that Wes, being an unduly modest man, should have been thrilled by the success of the record; he told Leonard Feather in a 1967 *Downbeat* Blindfold Test:

"Back in Riverside days, I recorded with small groups strictly for jazz fans. Later on I started these sessions with big bands, using a Latin beat or some kind of special rhythm background that helped to keep things moving. Then I did 'Goin' Out of My Head'. I had no confidence in it at all when Creed showed it to me, but he got the arranger Oliver Nelson, and told me, "Just play it in octaves" – and Wow! its gone over 80,000 and it's still moving."

Such sales must have convinced Wes of the merit of Taylor's directive 'Play it in octaves' as each successive Montgomery album exploited the technique further, effectively removing him from the mainstream of jazz and placing him in the category of popular or light music. The unique combination of Taylor's packaging and Wes' sensuous octave sound had become an instant recipe for success.

A simple recipe, yet one which worked only because of Wes' unfailing ability to play the right notes in the right places. Even with the constraints of octaves his improvisations were thoughtful, rhythmically vital and spontaneous, qualities which obviously contributed to the enormous sales of his records.

Reviewer Pete Welding wrote in a 1968 *Downbeat* review of a compilation of Wes' Verve material (The Best of Wes Montgomery Verve 8714):

"It's a pleasure to hear him just state the melody: his sound and control are lovely, and his sense of time, of note placement is uncanny."

Success spawns imitations and an entire spate of Taylor/Montgomery influenced albums quickly appeared, Kenny Burrell, Jim Hall, Joe Pass, George Benson, Jimmy Ponder, Wilbert Longmire and Gabor Szabo are just a few of the guitarists who received similar packaging with a noticeable reduction in improvisation. Of these perhaps Burrell and Hall's were amongst the most musically satisfying, whilst George Benson's were undoubtedly the most successful commercially.

Wes and Taylor quickly followed the success of 'Goin' Out of My Head' with two more albums in a similar vein. 'Tequila' and 'California Dreaming'. Both albums were recorded during 1966, 'Tequila' on the 17, 18 and 21 March and 'California Dreaming' on the 14, 15 and 16 September. Musically of the two albums 'Tequila' was the most successful, chiefly because of the quality of the material and the excellent, sympathetic rhythm section. This rhythm section consisted of Ron Carter (Bass), Grady Tate (Drums) and Ray Baretto (Congas) players who had gigged and recorded with Wes in the past, and more importantly, players who were both sensitive and supportive. Creed Taylor augmented this rock-steady unit with eight violins and four cellos, obtaining the services of Claus Ogerman for the arrangements. Although there were pop tunes on the album, 'What the World Needs Now' and 'The Big Hurt', Wes' loping blues 'The Thumb' and the title track ('Tequila') compensated for the commercial nature of the rest of the material, providing interest for the more jazz orientated of the Wes Montgomery enthusiasts.

The later album, 'California Dreaming', was musically less satisfying, marred by an over-abundance of pop tunes. ('Sunny', 'California Dreaming', 'South of the Border') even the presence of Herbie Hancock (Piano) and Don Sebesky (Arranger) could not rescue the proceedings, although Wes' playing did shine on some tracks.

Many jazz fans and critics, encouraged by Wes' fine playing on 'Tequila', were expecting even better things from the follow-up record. Unfortunately 'California Dreaming', a pastiche of the worst elements of Wes' previous commercial records, was not the album they were anticipating and although sales were good, the reviews were predictably bad. Harvey Pekar, reviewing the album for *Downbeat* wrote:

> "Now that Montgomery has attained some measure of commercial success, I wonder if he'll ever make another good album.
>
> "This LP is the worst I've heard by him. Compared with his best improvisation, his playing here is childishly simple and monotonous. The single-note lines that have been the most interesting aspect of his work are all but absent here.
>
> "At least he's consistent, though. There's not a good track on the LP. I can't blame Montgomery for wanting to make money, but I hope we haven't heard the last of him as a great jazz artist. Maybe he'll record serious music again under a pseudonym ..."[24]

rating it at one and a half stars (slightly better than poor). In all fairness to Wes the album was not really that bad, like most of the commercial period recordings, it had it's moments; the gorgeous unaccompanied chordal coda on 'You Crazy Moon' and Wes' fine playing on his own laid-back blues, 'Sundown' offered some comfort to the loyal Montgomery fan.

However, sadly, the classical Montgomery of 'Full House', 'Movin' Wes' and 'Goin' Out of My Head' was not to be heard again on record.* Creed Taylor moved to Herb Alpert's A + M records in 1966 taking Wes with him and although Taylor was to stay with A + M for the next three years, Wes did not stay the course, he died suddenly following a heart attack on 15 June, 1968.

Some sources suggest that Wes, suffering from, and taking medication for, a known heart condition collapsed on the steps of his home and died later that day in hospital. However, Serene Montgomery, Wes' widow recalls:

> "The way it happened on the morning of 15 June, 1968, was that Wes mentioned he didn't feel very well and sat down in the dining room chair. He fell from the chair and in a moment or two, he died in my arms."[25]

David Baker, a colleague and close friend, recalls that Wes took nitroglycerine tablets for angina and had stopped taking them shortly before his death after suffering from severe headaches. Another friend and colleague, Pookie Johnson, recalls that prior to his death Wes seemed in a bad way, complaining of headaches and continually falling asleep. Although the suddenness of Wes' death shocked the music business, it was obvious to those who knew him well that he was ill. Whatever the circumstances, Wes' death was a tragic and untimely loss to everyone.

Three albums emerged from the Taylor/Montgomery A + M collaboration; 'A Day in the Life' (6, 7, 8 and 26 June, 1967), 'Down Here on the Ground' (20 and 21 December, 1967 and 22 and 26 January, 1968) and 'Road Song' (7, 8 and 9 May, 1968).

Collectively these records are considered by many to be completely insignificant to Wes' recorded output as a jazz player, and it is true that they are not at all representative of the man's obvious talents.

Taylor's directive 'Play it in octaves' may well have changed to 'Play the tune in octaves and then drop out', for that was basically Taylor's approach to the A + M Records, if Wes got two choruses in succession he was lucky. Such an uninspired approach left little room for Wes' thoughtfully structured improvisations, tunes in octaves were unquestionable the raison d'etre of the A + M recordings.

Mark C. Grindley wrote in his book 'Jazz Styles'[26]

> "His reputation with non-musicians was earned by recording for Verve and A + M which did not reflect much of his great talent. He played tastefully on these records, but his work in the late 50s and early 60s is in a far richer jazz vein."

Roland Atkins' sentiments,

> "a lucrative yet sterile series of LPs on which he strums resignedly while violins twitter around him"[27]

were, unfortunately, shared by many and it is true that these octave-bound, over orchestrated records did nothing to resolve the commercial versus purist problem. Jazz fans were disappointed and saddened by such bastardisation of talent, annoyed that society and the music business in general could not

---

*Several bootleg, pirate recordings and private tapes have been released posthumously, details of these can be found in Appendix I The LP Recordings.

offer a man of such massive talent an assured, worthwhile living under conditions that allowed him his full creative potential.

Brian Priestly mirrored those thoughts when he wrote:

> "If Charles Lloyd is the "Dave Brubeck of the 60s", it seems quite fair to describe Wes Montgomery as the "George Shearing of the 60s". His last recordings are bought by people who could hardly be called hardcore jazz fans, and this is because he had evolved a commercial, stultifying pleasant "sound" which was being exploited at the expense of any creativity whatsoever. And, although the story of Musician Deserts Jazz for Financial Gain is a familiar one, the disappointment is considerable in the case of Montgomery, who was once an inventive and exciting improviser."[28]

Wes' duality of appeal held up well until the release of these A + M records. Both the jazz fan and the less discerning listener could find something to enjoy on the Verve recordings, with the possible exception of 'California Dreaming', which was, it seems, a little too commercial for some ears.

However, Wes was the artist and to some extent the successful artist calls the tune. One cannot help recalling his own words, "I'm playing popular music and it should be regarded as such."

Perhaps this is where the critics missed the point. The music on all three of the A + M records was not really jazz, in the accepted sense of the term, and could not therefore be assessed by the same criteria. In commercial terms A + M recordings were an unmitigated success 'A Day in the Life' had sold more than 250,000 copies at the time of Wes' death and had been number one in the *Billboard* album charts for 32 consecutive weeks.

To conclude this chapter and further illustrate some important points already made about Wes' commercial success I have included a fragment of a long conversation I had with the jazz guitarist Barney Kessell:[29]

AI: *Do you remember the Guitar Player Roundtable article about the state of the jazz guitar scene where you were in conversation with Howard Roberts and Joe Pass, when you spoke about Wes saying that 'He wasn't bitter, just realistic about his situation?'*

BK: Yes I do.

AI: *I've already quoted this in the book, but would really like to hear you expand on it.*

BK: I think he got in a trap, it was a trap that had some good things about it. He became well-known, he also made some money. He was able to, as a result of the success of his recordings, provide for his family, many things that not only did they need, but had not received in a long time, because he had not really done well, financially until he came into his own. So it was a joy to him to be able to provide for them when they really needed it.

He did enjoy playing for people and meeting people and was really glad to be in the position he was in, in a way, in another way, in arriving where people knew him they only accepted him conditionally, and this is different than accepting a lot of other people. They didn't accept Charlie Parker conditionally, they didn't accept Bill Evans conditionally. They'd only accept Wes Montgomery when he would play mainly 'Goin' Out of My Head' and 'Tequila' and everything else was really less accepted than that. They would rather hear them over and over again than hear other songs.

They certainly didn't really want to hear any of his original songs, or him playing a Duke Ellington medley or anything like that.

Most of the people wanted to come into a club and hear and see him physically play what he had on the record, even note for note. They wouldn't even want to hear him playing another solo, that made him a little sad, it didn't make him sad enough to want to stop, because he was very glad to be able to make a living.

Actually it got to where the record company and the public demanded less and less from him.

AI: *So Wes' style had really become a 'sound' which was being commercially exploited?*

BK: Yes, out of many things he could do, a couple of things that he could do sort of 'caught on' with the public. The people around him, who were really after money and selling and exploiting took these one or two commodities and simply said 'Let's stay with that and forget everything else'.

AI: *Wes specifically mentions you as one of his favourite guitarists in one of his interviews, saying that you play with a lot of feeling. Did you discern any of your own style in Wes' playing?*

BK: I can't really comment on that! He and I do share one thing, we grew up playing certain songs and music, playing in a similar groove, and what it is, it's a position musically that hovers between late swing and early be-bop, and we would respond to songs in a similar way.

AI: *If you were asked to put into a simple paragraph what you thought about Wes, either as a person or as a musician rather than as a guitarist, as I realise it would be unfair to ask one guitarist to comment on another's playing, what would you say?*

BK: Well, the first word that comes is warm, swinging, setting moods, sustaining the moods, and as a person – basically earthy, down to the ground and sincere. As far as I know, void of facades, void of acting in a way where he's impressing. He was not overly humble, nor was he overly overbearing or egotistic, but just warm. He was what I could call being a jazz musician at it's finest, having all the qualities that go into being a fine jazz musician.

I think he used the guitar as a tool, I just think he had the music inside of him and it didn't really matter that he didn't have a pick, or if he played the piano. He wanted to play music and didn't wait until he could find a tutor, or didn't wait until he could make sure that he had the right pick, or even think about that it was wrong not to play with one. He didn't worry about that he just wanted to get the music out.'

Prior to and even after his huge commercial success, Wes Montgomery was considered one of the most outstanding guitarists in contemporary jazz. He had won numerous awards, including the *Downbeat* Critic's Poll (1960-63; 1966-67) and *Reader's* Poll (1961-62; 1966-67); the *Playboy* 'All Stars "All Stars" ' Poll for six consecutive years, a Grammy Award ('California Dreaming') and a Gold Disk ('A Day in the Life').

Whilst in his home town, Indianapolis, a 34 acre city park was renamed Wes Montgomery Park in October 1972 with some ceremony. Also in that same city a special jazz concert is staged annually as a special tribute to the Hoosier guitarist. Artists who have appeared so far include, Freddie Hubbard, Joe Williams, Leroy Vinegar, Kenny Burrell, Slide Hampton, James Spaulding, Ted Dunbar, John Bunch, David Baker, Virgil Jones, Mel Rhyne, Benny Barth, Larry Ridley and of course Monk and Buddy Montgomery.

Indianapolis payed further tribute to it's famous guitarist when a local bank established the Wes Montgomery Scholarship. Founded in 1969 by Merchant's National Bank and Trust Company, a $1,000 college scholarship is awarded annually to male negro graduates of Attucks, Tech, Washington Wood, Manual, Shortridge and Northwest, who major in business studies.

To date, 21 students have been honoured and according to the present vice-president for human resources, Clifford B. Spears, 'Merchants has every intention of continuing to award the scholarships in the future'.

COMMERCIAL SUCCESS
1. Crossover Crusader, a rare interview with Creed Taylor and Mike Hennessey, *Jazz Journal International*, Vol. 32, No. 11.
2. The Thumb's Up or What the View is Like from the Top, Bill Quinn, *Downbeat Guitar Issue*, 27 June, 1968.
3. A Day in the Life, AMLS 2001.
Down Here on the Ground, AMLS 3006.
Road Song, AMLS 927.
4. Wes Montgomery's Greatest Hits A + M SP4247, Record Review by Don Morgenstern, *Downbeat*, 11 June, 1970.
5. The Small Group Recordings, sleevenotes by Chris Albertson, Verve Select Double 2632 064.
6. The Best of Wes Montgomery, Verve 8714, Record Review by Pete Welding, *Downbeat*, 7 March, 1968.
7. The Genius of Wes Montgomery, booklet which accompanies a three LP special edition box set, Riverside 109561-3.
8. Wes Montgomery, Pretty Blue, sleevenotes by J. R. Taylor, Milestone double LP M47030.
9. California Dreaming, Verve 8672, Record Review by Harvey Pekar, *Downbeat*, May 1967.
10. The Guitar Players, One Instrument and It's Masters in American Music, James Sallis, *Quill*, New York 1982.
11. The Small Group Recordings (see note 5).
12. Crossover Crusader, Creed Taylor, November 1979 (see note 1).
13. Jazz Roundtable, Barney Kessel, Herb Ellis, Joe Pass, Howard Roberts, *Guitar Player*, September 1972.
14/15. The Thumb's Up, or What the View is like from the Top, November 1979 (see note 2).
16. The Guitar Players, One Instrument and It's Masters in American Music (see note 10).
17. Jazz at Ronnie Scott's, Kitty Grime, Robert Hale Ltd., 1979. ISBN 0 7091 6907 8.
18. Johnny Griffin/M. Cullaz, *Jazz Hot*, February 1979.
19. Wes Montgomery, Natural Genius, John Duarte, *BMG*, August 1968.
20. The Last Words of a Great Jazzman, Wes Montgomery, Les Tomkins, *Crescendo*, July 1968.
21. Jazz Roundtable (see note 13).
22. Howard Roberts, L. V. Eastman, *Guitar Player*, April 1970.
23. George Benson.
24. Review of California Dreaming by Harvey Pekar, *Downbeat*, May 1967.
25. Serene Montgomery, Powers interview, *Indianapolis News*, 1 June, 1977.
26. Jazz Styles, Mark C. Grindley, Prentice-Hall Inc. 1978, ISBN 013 509877 7.
27. Modern Jazz, The Essential Recordings, Max Harrison, Alun Morgan, Roland Atkins, Michael James, Jack Cooke, *Aquarius Books*, 1978, ISBN 0 9046 19.
28. Jazz On Record, A Critical Guide to the First 50 Years: 1917-1967, Albert McCarthy, Alun Morgan, Paul Oliver, Max Harrison, *Hanover Books Ltd.*, 1968.
29. Interview with the author at the 11th Annual Barney Kessel Guitar Seminar (Nov 1983) courtesy of Maurice Summerfield.

INDIANA CONVENTION CENTER

100 SOUTH CAPITOL AVENUE

SUNDAY EVENING, FEB. 5, 1978 AT 7 P.M.

*THE MAYOR'S (WILLIAM H. HUDNUT III)
BLACK HISTORY COMMITTEE and WTLC*

Presents

"A TRIBUTE TO WES MONTGOMERY"

All Proceeds go to the Wes Montgomery Memorial Scholarship Fund

Featuring For The First Time in History "Together In Concert" The Jazz Giants of the Nation All From Indianapolis

- ★ FREDDIE HUBBARD
- ★ DAVE BAKER
- ★ LARRY RIDLEY
- ★ WILLIS KIRK
- ★ DAVID YOUNG
- ★ MELVIN RHYNE

- ★ SLIDE HAMPTON
- ★ VIRGIL JONES
- ★ LEROY VINEGAR
- ★ JAMES SPAULDING
- ★ PHIL RANELIN
- ★ TED DUNBAR

SPECIAL GUESTS:

1. JIMMY COE
2. LARRY LIGGETT
3. BUDDY PARKER
4. JAMES COMPTON
5. ERROL GRANDY
6. PAUL PARKER
7. LAVERNE NEWSOME
8. RUSSELL BROWN
9. DON MOORMAN BAND
10. FLOYD SMITH
11. POOKIE JOHNSON
12. EUGENE FOWLKES

TICKETS CAN BE PURCHASED:

ROSS & BABCOCK
109 S. Illinois

ROSS & YOUNG
Castleton Square

ALL L. S. AYRES TICKET OUTLETS

Reserved Seating
COST OF TICKETS

$6.00 ★ $5.00 ★ $3.00

THE MAYOR'S BLACK HISTORY COMMITTEE

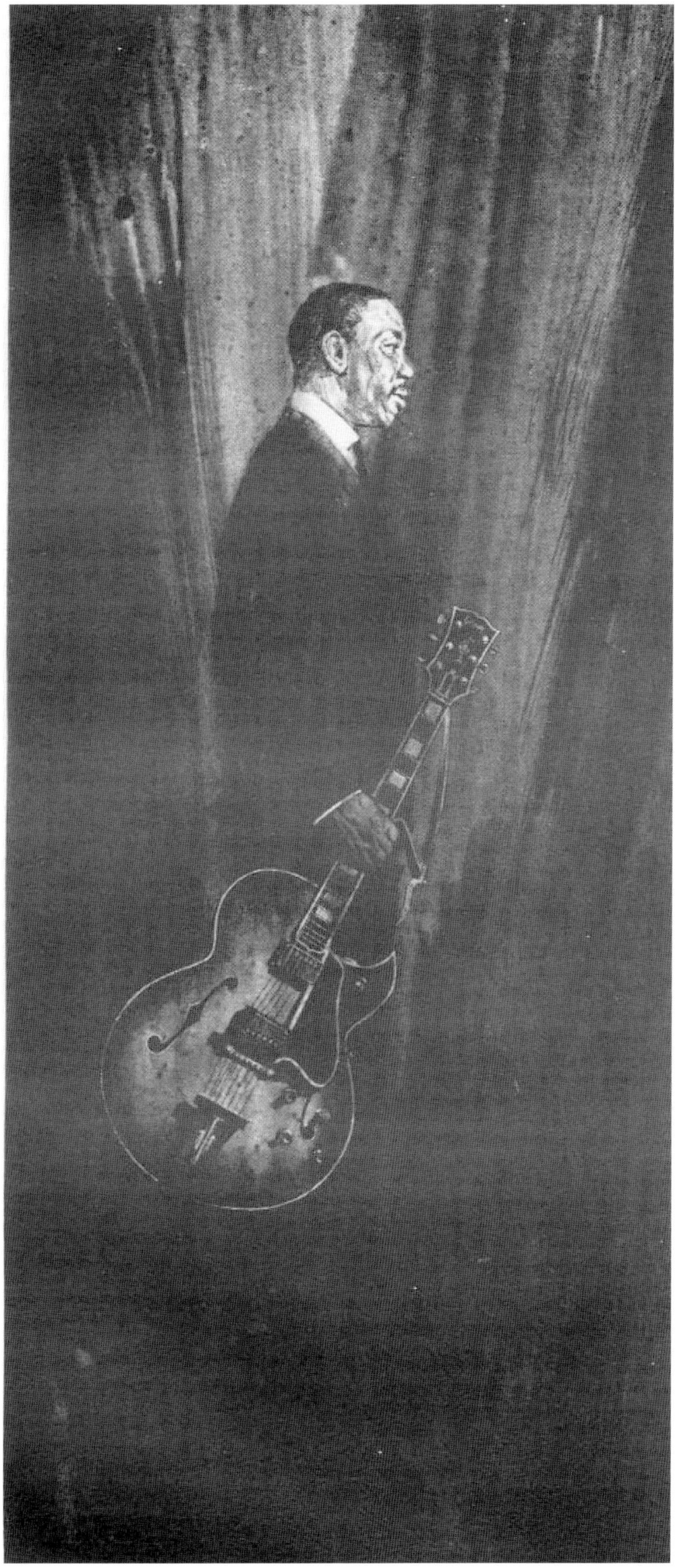

Wes Montgomery

"If Wes Montgomery were not self-taught," wrote one jazz critic, "someone would surely have told him that the way he uses octaves and chords is just not possible on a guitar!" Such astonishment among jazz men is not uncommon where Wes is concerned, because his astounding musical ability is equalled only by his enormous emotional range. The latest example of his incredible talent is Movin' Wes (Verve 8610) on which he plays his Gibson guitar with a blistering, driving, free-swinging style that ranges from the blues-inflected title song Movin' Wes to the virile and intense Caravan. He never lets down, and as you listen you begin to feel the demands he is making on his Gibson—you can hear the guitar's responsiveness and sensitivity. Wes Montgomery first played a Gibson in 1942, and now, more than 20 years later, this master of the jazz guitar continues to play Gibson—choice of the professional artist and acknowledged world leader in fine guitars.

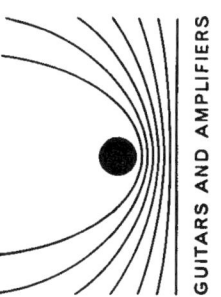

1965 Gibson Guitars advertisement.

GUITARISTICALLY SPEAKING

Wes Montgomery.

GUITARISTICALLY SPEAKING

"Wes Montgomery was the rarest of all musicians, an innovator. He extended the potential of jazz guitar playing and the norm will never again be the same ..."
Jim Hall[1]

Exactly how Wes arrived at the peak he had attained we will probably never know. There is always the thorny question of how much of his ability was natural and how much was the result of hard work, determination and willpower. To travel so far without any formal training, or help from tutor books and without the ability to read music or chord symbol notation, still remains an amazing achievement.

We do however have well documented evidence that Wes' ear was exceptional,

"Charlie Christian's records. I listened to them real good, and I knew that everything done on his guitar could be done on mine, because I had a six-string, so I just determined that I would do it. About six or eight months after I started playing I had taken all the solos off the record and got a job in a club just playing them ..."[2]

In a round table guitar discussion for Crescendo magazine (July 1965) Wes said that whenever he went to the movies he could hear the chord changes in the sound track.

His friends and associates also testify to his extraordinary aural ability:

"Wes didn't read music. He had a great ear and knew what he wanted to do."
Jimmy Stewart[3]

"Wes could always depend on his quick ear. He never learned to read or any theory to speak of, yet he consistently played over the heads of other guitarists, turning out remarkably sophisticated harmonies and unremittingly fresh lines."
James Sallis[4]

"On sessions he is quicker than many trained (and famous) musicians in assimilating a new sequence or arrangement."
John Duarte[5]

"He didn't read at all and was very self-conscious about it, but he was a natural musician."
Creed Taylor[6]

"Wes had big ears and an open mind ..."
Steve Khan[7]

"Although he could not read music he could remember any new piece of music after hearing it once, no matter how intricate."
Ivor Mairants[8]

"Wes had a marvellous ear and could play anything in any key."
Alonzo 'Pookie' Johnson[9]

Wes, like Django Reinhardt and Charlie Christian before him, *had* to make music and this was the over-riding factor in everything he had attained in the area of guitar technique. When specifically questioned about guitar technique and his unorthodox way of playing he replied:

"The player builds his confidence by working out his problems himself. Don't worry if you have limitations. The method and technique that identify me – playing with my thumb and the use of octaves – were born out of limitations. We all have them and must accept and build something meaningful out of them. What I do might not be right technically, but the music comes out all the same. Why? Because I had to play to tell my story."[10]

This compulsion to create, to tell a story, is what made Wes' playing so compelling. His technical skills and expertise were developed only because they were needed in order to say what had to be said, to do what had to be done for, as with other great jazz improvisers, his technique was a means to an end, not an end in itself. Whatever woodshedding Wes needed to do throughout the years to achieve that end was a demonstration of his *commitment* to jazz guitar playing.

It has often been said that Wes both played the guitar and made music instinctively. John Duarte wrote in a magazine article:

"He is not conscious of any organisation of his fingerboard, he merely knows where everything is."[11]

His harmonic knowledge must have been instinctive for without the luxury of even the most rudimentary theoretical knowledge how else could it be done?

"Astonishingly, the basic everyday knowledge of chord symbol notation, which most guitarists almost take for granted, remained a mystery to him."

In what sadly turned out to be one of his final interviews, Wes revealed, much to the surprise of many of his admirers;

"I don't know the chords from seeing their names on paper, I've got to hear it. By hearing it, I can get the idea."[12]

Wes must have relied on his exceptional ears and his inherent good taste to edit and censor his music as it was created. Howard Roberts, a highly respected jazz guitarist/educator, once suggested that a jazz guitarist should have a 'built-in, shock-proof crap detector'[13], certainly Wes must have had an effective one for we know that he was extraordinarily self-critical. He was continuously worried about performing and particularly anxious about his own playing.

The double LP set 'The Alternate Wes Montgomery'[14] gives us an indication of Wes the perfectionist, for there is enough out-take material to fill two complete records and none of it is in any way sub-standard Montgomery. Orrin Keepnews, the producer of the Riverside sessions, from which the material was collated, wrote in the album sleeve notes:

> "These are not takes which originally went unreleased because they weren't good enough. For the most part, they went unreleased because Wes Montgomery thought they weren't good enough – and that definitely is not the same thing."

We can be certain that he was always on his guard against performing music that was not truely satisfying, music that did not meet his own exacting standards!

Perhaps, being absolutely free from the constrictions and constraints of the burden of theoretical and technical knowledge, Wes was able to successfully arrive at a style uninhibited by convention.

Ronnie Scott, that great British tenor saxophonist, jazz entrepreneur and club owner described this very well when he wrote:

> "He played impossible things on his guitar because it was never pointed out to him that they were impossible."[15]

Complete choruses and melody statements played *entirely* in octaves were indeed considered impossible on the guitar before Wes did them.

Perhaps a little exaggerated, though quite indicative of Wes' enormous impact at the time, were Gunther Schuller's remarks:

> "Impossible to play octaves, a device which he did not originate but which he certainly imprinted on the consciousness of listeners everywhere. He perfected the style because, as a self-taught musician, he didn't know it was supposed to be unachievable."[16]

Wes' first melodic statement from Windy, from the album. A Day in the Life Of, A + MSP 3110.

Wes' adoption of the octave playing technique became such an integral feature of his style that his explanation of how he discovered it, to make his playing quieter, seems improbable, in it's over simplification:

> "The sound was too much even for my neighbours, so I took to the back room in the house and began plucking the strings with the fat part of my thumb. This was much quieter. To this technique I added the trick of playing the melody line in two different registers at the same time, the octave thing; this made my sound even quieter."[17]

This is the story that Wes used repeatedly, not only as the reason for his use of octaves but also for the use of his right hand thumb technique instead of the customary plectrum. However improbable the story may now seem, we must acknowledge that the environmental and social circumstances of Wes' formative years contributed something to the development of this unique playing style.

Wes gave an altogether different explanation of how he learnt to play octaves during a television interview with compere Jim Rockwell:

> "Tuning up one day – my guitar was always out of tune, I thought it was because I had a bad guitar in those days – it would be in tune down at the lower end, but up here within this range, it would be out of tune. So I used to take the 1st string and the 3rd string and go like that, and found out how close they were together and which one goes out, then I'd tune up, so whilst I'm doing that, I run a scale accidently, I said, 'Oh, that don't sound too bad,' so I put the two together and ran a scale again. I got so I could play a scale, then I said 'I think I'll play a melody line.' I couldn't play the melody line and every time I got the thing accomplished I couldn't do the next step. I kept on so I got that I wanted to play solo lines, which I couldn't do at that time. My hand used to get cramps and I took it off the guitar."[18]

Of course, Wes did finally achieve his goal of playing solo lines in octaves and the story that he related to Rockwell seems plausible. There is, however, probably truth in both stories, for although Wes stumbled on the octave technique whilst tuning, he may also have adopted it's use to make his playing quieter whilst practicing. What *is* evident from both stories is that he never intentionally tried to copy Django Reinhardt or any other guitarist who preceeded him with use of octaves.

Much has been made of his use of octaves, almost to the exclusion of acknowledging his obvious gifts as a single-line and chord player. Gradually octaves became *the* Wes Montgomery trade mark, his sometimes over-emphasis of this technique, not, I might add, always by his own choosing, became a calculated ploy to make his playing identifiable and immediately accessible even to the least experienced jazz listener. The use of an octave technique in itself was nothing startling or new, Django Reinhardt had used octaves as early as 1935 for his Hot Club of France recording of 'Djangology' (for eight bars) and the Hot Four recordings of 'China Boy' (for 16 bars).[19]

An extract from Django Reinhardt's 'Djangology' showing his use of the octave technique.

What Wes did was to develop a germ of an idea into an entire new concept of guitar playing, whereas the octave technique had only been used by acoustic jazz guitarists to achieve greater volume, or by electric guitarists for the occasional thickening of texture or dynamic. Wes' concept was completely different from both of these ideas, he developed octave playing in an entirely new way, to create interest and to add drama and tension to his improvisation.

He did this by juxtaposing choruses played in octaves with choruses played in chords and choruses played in single notes. This was to become the formula of the classic Wes Montgomery solo, and fine examples of it can be found in many of his recordings.

Indeed, Wes worked hard to cultivate this approach, for he was critically aware of the need for form and variety in improvisation.

> "My aim is to move from one vein to the other without any trouble. Like, if you're going to take a melody line or a counterpoint or a unison line with another instrument, do that, then maybe next time you'll play phrases and chords, or maybe you'll take an octave or something. That way you'll have a lot of variations there."[20]

Wes really admired jazz players who constructed their improvisations thoughtfully.

In one of Leonard Feather's Blindfold Tests, he said of fellow jazz guitarist, Howard Roberts:

> "He sort of mixes it up, he'll play a subtle line, then the next line will be a double line, come back to a subtle line, then he'll mix the chords next. It's a nice pattern."[21]

Like the very best examples from Louis Armstrong and Charlie Parker, Wes' single-line, octave, chords formula endowed his solos with a special class, each note was purposely and meaningfully placed, providing an inevitability which was at no time predictable or inhibited. Les Tomkins wrote in Montgomery's obituary:

> "The key factor to his success was that he never allowed his virtuosity to distract him from the basic business of swinging like mad. Along with Garner, Rich and a few others, Wes was one of the absolute 'naturals' possessing a God-given instinct for doing the right things in the right places."[22]

During the final period of his life Wes was encouraged, by finance conscious record companies and producers, to abandon his classic three-tier improvisational structure in favour of octaves.

Sadly the over emphasis of this technique on his last three albums became almost irritating, particularly to those who were aware of the man's true capabilities. In short octaves were used to the exclusion, almost totally, of any single-line or chord playing denying Wes the opportunity for creative licence.

As a result the commercial presentation of late period Montgomery reduced a superb improvisational style to a marketable parody of it's former self; as James Sallis cryptically remarked:

> "Grinding fine beefsteak into hamburger simply makes little sense."[23]

The following analysis of the tunes from Montgomery's last LP illustrates the extent of his over-use of octaves, sadly at the expense of abandoning the single-line, octave, chords formula which had, a few years earlier, firmly established him as one of the great jazz improvisers.

WES MONTGOMERY: ROAD SONG
A + M (CTI) AMLS 927

Side 1

1. **Road Song**
Chord vamp introduction.
Tune in octaves with rhythm chord fills between each statement.
One chorus of improvisation in octaves.
Chord vamp under full orchestra for a chorus (chords more exposed in the middle eight).
Return of full statement of the tune in octaves.

2. **Greensleeves**
Baroque style orchestral introduction.
Tune in octaves.
Three choruses of improvisation in octaves.
Tune twice in octaves.
Orchestral coda in baroque style.

3. **Fly Me to the Moon**
Orchestral introduction in baroque style.
Tune twice in octaves.
Three choruses of improvisation in octaves.
Tune twice in octaves.
Orchestral coda in baroque style.

4. **Yesterday**
Baroque style orchestral introduction.
Complete tune in octaves.
Half a chorus of improvisation in octaves.
Orchestral middle eight.
Tune in octaves.

5. **I'll be Back**
Tune in octaves (twice).

Chorus of improvisation in octaves.
Tune in octaves.

Side 2

1. **Scarborough Fair**

Tune in octaves.
Orchestral statement of tune in baroque contrapuntal style.
Improvisation in octaves over ostinato pattern.
Fade.

2. **Green Leaves of Summer**

Orchestral introduction in baroque style.
Tune in octaves.
Improvisation in octaves (two choruses).
Orchestral middle eight, punctuated with octaves.
Tune in octaves leading to octave improvisation over ostinato and fade out.

3. **Serene**

Chord melody introduction.
Tune in octaves (twice).
Orchestral fill.
Tune in chords.
Chord melody coda.

4. **Where Have All the Flowers Gone?**

Orchestral introduction (quote from Haydn's St Anthony Choral).
Tune in octaves (twice).
Orchestral fill.
Improvisation in octaves.
Orchestral ostinato (quote from Haydn), with improvised octave punctuations.
Fade.

His use of octaves were, at their best, part of a beautiful improvisational structure and, at their worst, a timbre of sound for blatent commercial exploitation. As we have previously seen in a discussion of Wes' commercial success he, like most other musicians, needed to earn a living, not only for himself but for a wife and seven children, and in no way did he ever feel that by playing in octaves he was compromising his art, indeed was he? The georgeous sound was there, the inexplicable good taste was there, even the overall magic and appeal was there, but alas the ideas were subdued and the extended improvisations gone. As a result, Wes lost one audience and gained another!

To cover new ground on any instrument requires determination and perserverance and Wes' philosophy of 'You only take off it what you put in'[24] tells us that beneath the flowing style was a technique dearly bought. Wes, like all great musicians, had a technique so completely integrated with his musical concept that one was under the impression that everything he did was easy. He would never parade his facility, he was too much of a self-effacing person to consider doing so even for a moment. He was therefore never considered primarily as a guitar technician. John Etheridge wrote in his Guitar Magazine series Electric Guitar Greats (Oct. 1980 No. 4).

> "... He was no slick technician on the instrument, rather a true virtuoso, possessing all the tools needed to do the job and no excess baggage."

Indeed it would be very easy to draw parallels in this respect between the work of Wes and that of the younger jazz guitarist Pat Metheny.

An uncredited Guitar Player feature from October 1968 gives us an indication of Wes' exhausting and intensive application to the mastery of his instrument:

> "Methodically, patiently, painfully he laboured on his guitar, humiliated by it's complexity and angered by his inability to respond to the harmonic patterns within his mind ... He missed no opportunities to observe any local or touring bands providing the instrumentation included a guitar, and his concentration was always on the hands of the guitarist to the exclusion of all others. It was the neck of the guitar he told himself, the secret was in the neck. He studied for eight months with supressed intensity, determined to justify his purchase."[25]

Wes wanted to play the guitar to express the sounds that he could hear inside his head, it was never his intention to become a hot player and seek fame through meaningless displays of guitar pyrotechnics. Jimmy Stewart, who collaborated with Wes in writing the Wes Montgomery Jazz Guitar Method, wrote in the preface to the work:

> "Wes worked from the inside outward. His problem was to express the sounds he already heard, and therein lay his uniqueness" ...[26]

The most striking aspect of the sound that Wes transferred from his head to his instrument was his manner of obtaining it, with the thumb. Jazz guitarists usually use a plectrum which is moved up and down across the strings to achieve rapid horn-like streams of notes. Amazingly Wes was somehow able to obtain the same results using the fleshy part of his right-hand thumb, much to the astonishment of his peers. The late George Barnes (1921-77) a fellow jazz guitarist commented:

> "I watched him in amazement, he strokes both up and down with it. Not only that, he can play a fast tremelo (extremely rapid note repitition) with it."

As a gesture of respect and esteem Jim Hall, already an established jazz guitarist himself, half jokingly said,

> "I spent an entire afternoon in San Fransisco trying to catch Wes' thumb in a car door."

That well known observer and analyst of guitarists' techniques John Duarte, wrote in an article about

Wes' thumb in BMG Magazine (June 1965) shortly after the guitarists appearance at Ronnie Scott's (England).

> "The famous right-hand thumb is fairly long (it is just as 'curly' as Segovia's) the tip joint is comparatively long and the root of the thumb is farther then average from the hand. Throughout single note passages and in much of his octave and chord work, the fingers are spread (virtually flat) over the scratch plate resting lightly on the edge of the plate on the guitar beyond. They are not rivetted in position but they move in a limited way. Single notes receive only downward strokes of the thumb, though chords and octaves are played in both directions – but only when velocity demands it ...
>
> The action of striking is a curiously mixed one. It bears a superficial resemblance to the classic guitarists apoyando, the supported stroke, in which the thumb is pushed through so it comes to rest against the next string. The thumb operates with the tip joint in a plane almost parallel to that of the strings, so it is the fleshy side that meets the string rather than the nail ..."

Wes became affectionately known as the 'Thumb' to his friends and fellow guitarists, and the use of the right-hand thumb has since become an accepted supplement to the standard norm of jazz guitar technique. George Benson, Joe Pass, Jimmy Ponder, Les Spann and Jim Mullen are just a few of today's guitarists who are using the thumb technique alongside more traditional methods.

> "What Montgomery brought to the legend and the literature of the guitar is by now so fully incorporated into the body of jazz language that it is difficult to realize the force of its initial impact. But his relatively brief career left a mark comparable to that of Charlie Christian and Django Reinhardt on virtually all guitarists who came after him."[27]

It could even be argued that besides the octaves the main reason for Wes' enormous popularity was the warm sensual timbre produced by the thumb.

Playing with the thumb was not however an exclusive Wes Montgomery discovery. We know that acoustic guitarist Teddy Bunn (1909-1978) sometimes improvised using the right-thumb in a 1930s group, Spirits of Rhythm, it is also highly probable that a few negro blues guitarists/singers used this technique as far back as the 1920s. Wes, of course, usually told the story which was written earlier in this chapter to account for his adoption of the thumb technique, but the story he related to Ralph Gleason in a 1961 Downbeat interview seems far more likely:

> "I didn't like the sound of the pick, I tried it for I guess, about two months. I didn't even use my thumb at all. So I said "Well, which are you going to do?" I liked the tone better with the thumb ..."[28]

The fact is, Wes just couldn't get on with the pick at all, he often remarked that it felt awkward and clumsy and that he was forever dropping it. He somehow felt that the thumb brought him into closer contact with the instrument, and, as we have seen he liked the fullness and warmth of tone produced by the thumb far more than the harder percussive sound of the pick. Preferring the sound of the thumb and not knowing that he was not supposed to use it exclusively Wes decided to pursue this technique and make it his own, totally unaware of the notion that he was breaking new ground.

It seems incredible that the two facets of the Montgomery style, octaves and the use of the thumb, were initially developed by trial and error and not through a conscious act. Certainly, in Wes' case, a lack of guidance contributed much to the formation of a totally unique style, a lesser talent would probably never have got off the ground given similar circumstances.

We know that Wes' instrumental facility stemmed from the need to play which was instilled in him through his early influences. Of these influences the guitarist, Charlie Christian, at that time playing electric guitar (one of the first) with the Benny Goodman band, was undoubtedly the most important: Wes wrote in the introduction of his Guitar Method:

> "In every museum throughout the world you will find aspiring painters patiently copying the masters. Similarly, young musicians play records of their favourite musicians in order to absorb techniques and personal expressions. For example, when I first started to play, I wore out parts of Charlie Christian's recordings."[29]

When asked what initially attracted him to jazz guitar playing Wes replied:

> "'Charlie Christian, like all other guitar players.' There was no way out. That cat tore everybody's head up. I never saw him in my life, but he said so much on records ... 'Solo Flight', boy that was too much, I still hear it. He was IT for me."[30]

Wes also made similar comments to the jazz critic Max Jones in a 1960s *Melody Maker*.

> "I never planned to be a musician, had no thought of doing that, Charlie Christian was my inspiration. I heard his 'Solo Flight' (with Benny Goodman in 1943) and something about it made an impression. I should explain that I wasn't buying records at the time and wasn't exposed to jazz. I went to dances like any young man, but that was all. But when you hear something that sounds good you want to hear it over, and that happened to me with 'Solo Flight'. And when you hear it over and it still sounds good, you want to make something like it. So I thought 'Why not?' ... I had nothing but time, so I bought a guitar and started teaching myself."[31]

The following is an extract from Charlie Christian's monumental guitar solo from the 1941 Benny

Goodman Band recording of 'Solo Flight', a major influence on Wes Montgomery.

Charlie Christian obviously had a tremendous impact but nevertheless Wes did not remain impervious to his surroundings. Although Christian provided the early inspiration to play jazz guitar, Wes obviously had his own ideas about improvising, hearing complex melodic lines and harmonies in his mind, many of which were logical extensions of the Christian solos he had already mastered. Only a few months after Wes had had his initial encounter with Charlie Christian he learnt all of the recorded solos note for note and it soon became apparent that he couldn't copy his mentor forever.

Fired with enthusiasm for his instrument and wanting desperately to improve his playing Wes contacted Alex Stevens who was in Wes' own words "the toughest cat I had heard around our vicinity" for lessons. Fortunately, as it turned out, Wes was unable to obtain his services and was left to master the guitar though trial and error, listening to records and watching every jazz guitarist that passed through Indianapolis.

By that time Wes had heard Django Reinhardt, Les Paul and an obscure guitar player from Chicago, George Henry, who was the first person he had heard playing Charlie Parker's be-bop concepts on the guitar. Throughout his entire playing career Wes was an indiscriminate listener who enjoyed pianists and horn players as much as he did guitarists.

Later on John Coltrane became an important influence:

"John Coltrane has been a sort of God to me"

he once remarked. Miles Davis and the great ballad singers, Sinatra, Nat Cole and Tony Bennett were also significant influences.

Many of Wes' Verve recordings display a tender lyricism which is more usually associated with ballad singers, the tune 'People' from the album 'Movin' Wes' is a fine example of this.

Miles Davis and John Coltrane influences are particularly discernable in the up tempo tunes like 'Tear it Down' (Bumpin') and 'Impressions' (Willow Weep for Me).

It would be extremely difficult if not impossible to pin down Wes' influences more specifically, for he was a very open-minded person both about music and life in general. His two years with the Lionel Hampton band, rubbing shoulders with seasoned performers like Fats Navarro, Charlie Mingus and Milt Bruckner, had to have a maturing effect on his playing, as did his sojourn on the road with the Brownskin Models and Snookum Russell. Wes was a highly perceptive individual, his assessments of other musicians were remarkably discerning and accurate, he may have fashioned his playing style from an ignorance of technical know-how, but he was acutely aware of what was going on musically in the jazz world.

Steven Khan summed this up nicely in his sleeve notes for Groove Brothers:

"Wes had big ears and an open mind, and it seemed to me that he never stopped growing."

When asked by Ralph J. Gleason to name his half-dozen favourite guitarists Wes replied:

"Barney Kessel is one. He's got a lot of feeling, he's got a good conception of chords in a jazz manner. And he's trying to play a little flamenco. He's trying to do a lot of things, not just standing still at one particular level. He's trying to get away from the guitar phrase, to get into the horn phrase. Tal Farlow strikes me as a different cat altogether. To me, he doesn't have as much feel as Barney Kessel, but he's got more drive in his playing, and his technique along with his drive is pretty exciting. And he's got a better conception of modern chords than the average guitar player. Sometimes he gets kind of sloppy like a lot of guitar players, that's why a lot of cats have put him down. But I guess nobody has got it all, but he's got a lot of *drive,* though, and he's fast. Now, Jimmy Raney is just the opposite of Tal Farlow. It seems like they have the same ideas, the same changes, the same type runs, the same kind of feeling, but Jimmy Raney is so smooth he does it without a mistake, a real soft touch, it's the touch he's got."[32]

Wes' style was a culmination of all he had heard through the years, a unique playing technique, infallible good taste and lots of gigs!

Although he was aware of what was happening musically on the jazz guitar scene, by today's standards he was never really very equipment minded, though he did have a lot of trouble finding a suitable amplifier. Wes alternated between Standel transistor and Fender valve (tube) amplifiers, though he was never quite satisfied with either, Rudy Van Gelder kept an old Fender Deluxe amplifier permanently in the New Jersey studios where Wes recorded his albums for Creed Taylor, and it is probable that Wes used it exclusively on those recordings. He was constantly complaining about amplifiers. The comment he made to Ralph J.

Gleason in a *Downbeat* interview (July 1965) was a typical overture of his dissatisfaction:

> "I think every instrument should have a certain amount of tone-quality within the instrument, but I can't seem to get the right amplifier ..."

Serene recalls:

> "Wes was always burning up his amplifiers, he had a room full of those things."

Fortunately Wes had better luck with his guitars. He was a Gibson man through and through, favouring the L5 CES (Cutaway Electric Spanish) model. Some early publicity photographs show him playing an L4 with a Charlie Christian bar pick up, others show him with a 175D and a 125D. As early as 1960 Wes was shown in a *Downbeat* Gibson advertisement endorsing an L5 CES, the instrument he was to adopt and use exclusively for the remainder of his career. If the LP sleeves and the publicity photographs give an accurate indication of Wes' collection of L5s he must have had at least six:

1. Pre 1958, Venetian cutaway with Alnico pick ups ('Pretty Blue' Milestone 47030).[33]

2. 1958/60 Sunburst, Venetian cutaway with PAF humbucking pick ups ('A portrait of Wes Montgomery Pacific Jazz' Milestones Series ST 20137).[34]

3. 1958/60 Blonde, Venetian cutaway with PAF humbucking pick ups ('Wes and Friends', Milestone Double M-47013).

4. Early 60s Sunburst, Florentine cutaway with PAF humbucking pick ups ('Movin' Wes' Verve 2304 377).

5. Mid-sixties Sunburst, Venetian cutaway with one humbucking pick up. A custom built L5 with a diamond and the name Wes Montgomery inlaid in mother of pearl beneath the scratch plate (where the three way toggle switch is usually situated). ('Wes Montgomery Jazz Guitar Method'.)*

6. Mid-sixties Sunburst, Venetian cutaway with one humbucking pick up. Another custom built L5 with a mother of pearl heart fingerest inlaid beneath the scratch plate (name running vertically through it). The Genius of Wes Montgomery box set.)

Wes strung his L5s with Gibson HiFi, flatwound strings, gauges:

String	Gauge
E	.014
B	.018
G	.025 wd.
D	.035
A	.045
E	.058

With the exception of two single pick up L5s all of Wes' guitars were standard stock production line models with no modification whatsoever. The two single pick up models were custom built to his requirements and besides the pearl inlays they differed from standard in two ways. Firstly, they had one humbucking pick up instead of the usual two, and secondly, these pick ups were mounted back-to-front (pole pieces on bridge side of the pick up instead of the usual neck side). Whether Wes requested this or whether it was a construction oversight is not known.

The use of the thumb coupled with heavy gauge, flatwound strings on a deep body guitar would almost certainly produce a very mellow bassy tone. By turning the pick ups round, the pole pieces (six string screws in the face of the metal) would be nearer to the bridge of the guitar resulting in a much brighter sound. It seems likely that Wes either specially requested this or turned them round himself to compensate for the bassy sound of the thumb and to achieve the full yet biting sound for which he was famous.

To enhance this incisive yet full and throaty sound Wes used metal 'tune-o-matic'[35] bridges on all his guitars. During the sixties the purchaser of the Gibson L5 CES had the choice of two types of guitar bridge, a standard wooden one (usually ebony or rosewood), or a metal 'tune-o-matic'. Although the difference in sound produced by these two bridges was small, there was a perceivable difference.

Wooden bridges were used traditionally for unamplified instruments producing a lot of volume and, characteristically, a woody tone, whilst the newer metal bridge, designed specifically as an aid to intonation, produced a brighter, thinner and quieter sound. Amplification, of course, had long negated the need for a wooden bridge but, although wooden bridges were notoriously poor for accurate tuning, jazz guitarists continued to use them. Under these circumstances it is interesting to observe that Wes employed the new type of guitar bridge on all of his instruments.

Apart from these minor but interesting modifications, he preferred not to customize his guitars:

> "I got a standard box – I don't never want nothing special. Then, if I drop my box, I can borrow somebody else's"[36]

Although he never really became too involved with the new developments in electronics or instrument technology he was an excellent observer and once

---

*This instrument is currently on display at The Children's Museum, Indianapolis. Courtesy of Serene Montgomery Woods.

remarked "Nothing new gets by unnoticed". He remained to the end a straight 'no gimmicks' player, conservative about electronics at a time when fuzz boxes, echo chambers, feedback and other divices were rapidly gaining popularity.

When he decided to use an electronic effect, as he did on 'Portrait of Jennie' and 'Oh You Crazy Moon' ('Willow Weep for Me', Verve Select 2317 023) or 'Round Midnight' ('Kings of the Guitar', Beppo BE KOG 14800), it was with impeccable taste and timing.

Of the effects available at that time Wes had a particular fondness for a combination of reverb and tremelo, devices which were standard additions to both Fender and Standel amplifiers. These effects, used in tandem, produced a swirling dreamlike effect not unlike vibes or the rotating Leslie speaker. Wes particularly liked this combination for ballads, an excellent example can be heard in the Beppo recording of 'Round Midnight', where he used tremelo and reverb (together) with tremendous effect by judiciously adding it only to the initial and final statements of the tune, switching to a straight guitar sound for the improvised choruses in between (these effects can be turned on and off quickly by means of a footswitch).

Wes would only switch on these effects when it was appropriate to do so, he instinctively chose the right moment to enhance the music; for the theme of a ballad, the chord solo of a medium tempo tune, unaccompanied introductions and endings, in short whenever it would add something positive and meaningful.

Although there is no doubt that Wes' tasteful use of electronic effects did enhance the music, he did not use them habitually, out of four recorded versions of Thelonious Monk's tune 'Round Midnight' two are played with effects ('Kings of the Guitar' and 'Live at Jorgies and More', VGM 0088) and two without ('Solitude', Affinity AFF18 and 'Wes Montgomery Trio', Riverside RLP1156) which demonstrates that Wes followed his intuition with the use of effects much as he did for the rest of his playing. In every event Wes' playing was never predictable, using the same effect for the same tune over and over was just not his style.

The unique manner of Wes' playing (thumb and octaves) has unfortunately tended to overshadow the other aspects of his playing, particularly his innovative approach to chords. He was extremely inventive with his chords, but his voicings were so tasteful and appropriate that their beauty was not immediately noticeable, particularly on first hearing.

Good music yields more rewards with each renewed listening, the subtleties and mysteries unravel a little further each time, this is particularly true of Wes' chord playing.

It requires concentration and an appreciative ear to follow. During the late forties and early fifties several guitarists made major advances in chord playing techniques. Of the electric guitarists Barney Kessel showed us how to play melodies in chords like a pianist, Johnny Smith demonstrated the beauty and usefulness of close harmony chords (and long stretches) whilst Tal Farlow went on to demonstrate the tremendous effect of moving voices within chords, whilst comping.

Wes had latched on to all of these methods, taking the best ideas from each. He tended to favour chords built on the first three or four strings of the guitar and had a special way of voicing the chords of a specific chord family (i.e, Major 7th or Minor 7th) to create tension.

The following examples illustrate the type of sequence that Wes used for comping over a static Minor Seventh harmonic situation.*

These short progressions or vamps were quite new and innovative to guitarists at that time, though pianists had used them for some years, particularly those pianists who had passed through the Miles Davis groups and we know Wes was a devoted Miles Davis dedicatee. In the late forties and early fifties, Wes' formative years, guitarists were by and large either following Freddie Green's (Count Basie) example of four-to-the-bar rhythm guitar, or Tal Farlow's close harmony moving-voices concept.

Wes' style contained elements of Tal's 'moving-voices' approach whilst allowing for a greater freedom of pitch. His chord shapes were more detached than Farlow's and no longer required to stay under-the-hand, and in one area of the guitar

---

*See Appendix[3] for further selection of Wes' favourite chord shapes.

fingerboard to make the voicings follow one another.

In true Montgomery tradition Wes would change from biting four string chords to lush six string ones with chameleon-like rapidity and could produce beautiful chord melody arrangements using the entire range of the guitar. While We're Young, from the album 'So Much Guitar' (Riverside RLP 9382) is a beautiful example of Wes using the complete range of his instrument demonstrating his mastery of the chord melody style, a style with which he was not generally associated but could deliver with eloquence.

Wes' chord playing asserted quite an influence on the next generation of guitar players. His use of simple yet fresh sounding chord shapes appealed to the young jazz players who were looking for something a little different and more up to date.

Many of the day's established players like Jim Hall, Kenny Burrell and later on George Benson also absorbed elements of his chordal style, particularly the simple, yet refreshing use of the diminished seventh chord.

Like his chord playing, Wes' single-line work had long been overshadowed by the use of octaves, but he was nevertheless one of the few guitarists to keep pace with the horn players. He had followed and absorbed the modal experiments of trumpeter Miles Davis and had learnt the art of side-slipping, momentarily playing outside of the chord changes, from saxophonist John Coltrane. He felt that Coltrane was the only coloured player with the technical facility of the great white classical musicians and greatly admired his work:

> "There is only one coloured musician with that facility and that's Coltrane. I have listened to him a lot and I'm sure of it. I even took his album 'Giant Steps', and played it an 16 rpm to study what he was doing and every note he hit was correct. I think he is greater than Charlie Parker in this respect because Bird died before he could finish what he was doing. But Trane has had the time and opportunity and he is the only one with that facility.[37]

He also listened to tenor saxophonist Sonny Rollins, whose concept of thematic development he liked and used in some of his solos. These influences converged to make Wes one of the most up-to-date single-line players of his day.

His lines were more horn-like than guitaristic because he did not play off chord shapes or scales. Although his single-line playing was agile, his technique was, in conventional terms, sloppy and undisciplined. While he had no rationalised positional approach to the guitar finger-board, he was able to play everything he wanted to, finding his notes wherever convenient. Despite its clumsiness, this technique helped him to avoid cliches and set finger patterns.

Wes was not really concerned about his playing technique and felt that had he tried to correct it, he would have lost everything he had already achieved, though he did show some insecurity when questioned about the learning of new guitar techniques "I figure before I start on anything else I have to clean this one up and that's got a long way to go".[38] Though he sometimes felt insecure about his technique he brushed this aside, reasoning that coloured musicians seldom had the technical facility of the 'schooled' white players, though they did have a lot of feeling.

> "The ofay cat has the technical facility and the Negro has the feeling for jazz. But take an instrument like guitar. In every part of the world white cats would pick it up 500 or 600 years ago and they had all that time to get ready. The Negro had to wait for it to be dropped in his lap 50 years ago but after a while he was playing it and getting a whole lot of feeling out of it. But he couldn't get that technical facility. And in fact, I've never heard a coloured guitar player who could come up to the technical standard of some of the great white guitarists. For that reason I don't bother too much about the technical side of the guitar. I just concentrate on feeling."[39]

Wes once told a reviewer (John Duarte),

> "I don't practise at all. If I can do it, I don't need to practice it. If I can't do it I ain't risking it!"[40]

What Wes Mongtomery did was enough to influence an entire generation of guitar players.

GUITARISTICALLY SPEAKING
1. The Wes Montgomery Guitar Folio – Steve Khan, Gopan Enterprises 1978.
2. Wes Montgomery 1925-1968, a rare unpublished interview with Ralph J. Gleason, *Guitar Player* July/August 1973.
3. Jimmy Stewart – Bill Lee, *Guitar Player* December 1970.
4. The Guitar Players, One Instrument and It's Masters in American Music, James Sallis, Quill Publications, New York 1982.
5. Wes Montgomery by Jack Duarte, *B M G Magazine*, June 1962, Vol. LIX, No. 686.
6. Crossover Crusader – A rare interview with Creed Taylor and Mike Hennessy, *Jazz Journal International*, November 1979, Vol. 32, No. 11.
7. Wes Montgomery, Groove Brothers – Sleevenotes by Steve Khan, Milestone Stereo M-47051, 1974.
8. Ivor Mairants, My Fifty Fretting Years – Ashley Mark Publishing ISBN 0 9506224 3 5.
9. Interview with the author – April 1984, Indianapolis.
10. Max Jones, *Melody Maker*, 3 April, 1965.
11. Wes Montgomery by Jack Duarte – *B M G Magazine*, pp 325, July 1965.
12. The Last Words of a Great Jazzman – Wes Montgomery – an interview with Les Tomkins, *Crescendo, July 1968*.
13. Howard Robert's Binary Bag – Harvey Siders, *Downbeat*, 11th Annual Guitar Issue, 29 June 1967.
14. The Alternative Wes Montgomery, 14 Previously Un-issued Takes – Milestone C A 94710, 1982.

15. Jazz at Ronnie Scott's – Kitty Grime, Robert Hale Ltd., 1979, ISBN 0 7091 6907 8.
16. Jazz Review – Gunther Sculler.
17. The Thumb's Up or What the View is Like from the Top – Bill Quinn, *Downbeat Annual Guitar Issue*, 27 June 1968.
18. Interview with Jim Rockwell during a 1968 TV appearance in Detroit – Live at Jorgies and More, Vol. 2, *VGM*, 008.
19. Stephane Grapelli's Hot Four – Decca F-5824 Recorded 21 October 1935.
20. Wes Montgomery 1925-1968 (see 2).
21. Wes Montgomery, Blindfold Test, Leonard Feather – *Downbeat 11th Annual Guitar Issue*, 29 June 1967.
22. A Genius of Jazz Guitar – Les Tomkins, *Crescendo Magazine*, July 1968.
23. The Guitar Players – James Sallis (see 4).
24, 25. The Memorable Montgomery – *Guitar Player*, October 1968, Vol. 2, No. 5.
26. The Wes Montgomery Guitar Method – Robbins Music Corporation, New York 1968.
27. Wes Montgomery, Movin' – Sleevenotes by Maggie Hawthorn, Milestone double LP – 47040, 1977.
28. Wes Montgomery by Ralph J Gleason – *Downbeat* 20 July 1961.
29. A Word from Wes – Montgomery Guitar Method (see 26).
30. Wes Montgomery 1925-1968 (see 2 and 20).
31. Max Jones interview with Wes Montgomery – *Melody Maker* 1965.
32. Wes Montgomery 1925-1968 (see 2, 20 and 30).
33. Circa 1953 Gibson engineers Seth Lover and Walt Fuller developed a new pick-up known today as the 'Alnico' because of its six oblong alnico magnets placed directly beneath the strings. The alnico was more powerful and responsive than its predecessor the P90 and was therefore only used on top quality instruments.
34. PAF pick-ups were fitted as standard to Gibson electric guitars between 1957 (late) and 1962 (early). PAF is a simple abbreviation for Patent Applied For.
35. The Tune-O-Matic bridge was developed at Gibson by Ted MacCarthy in 1953. The bridge had six adjustable string saddles which enable the pitch of the string to be raised or lowered offering greater accuracy for intonation. The Tune-O-Matic bridge was fitted on certain Gibson guitars from 1957 onwards.
36. Guitar Discussion – Wes Montgomery, Jack Duarte, Ike Isaacs and Cedric West *Crescendo Magazine* – July 1965.
37-39. Wes Montgomery talks to Valerie Wilmer – Musicians Talking – *Jazz Monthly* – May 1965.
40. Wes Montgomery by Jack Duarte – *BMC Magazine* – August 1965.

Wes Montgomery Swimming Pool, Indianapolis.

PHOTO: DR LEO HARPER

IMPRESSIONS

Cedric West and Wes Montgomery.

IMPRESSIONS

Music is the least tangible of all the art forms, it affects each of us in a variety of ways and the emotion imparted during a musical performance can convey something entirely different to each individual. As a result of this, a phenomenon associated specifically with expression in musical performance, it is possible for the listener or the critic to react by grossly over-stating the case, spicing comments with highly subjective value-judgements and superlatives. Of course, it would be extremely easy to do so myself, for Wes Montgomery has not only been a personal inspiration but a spiritual influence.

Therefore, my writing within these covers will be inevitably biased, though my primary aim has been to provide empirical evidence where possible to substantiate the work and to allow for a certain element of objectivity. To introduce an even greater degree of impartiality into the book I have for this chapter collected and collated a series of impressions of Wes Montgomery from friends, critics, musicians, relatives and admirers.

The contents of this chapter are therefore intended to provide an unbiased celebration of the man and his music, a tribute which should give some insights into Wes' character, personality and musical conception. For the most part, the contributors have met Wes at some time or another and are therefore contributing to the chapter with a knowledge and authority of Wes' aura, charm and humility.

Other guitarists are perhaps the most privileged of the Montgomery connoisseurs as they are in the enviable position of being able to assess the man's contribution not only to jazz, but also to the development of the electric guitar as a jazz instrument, therefore many of the contributions are from guitar players.

One of my greatest regrets is that whilst playing guitar in a Soul band during the nineteen-sixties I, for reasons which escape me, foolishly missed attending one of Wes' engagements at the Ronnie Scott Club. To compensate for that misfortune I will begin the chapter with some impressions from British musicians and admirers who were lucky enough to witness Wes playing during his month at Ronnie Scott's Club.

Ray Dempsey
I'm speechless. Some of his chords were fantastic. *Everything* was fantastic.
1965[1]

Tommy Whittle
Wes has been a great favourite of mine for a long time. For me, his playing has everything. It is completely natural, logical and uncontrived. Right from his statement of the theme, it's as if a beautiful carpet of sound is being unrolled. Above all, he has a personal style which is everlasting, regardless of superfluous fashions and trends.
1965[2]

Rich Laird
(Wes' bassist at Ronnies')
It's true to call him incredible. It seems that everything he touches turns to gold. Of the guys from the States who have appeared in the Club, on any instrument, Wes generates the most *happy* feeling.

It's a lot of kicks to dig the chording he plays behind my solos. It's so *right*. Also he seems to play very much *with* the group. It's not like just a soloist out front. The quartet is working as a quartet.
1965[3]

Ronnie Stephenson
(Wes' drummer at Ronnies')
Well, you can say its bloody marvellous. It's easy — like it was working with Johnny Griffin. What I mean is: there's no worrying about which direction he's going to take. No question of trying to set a mood — he does that. You just grab hold of his coat-tails, and off you go. This is one of my most enjoyable gigs in the club.
1965[4]

George Kisch
He's a bloody genius. This is something we've never heard before, and are not likely to hear for the next twenty years. His timing is fantastic. So is his whole conception, the way he builds a tune. Each chorus is always better than the one before.

I think Wes is the kind of man who, had he taught himself any other instrument, would be just as brilliant.
1965[5]

Crescendo Magazine
Wes Montgomery, guitarist extraordinary, has made a powerful impact upon the London jazz scene. Down in Ronnie's we have never seen, or heard a more enthusiastic crowd — literally shouting for joy at the peaks of his performance.

Anybody looking for a good guitar player would have a choice of several in the audience any night,

often listening through all three swing-filled sets. Many of them have been so overwhelmed as to be unable to describe their feelings adequately.
May 1965

Keter Betts
He's got something that only God can give a man.
May 1965[6]

Big Jim Sullivan
With all due respect to the supporting trio – they're doing a marvellous job, but he doesn't need anybody. He could just sit there and play, and create that wonderful atmosphere all by himself.

He has such immaculate taste. He doesn't put a note wrong. There's nobody who could do what he's doing. He just plays the feeling derived from his own character and he obviously knocks himself out, as well as his audience.

I didn't think it was possible to play at that speed with his thumb, but I saw it with my own eyes.
May 1965[7]

Harry South
He's been very misrepresented on records, from the ones I've heard anyway. He's much more of a groovy down-home swinger than I realized before.

Guitar players, however good, usually haven't got the power to get across they way a horn does but Wes can do it!
1965[8]

Ronnie Scott
Wes was stocky, supremely good humoured and easy-going and a grandfather three times over, one of those rare creatures, the utterly natural musician. He played impossible things on his guitar simply because it was never pointed out to him that they were impossible.
1979[9]

John Duarte
Throughout his stay at Ronnie Scott's Wes played the language of pure Jazz. Guitar clichés were absent from his playing for the simple reason that, as wonderfully as he exploits the guitar – more than anyone else to date – he is not a guitarist, strictly speaking.

His prime motivation is that of playing jazz and he chose to apply it from the guitar – unhampered by any notions of the guitar acquired from study or through the ministrations of a teacher.

It is perhaps his music-making that is the most remarkable of his facets. So powerful is the creative urge that he thrusts past technical barriers as though they do not exist. The guitar is simply the medium for the music.

Ask any great jazz guitarist who his favourite musicians are and he will begin by citing saxophone players, followed by other wind players. He will have plenty of well-loved guitarists but the first choice will be the 'horn' players because their phrasing and expression are flexible, vocal and untrammelled by strong clichés.

Wes Montgomery is no exception.

For once, though the boot has changed feet. During Wes' stay at Ronnie Scott's Club, not only guitarists flocked to pay their homage, the wind players kept them company. Such tribute must have been rare since the death of Charlie Christian.
1965[10]

Ivor Mairants (1965)
What can one say on hearing Wes Montgomery perform at Ronnie Scott's Club? From the first moment his physical playing bursts in on you, you know you are listening to jazz, clean and uncontrived. Jazz which has life, gaiety, sparkle, rhythmic abandon and a new world of Ideas!

With the greatest respect and admiration for the other wonderful jazz guitarists who stem from the States (and including the great Django) I consider Wes Montgomery the greatest jazz guitarist up to the present time. He certainly ranks with Charlie Parker as an innovator in tone, style and technique.

This man of medium build and pleasant countenance enjoys playing and it is evident he is as excited as the listener in building up his storms of jazz extemporisation. The strength of his attack is phenomenal and I can only compare it to Oscar Peterson's similar build-ups on piano.

The simplicity and warmth in the melody line of 'I Remember You' was completely free from the nauseating effects of schmaltz and melted one's feelings in relaxed pleasure.

Montgomery does not use a plectrum but his right-hand thumb to sound the strings. He strikes in a downward direction so that his thumb rests against the next highest string, similar to an apoyando thumb stroke on the Spanish guitar. The remainder of his right hand usually rests across the pick guard.

At times he also uses up strokes, particularly when playing chords in triplets and semiquaver rhythms.

He does not use the thumb nail (which is short) but the ball of the thumb. He admires classical guitar playing and tried to grow a firm thumb nail, without success. He said "Now I'm getting older, it seems even harder to grow strong nails". Coming from Wes, this struck me as being a big joke.

His left-hand technique is also unorthodox, which hardly matters. I am stating this fact to show that exceptional people can be successful using their own particular methods. (One had but to bring to mind Django and Charlie Christian!) For runs, Wes does not use his little finger at all. He uses his little finger only for octaves wherein he has a special locked-hand technique that enables the fourth and first fingers to be used on 1st and 3rd strings (or 2nd and 4th) and the third and first fingers on the 3rd and 5th (or 4th and 6th).

For the many chord changes he plays he uses every finger with great facility which enables extreme single-finger manoeuvrability in changing semitones within the chords. Although he employs a great deal of slurring, both in single notes and octaves, I must reiterate this does not give the slightest schmaltzy effect because the finger slur is used only as an essential to jazz phrasing and for no other effect. It sound more like a legato phrase produced on the saxophone as compared to a group of tongued notes.

It is impossible to produce the Wes Montgomery sound by using a plectrum. To my ear it is the most attractive I have ever heard although in all fairness I must say that Kenny Burrell, whom I heard in New York, produced a nice fat warm note with a pick. Wes Montgomery has advanced the conception of jazz on the guitar more than any other player since the instrument has been used for jazz playing.
May 1965[11]

Ivor Mairants (1983)
The basement premises of the old Ronnie Scott's Jazz Club in Gerrard Street were packed: all the seats were taken and the rest of the floor space was covered with human beings standing body to body craning their necks for a glimpse of the miracle man with the guitar, sitting on the three foot high platform smilingly creating the sounds of 'The Incredible Guitar of Wes Montgomery'.

It was utterly amazing to hear the inventions continue chorus after chorus without resorting to repetition. Chord solos were interchanged with single string melodies which, in turn, modulated to octave acrobatics. His music seemed to flow with the freshness and vigour of a sparkling waterfall, and although we had previously marvelled at his recordings they were not eqivalent to the live performance.

His playing was so inspired and inventive that I could not refrain from mentioning to the friends around me that he was the greatest player I had ever heard. Both my impression and my opinion remain to this day.
July 1983

Richard Cobby
It was several years after becoming A 'Wes fan' that I had the opportunity of meeting him and hearing him in action at Ronnie Scott's Club.

Everything about that occasion was so memorable. His manner was relaxed and informal yet there was such melodic power created by every note and chord he played. No matter what the tempo, one couldn't help getting caught up with the spellbinding atmosphere of the music combined with watching Wes' fingers seemingly glide effortlessly over the strings of his Gibson. Every note, even in the very fast octave runs was made to be so important. This to my mind was real genius at work.

Having been so completely captured by the tremendous sound that Wes achieved, I asked him in a meeting afterwards, some details about his amplifier. This he informed me was a Standel 100 watt Custom model with a JBL 18" speaker. Several days afterwards, unable to resist the challenge of the Wes Montgomery sound I found myself in Ivor Mairants Musicentre ordering exactly the same model. Only recently was I forced to part with it and since that time the speaker cone has been rewound and it has had a new grill cover, apart from which it is still as good as new.
December 1983

Ike Isaacs
Wes visited my wife and I on a few occasions and played for us. We got to know him as a person and were really thrilled at the wonderful philosophy of music and life that he had, which was really uplifting.

My brother, who is a classical violinist came along to Ronnie Scott's Club to hear Wes play and came out of the concert saying that it was as great an experience as listening to Pablo Casals or any of the really great classical artists, the ambience and the feeling was as spiritually high and supercharged. He also remarked that the experience lingers on giving a feeling of being spiritually cleansed, which is exactly the sentiment that I endorse. Wes' playing did give you that feeling of something beautiful, his music was really a great expression of his innermost character.
Spring 1984.

Steve Khan
I'll never forget sitting on the floor with the volume turned way up and being blown away by Wes' interpretation of Duke Ellington's classic 'Caravan'. That experience literally changed my whole life by opening me up to the world of improvised instrumental music, otherwise known as jazz. I still owned a set of drums, so hearing Grady Tate on the recording was at the same time both uplifting and the final blow to my hopes of becoming a drummer. From that point on I sought out any record by Wes and anything that had Grady as the drummer, thus starting a chain reaction that led me to an

over-whelming number of great jazz names: Miles Davis, John Coltrane, Sonny Rollins, Bill Evans, Jim Hall, Grant Green Oliver Neslon ... It was an incredible period of listening and exploring, and out of all this, at the age of twenty, came the decision to try my hardest to become a jazz guitarist. Wes Montgomery, the man and his music, became the total inspiration for what I was attempting to do.[12]

Monk Montgomery

Everybody liked him, got along with him and loved to work with him. He was wonderful to be with. He wasn't only my brother, he was my best friend. We never had an argument or a fight, even working together all the time. He had a lot of humour; you'd think he could have been a comedian. Of course, we were so used to it, we didn't realise until he was gone how important it was.

Larry Coryell

I first heard Wes Montgomery on the radio around 1959 or 1960 in a broadcast on a late night jazz show out of Salt Lake City, Utah. I was living in south-eastern Washington State at the time. I don't remember much about what I heard at the time except it sounded mellow and comforting.

I moved to Seattle, Washington in 1961 to attend university and shortly after that the Montgomery Brothers group came to play a club called the Penthouse. I had bought some of Wes' records by this time and tried to learn some of his solos: 'D Major Blues' (or was it Blues in D?) and 'West Coast Blues'; this was the best jazz guitar playing I had ever listened to. He seemed more modern than the other guitarists playing at that time.

When I saw him play I was impressed with his right thumb; I was floored by how it seemed to shine. I followed him down the street after the gig that night and called out the changes to 'West Coast Blues' and asked him if that was correct, and he seemed to like me or, to put it better, to put up with me. Then I stowed away on a boat cruise that he took on his day off and hounded him the whole time, asking him questions. He was self-effacing. Modest. Said he used to play better when he lived in Indianapolis. He was a humble man. Very kind. He asked me to bring up my guitar just before the boat docked and I played his solo from 'West Coast Blues' up to the octaves. Then he took my guitar and my pick and played a little bit with a pick. He shared with me that he thought his soon to be released record ('Full House') was his best recorded work to date.

Later on when he 'went commercial' we met again in New York at Rudy Van Gelder's studio. My hair was extremely long at that point, but he still remembered me from Seattle. Little did I know that his career was ending. This was in 1966.

In 1967 we were touring together for George Wein and we sat together on a plane flight to North Carolina and he told me how much he liked my work on a Don Sebesky record. To get a blessing from him was "The Ultimate".

There will never be another musician like Wes Montgomery. Non-guitarists (piano players, horn players, etc) liked his octaves the best of all his musical talents. He was melodic and steeped in the blues. I see now how he carried on the Charlie Christian legacy. His music was like his personality; warm, happy and humble. His records sound fantastic today. I gigged in Indianapolis and talked with some of the people who saw him when he was a 'local'. The extent to which his artistry holds up today is amazing. I hope I can accomplish one-tenth of what he did with the guitar. He was truly one of the greatest jazz musicians who ever lived and by far the most important jazz guitarist of his generation.

I loved Wes. I miss him.
July 1983

Joe Pass

First let me say, to me Wes was an honest and natural jazz musician and my favourite player – not only because of his unique octave style, but because everything he played was improvised and swung and was jazz all the way. I found him to be a quiet and shy person.

We visited one time – he came to dinner and we talked at that time, maybe six months or so before he died, he was complaining about his travelling around for the record company – or his management – because of the hit record he had. I remember he said he didn't play or jam in the day time, so he could save all of his playing for the gig and not leave it in his hotel room.

My impression of Wes as a player was that he put himself into his music and the guitar was just an extension of him and he worked very hard when he played, I mean emotionally and it took a lot out of his physical self.

To me he was the Best of the jazz guitar players.
October 1984

Barney Kessel

He really did seem to be a warm person, he played mostly by feeling and instinct, he was not really a scholar in terms of working on things the way a student might, but he was a student in that he was always interested and curious. I think, really, the feeling that he perpetrated was the best thing about his playing, his 'groove', whereas some people are really a fountain-head with a different harmonic approach, or they're different because they're actually playing different kinds of material.

I think that with Wes it was not that what he was doing was really that new, it was the fact that he was playing these things, lines with octaves, with a warmth and swing. Also Wes had a very high expectation of himself and would not put things out that didn't come up to a certain standard.

I did not meet him many times in my life, but I once loaned him a guitar for a date that he did for Pacific Jazz with his brothers when they were called the Mastersounds, that's when I first met him. He was a very warm, very nice guy. Although I didn't see him many times, whenever I did I felt the warmth and sincerity of him.

At one time, I was on the road and I mentioned that I came through just to hear him. He and his brothers were playing some place in California and he said "Where's your guitar, Barney?" I said "It's in the car" and he said "Why don't you come play it?" and I said "No" and they just absolutely would not accept that I wasn't going to play, so they just went out to the car, the three of them, and carried my guitar in, and that was the only time I ever played with Wes, though I have played with his brothers, Buddy and Monk on many occasions since.
November 1983

Herb Ellis

I never got to play with Wes, but I met him and he was a splendid gentleman, a devoted player and a very warm guy. He was a lovely man, as was his playing and for the short time that he was around I really liked him. I loved that sound that he got from using his thumb and would have played that way myself but by the time I heard him it was too late to re-vamp my own playing though I did try to emulate his sound on my Verve LP 'Thank You Charlie Christian', and I also experimented for a time with a felt pick.

Wes, I have nothing but great things to say about him.
May 1984[14]

Movin' Wes

I first heard Wes when I was fourteen. I had been playing the guitar for two years and had recently discovered Django, Merle Travis, Chet Atkins, Segovia and B B King. When a guitar playing friend told me he had just heard a guitarist called Wes Montgomery on the radio (Alan Dell show I think) playing a tune called 'Caravan' using his thumb instead of a plectrum!

Having an insatiable curiosity about anything to do with the guitar and its players I immediately rushed to the local shop to order a Wes Montgomery record with 'Caravan' on it. Four weeks later my record 'Movin' Wes' arrived, though it was a week later before my paper round had yielded enough money for me to pay for it. I rushed home to play it. The first experience of hearing the thrill of Wes' spine tingling improvisations, his sumptuous tone and the magical shape and direction of his choruses is still with me now and after almost twenty years 'Movin' Wes' remains to me the ultimate all round guitar album (I'm on my third copy).
Adrian Ingram, 1983

Kevin Eubanks

It's impossible to put into words what Wes' playing means to me, I can't describe the feel that he has and the effect it has on me, it's incredible, he really was an amazing guitarist.

People talk a lot about guitar technique, especially playing fast, but Wes had it all, octaves, chord solos, single line, everything.

His solos were beautifully constructed and that's something that you can't learn, it has to come from inside. Wes' playing was warm and instinctive.

His solos reminded me of J. J. Johnson's (trombone), beautiful playing.

I've spoken with my buddy, guitarist Ted Dunbar who was quite tight with Wes and he said that Wes' agents had him rushing everywhere and working so hard that he was thinking of quitting just before he died. Ted thinks that his heavy schedule probably contributed to his heart attack.

There really isn't anyone playing jazz guitar like Wes today but if you sit down with George Benson and get him to play some jazz, a standard or something he comes pretty close. There aren't many players like those cats around!
November 1983

Robert Yelin

In July of 1964, I went down to one of New York's most famous jazz nightclubs, the Half-Note, to see the Wes Montgomery trio. I had been playing guitar for nearly five years and was a slowly, budding jazz guitarist. Wes was one of my favourite jazz guitarists and one I had never seen play before I was really excited about meeting him and seeing him play. (This was before his great popularity brought on by his 'commercial' albums for Verve and A & M Records).

One reason for going to see jazz guitarists play is to cop some runs and chords. Wes' playing was so unique that I couldn't copy anything he played. I could play some octave lines but nothing as intricate or as well executed as Wes.

Two things really stick in my mind when I think back to my conversations with Wes. I complimented him on his gorgeous playing on an album he recorded for Riverside called, 'Fusion'. This was a recording with a large orchestra with beautiful arrangements by Jimmy Jones. The album was comprised of mostly ballads. Because the album only received 2½ stars in a *Downbeat* record review, Wes told me he was never going to record ballads again! (The highest rating for a record in *Downbeat* is five stars.)

One of the things that most young jazz guitarists get caught up in is wanting to know what kind of guitar the famous jazz guitarists use. When I saw Wes, I noticed he was playing a Gibson L-5 model electric guitar ... no small coincidence ... it was just like mine ... and Kenny Burrell's too! (Kenny has the bar pickup, though ... Wes and I had the humbuckers). I complimented Wes on his guitar, the strings, the action and the great sound he got from his favourite amp, a Fender Twin Reverb. When I asked Wes this question, "Do you pick every note with your thumb or do you slur more than one note with each picking stroke of your thumb?" Wes replied, "How would you like it if you had a large family to take care of and someone snuck up behind you and kicked the stool out from under your ass!" Wes, then smiled. What he was really saying was that he wasn't going to give out the technical knowhow of how he plays For good reasons, he was afraid of having other good jazz guitarists playing his style and taking his popularity and work away.

Though Wes was a one-of-a-kind, consumate jazz guitarist, he showed a great deal of insecurity in his playing seen by his reaction to the *Downbeat* record review and his response to my question of how he picks with his thumb. I had also come to notice, with other meetings with Wes, that he was very shy.

The night I had seen Wes play at the Half-Note, was during a brutal heatwave. It had been around 100 degrees with a very high humidity for about a week. The Half-Note was small and couldn't seat a lot of people. And during a heatwave, with a full house, the Half-Note was no place to be to cool off. Yet, on the night I had seen Wes, the club was packed! Wes's talent not only brought out the jazz fans but many top jazz musicians. In the audience with me were such jazz notables as, Carmen McRae, Ornette Coleman, Steve Swallow, Wayne Wright (guitarist), Herman Wright and Roger Kellaway. The highpoint of the night was when Carmen McRae came up on stage and sung with Wes's trio. She chose a song that Wes didn't know and the audience didn't seem to know either. I remember her calling out to Wes, "Bb!" Not only did Wes accompany her flawlessly with chords, but his solo was mesmerizing! It seemed like when the song was over, the applause never ceased to stop!

The sidemen Wes had with him were Mel Rhyne on organ and George Brown on drums. Mel had been with Wes for many years. His playing was only heard on the Riverside records. I asked him if he noticed any flaws in Wes's playing, he replied, "He speeds up the tempo and it's hard to catch up to him!"

The main reason I remember the details so well from my 1964 meeting with Wes was that I co-authored an article on him for a local newspaper. The part of Wes's music that I enjoyed the most was the happy feeling he portrayed in his playing. It sounded like he 'was having a ball' and you were right beside him having a great time, too! Maybe that is why, Wes's death has always bothered me more than any others I have experienced in my lifetime! I cherish his music and I'm extremely grateful that Wes made many different albums, and I own at least one of each!
April 1984

Orrin Keepnews
Whether or not they realize it, almost everyone who ever heard Wes knew him to some extent – I can verify that the warmth and directness and spontaneity and love you seem to hear in his music was really there. What is on his records is actually an honest projection of things that were in him. He was a man, with some routine traits and some faults and a few peculiarities and this one large touch of genius. He was also as I'm trying to stress right here, a very rare and beautiful human being whose music sounded like his soul and who, as far as I know, never deliberately gave anybody a hard time.

Since we were no longer working together, we didn't see too much of each other during the last three years of his life. But the feeling of closeness remained for both of us – I'd have to say that there haven't been over a half-dozen people in the world who have meant more to me.

Martin Taylor
When you hear Wes play the first thing that hits you is his honesty. He was true to himself and that's how he managed to create a new sound and style that was pure Wes.

Even on his later commercial recordings he didn't lose sight, everything he played was Wes. All of us are deeply indebted to him.
March 1985

Serene Montgomery
"Webster defines talent as, 'a special, often creative or artistic aptitude' ... a gift."

This sums up what my husband was to me, his family and to all of you who knew and loved him, not only as the greatest guitarist in the world, but as a sincere, warm and kind human being.

This gift Wes had came from God!
1978[15]

Tommy Tedesco

The first time I heard him on the radio I had no idea who it was. His jazz was brilliant. I sat in the car for 15 minutes until the announcer said his name. Now I had a double shock because I had never heard of his name before this time. Needless, to say, I asked many of my guitar friends who were up to 'what's happening' and they filled me in on every detail of this newcomer from Indianapolis. He became one of my favourite guitar players of all time. I feel very fortunate to have met many of my favourite guitar players but unfortunately I never had the opportunity to meet Wes. It's ironic that I am reminded of Wes every time someone writes in octaves in the studio.

July 1984

Emily Remler

During my years at Berklee College, I decided I wanted to play exactly like Wes Montgomery, and was so loyal I rejected all other approaches. Not only were the legendary octave techniques incredible, but I found in his playing a thematic, motific, logical form in his solos. (You could sing the melody through solos.) Many of his compositions were question-answer form (which someone had told me originated from African groups answering each other passing info. from song-singing while at work). For a few years I became obsessed, had Wes' picture hanging on my wall – I wanted him to play through me! I had never heard a happier, cleverer, sentimental and bad bluesy M F at the same time. He took Charlie Christian and B B King monstrous steps ahead, and his natural relaxation made my stomach thrill with anticipation. I have not heard any one yet who can compare with his rhythmic approach – be it Latin, Salsa, swing or just plain Wes. In short, he was not only a great guitarist, but went past guitar because he was a true natural musician.

May 1985

IMPRESSIONS
1.-8. Montgomery The Magnificent – Crescendo International, May 1965.
9. The Band in The Hand – Jazz at Ronnie Scott's Kitty Grime – Robert Hale Publishers, 1979, ISBN 0 7091 6907 8.
10. Wes Montgomery by Jack Duarte–*BMG Magazine* July 1965.
11. Wes Montgomery by Ivor Mairants, *BMG Magazine* May 1965, Vo. LXII No. 721.
12. Sleevenotes from Groove Brothers – Milestone M47051, 1979.
13. Sleevenotes from Movin' – Milestone M47040, 1977.
14. Interview with Herb Ellis and Dil Shaw, Halifax, May 1984.
15. A Tribute to Wes Montgomery, William H. Hudnut, III. The Mayor's Black History Committee and WTLC presents– Mrs Montgomery and children.

Wes Montgomery display at Indianapolis Children's Museum.

Cover of concert programme 'A Tribute to Wes Montgomery'.

WES MONTGOMERY

The powerful genius of Wes Montgomery still lingers over the music world of our times, and will continue to exert its unmistakable influence on creative music of the future. No other guitarist has had so long and lasting an effect on the minds and sensitivities of fellow musicians. We still remember the electrifying responses of our bodies and minds when we listened to Wes' genius turn the guitar into a living and vibrating extension of himself. He remains a phenomenon, an original artist that had an immediate and remarkable effect on all who heard him.

By late 1960, it was already old and accepted news that the normally restrained Ralph J. Gleason had bluntly labeled Wes as "The best thing to happen to the guitar since Charlie Christian." Honors continued to be heaped on him. Another New York Times critic had nothing but praise for his genius, saying . . . "Montgomery consistently is capable of producing impossible guitar music." Since the early '40's, Charlie Christian, the great pioneer modernist, had been such an overwhelming influence that all jazz guitar had become a reflection of his playing, but with the appearance of Wes on the scene, a new technique was born. Wes used only his thumb as a plectrum, mixing chords and rapid single note lines, so his playing did not have the looping flow associated with Christian. Instead, it had a fierce jabbing intensity, common to such present day gifted saxaphonists as John Coltrane and Sonny Rollins. By this means, he changed the guitar from an instrument producing a relatively delicate sound to a remarkably strong, full-throated ensemble and solo voice at the same time."

Thus, the truly amazing artistry of Montgomery emerged, although he did not appear on the national scene until he was in his mid-thirties. This was in part due to family responsibilities and, in part, to a natural diffidence which was quickly overcome by his many friends and admirers. His amazing talent enabled him to short-cut the often exasperatingly long route from discovery wide recognition. In his first year, he was "New Start" winner on guitar in the 1960 Down Beat International Critics Poll. He then topped all guitarists as the critics' choice and was voted first place and second place, respectively, by Metronome and Down Beat readers in their 1960 ballotings. Late in 1960, he rejoined Monk and Buddy, and the club-to-club travels of the combined Montgomerys brought Wes face to face with a nation-wide audience for the first time, and his climb to major stardom was accelerated.

Although Wes' unbelievable creativity on the guitar caught everyone's attention, his greatest contribution to jazz has been in the fire and deep soul with which he performed. In the words of Ralph J. Gleason . . . "Make no mistake, Wes Montgomery is the best thing to happen to the guitar since Charlie Christian. He has the electric quality, that special gift of making whatever he does come alive that marks the true artist. He has terrific swing, the ability to build solos dramatically and beautifully to climax after climax, and everything he plays has a sense of rightness about it . . .''

The genius of WES MONTGOMERY will continue to remain a lasting inspiration to us all . . .

Extract from Concert Programme 'A Tribute to Wes Montgomery'.

Wes Montgomery

MRS. MONTGOMERY AND CHILDREN

"Webster defines talent as, 'a special, often creative or artistic aptitude' . . . a gift.
This sums up what my husband was to me, his family and to all of you who knew and loved him, not only as the greatest jazz guitarist in the world, but as a sincere, warm and kind human being.
This gift Wes had came from God!"

Serene Montgomery

Extract from concert programme 'A Tribute to Wes Montgomery'.

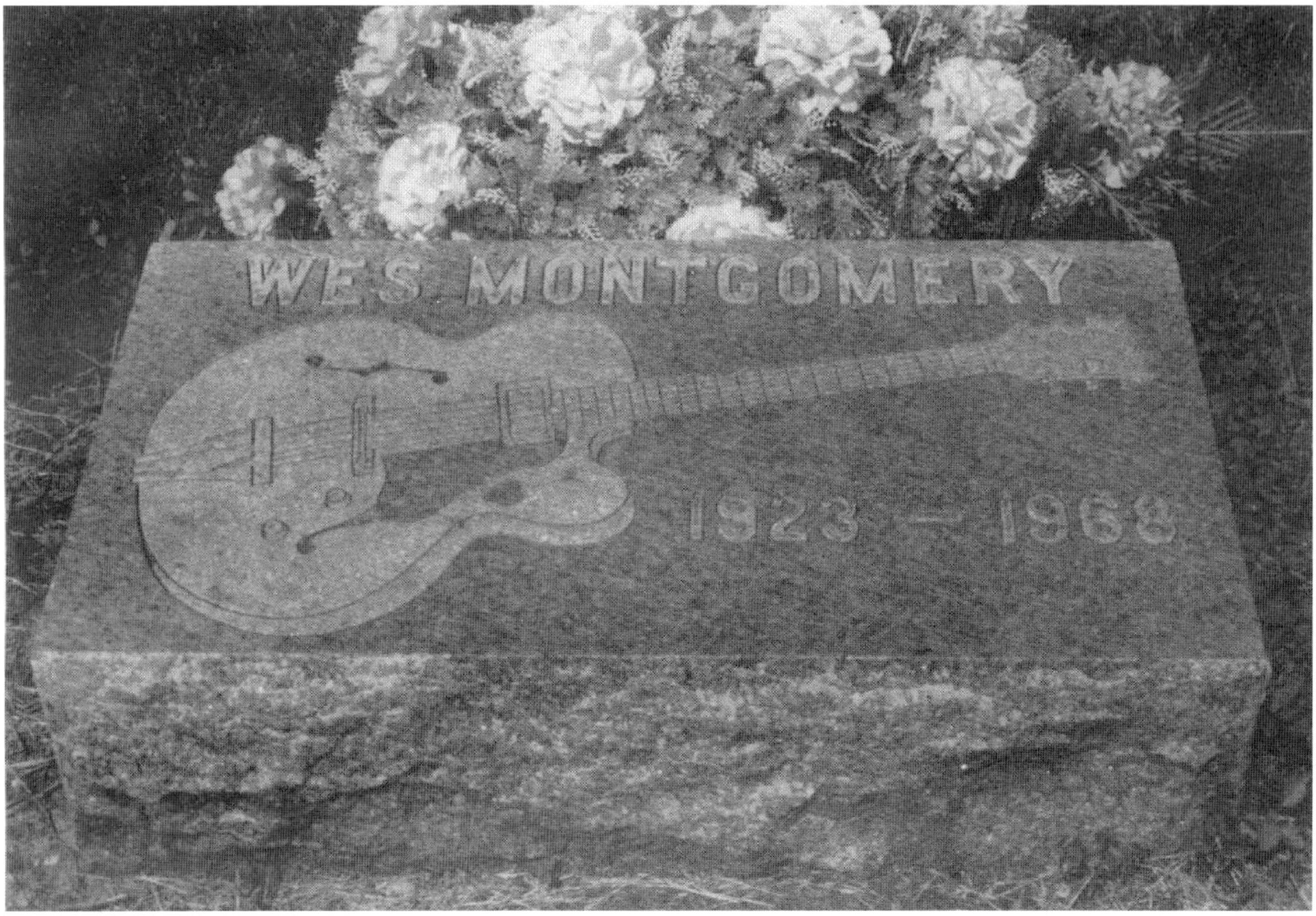

PHOTO: DR LEO HARPER

Memorial Stone - Wes Montgomery's grave - New Crown Cemetery, Indianapolis.

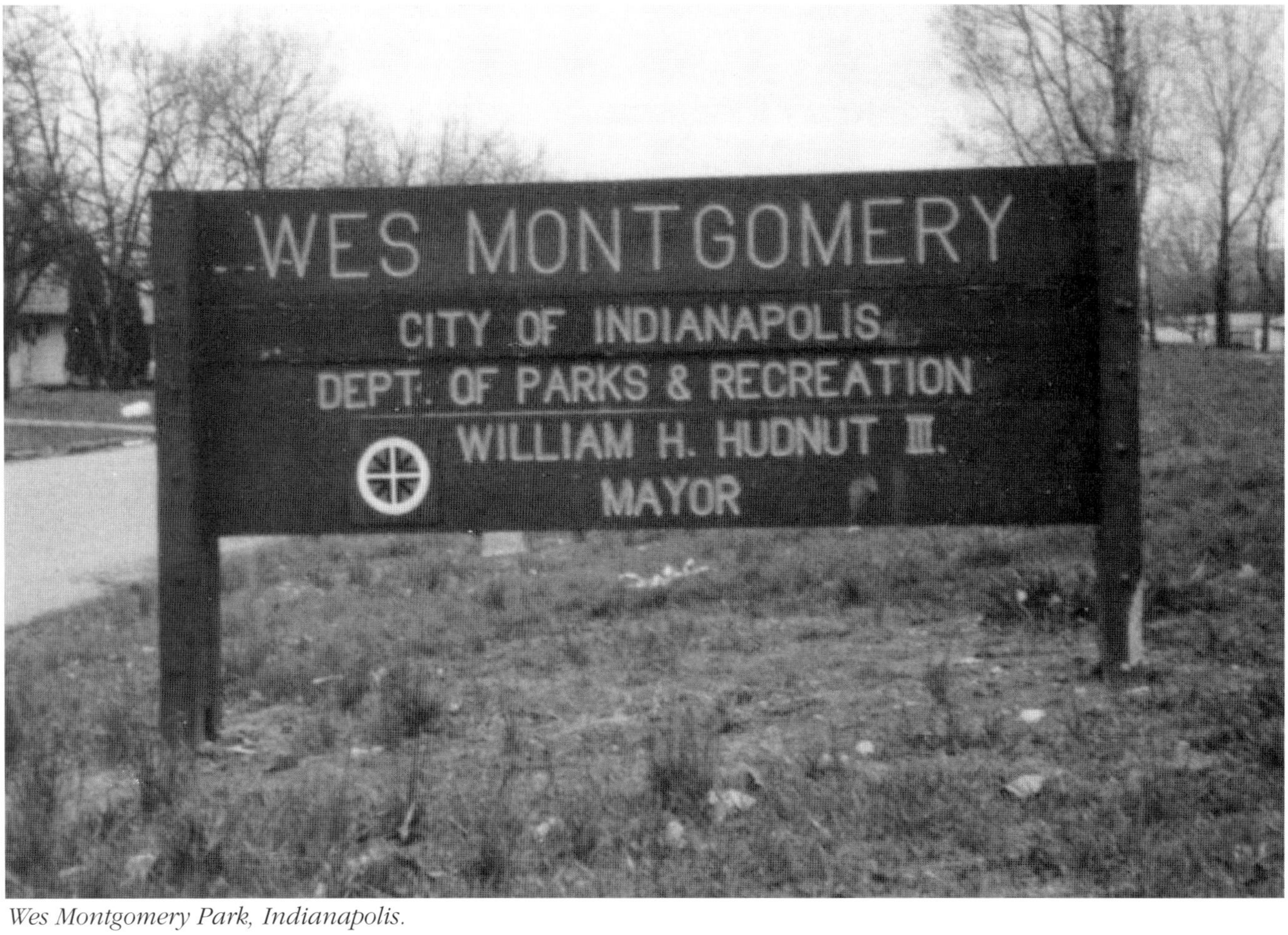

PHOTO: DR LEO HARPER

Wes Montgomery Park, Indianapolis.

APPENDIX 1
RECORDINGS

In the first edition of this book, and its subsequent reprints, my aim was to provide details of each recording in chronological order whilst, at the same time, noting the numerous appearances of each tune on a myriad of reissues, 'tasters', samplers and compilations. With the introduction of the CD and DVD formats this repackaging has not only gained pace, but it is also constantly evolving. The appearance of many known, yet hitherto commercially unavailable, sessions, owned by private collectors or circulated as bootleg tape recordings and videos, has led to a full-scale revision of the existing discography.

Rather than attempt to list every possible place a Wes Montgomery recording can be found I have chosen to provide a more traditional discography, which is supported by comprehensive details of currently available film footage and designated publications (e.g. tutors, transcriptions, lessons etc.) It is probable that the scenario will have changed again by the time this new edition of my book has been printed. Nevertheless, I believe this revised discography is far more comprehensive in scope than the previous version and should prove an invaluable source of information for the serious collector of Wes Montgomery's audio and visual recordings.

Adrian Ingram June 2008

RECORDINGS

AUTHOR'S NOTE -The number of the initial pressing is listed first, followed by subsequent pressings and CD reissues. CDs are identified, either by the incorporation of the letters CD in their designation, and/or are placed at the end of each bracketed number in the 'issued as' section. CD issues are also marked in bold.

1948

Lionel Hampton And His Orchestra

Teddy Buckner, Wendell Culley, Duke Garrette, Jimmy Nottingham, Leo Shepherd (tp) Lester Bass (btp) Sonny Craven, Britt Woodman, Jimmy Wormick (tb) Ben Kynard, Bobby Plater (as) John Sparrow, Billy Williams (ts) Charlie Fowlkes (bars) Lionel Hampton (vib, p, d, vo) Milt Buckner (p) Wes Montgomery (g) Charles Mingus (b) Earl Walker (d)
radio broadcast, Geneva, NY, July 1, 1948

1.Adam Blew His HatWeka [Swt] Jds 12-1; Cicala Jazz Live [It] BLJ 8015; Alamac QSR 2419; **Forlane [F] UCD 19008**

Issued as:
Lionel Hampton And His Orchestra 1948 (Weka [Swt] Jds 12-1)
Lionel Hampton In Concert (Cicala Jazz Live [It] BLJ 8015)
Lionel Hampton And His Orchestra 1948 (Alamac QSR 2419)
Lionel Hampton/Gene Krupa (Forlane [F] UCD 19008)

Lionel Hampton And His Orchestra

Teddy Buckner, Wendell Culley, Duke Garrette, Jimmy Nottingham, Leo Shepherd (tp) Lester Bass (btp) Sonny Craven, Britt Woodman, Jimmy Wormick (tb) Ben Kynard, Bobby Plater (as) John Sparrow, Billy Williams (ts) Charlie Fowlkes (bars) Lionel Hampton (vib, p, d, vo) Milt Buckner (p) Bobby Tucker (p -1) Wes Montgomery (g) Charles Mingus (b) Earl Walker (d) Billie Holiday (vo -1) Wynonie Harris (vo -2)
radio broadcast, Geneva, NY, July 7, 1948

1.I Cover The WaterfrontWeka [Swt] Jds 12-1
2.Good Rockin' TonightWeka [Swt] Jds 12-1; Cicala Jazz Live [It] BLJ 8015

Issued as:
Lionel Hampton And His Orchestra 1948 (Weka [Swt] Jds 12-1)
Lionel Hampton In Concert (Cicala Jazz Live [It] BLJ 8015)

Lionel Hampton And His Orchestra

Johnny Board (as) replaces Tucker, Holiday, Harris
radio broadcast, Geneva, NY, July 21, 1948

1.Brant Inn BoogieWeka [Swt] Jds 12-1; Cicala Jazz Live [It] BLJ 8015; Alamac QSR 2419; **Forlane [F] UCD 19008**

Issued as:
Lionel Hampton And His Orchestra 1948 (Weka [Swt] Jds 12-1)
Lionel Hampton In Concert (Cicala Jazz Live [It] BLJ 8015)
Lionel Hampton And His Orchestra 1948 (Alamac QSR 2419)
Lionel Hampton/Gene Krupa (Forlane [F] UCD 19008)

Lionel Hampton And His Orchestra

same personnel
Radio broadcast, Peoria, IL, August 4, 1948

1.	Body And Soul	Weka [Swt] Jds 12-1; Cicala Jazz Live [It] BLJ 8015; Alamac QSR 2419

Issued as:
Lionel Hampton And His Orchestra 1948 (Weka [Swt] Jds 12-1)
Lionel Hampton In Concert (Cicala Jazz Live [It] BLJ 8015)
Lionel Hampton And His Orchestra 1948 (Alamac QSR 2419)

Lionel Hampton And His Orchestra

same personnel
Radio broadcast, Denver, CO, August 11, 1948

1.	Satchmo's Blues	Weka [Swt] Jds 12-1; Cicala Jazz Live [It] BLJ 8015; Alamac QSR 2419; **Forlane [F] UCD 19008**

Issued as:
Lionel Hampton And His Orchestra 1948 (Weka [Swt] Jds 12-1)
Lionel Hampton In Concert (Cicala Jazz Live [It] BLJ 8015)
Lionel Hampton And His Orchestra 1948 (Alamac QSR 2419)
Lionel Hampton/Gene Krupa (Forlane [F] UCD 19008)

Lionel Hampton And His Orchestra

Lester Bass (tb) Ben Kynard plays (bars). Benny Bailey, Walter Williams (tp) Al Grey (tb) Roy Johnson (b) replaces Teddy Buckner, Nottingham, Craven, Woodman, Fowlkes, Mingus
Radio broadcast, Little Rock, AR, October 15, 1948

1.	Dues In Blues	Weka [Swt] Jds 12-1; Cicala Jazz Live [It] BLJ 8015; Alamac QSR 2419; **Forlane [F] UCD 19008**

Issued as:
Lionel Hampton And His Orchestra 1948 (Weka [Swt] Jds 12-1)
Lionel Hampton In Concert (Cicala Jazz Live [It] BLJ 8015)
Lionel Hampton And His Orchestra 1948 (Alamac QSR 2419)
Lionel Hampton/Gene Krupa (Forlane [F] UCD 19008)

Lionel Hampton And His Orch estra

Benny Bailey, Wendell Culley, Duke Garrette, Leo Shepherd, Walter Williams (tp) Lester Bass, Al Grey, Jimmy Wormick (tb) Johnny Board, Bobby Plater (as) John Sparrow, Billy Williams (ts) Ben Kynard (bars) Lionel Hampton (vib, p, d, vo) Milt Buckner (p) Wes Montgomery (g) Roy Johnson (b) Earl Walker (d) Betty Carter (vo -1)
Radio broadcast, unknown location, circa October, 1948

1.	Jay Bird	Weka [Swt] Jds 12-1; Cicala Jazz Live [It] BLJ 8015; Alamac QSR 2419; **Forlane [F] UCD 19008**
2.	Beulah's Boogie	Weka [Swt] Jds 12-1; Cicala Jazz Live [It] BLJ 8015; Alamac QSR 2419

| 3. | Calling Dr. Mancuso | Weka [Swt] Jds 12-1; Cicala Jazz Live [It] BLJ 8015; Alamac QSR 2419; **Forlane [F] UCD 19008** |
| 4. | Re-Bop | - |

Issued as:
Lionel Hampton And His Orchestra 1948 (Weka [Swt] Jds 12-1)
Lionel Hampton In Concert (Cicala Jazz Live [It] BLJ 8015)
Lionel Hampton And His Orchestra 1948 (Alamac QSR 2419)
Lionel Hampton/Gene Krupa (Forlane [F] UCD 19008)

1949

Lionel Hampton Nonet

Benny Bailey, Duke Garrette (tp) Johnny Board (as) Gene Morris (ts) Lionel Hampton (vib, vo) Albert Ammons (p) Wes Montgomery (g) Roy Johnson (b) Earl Walker (d) Betty Carter, Sonny Parker (vo -3)
NYC, January 24, 1949

1.	Chicken Shack Boogie	MCA [F] 510.181
2.	New Central Avenue Breakdown	Decca DL 4296
3.	Benson's Boogie	MCA [F] 510.181

Issued as:
Lionel Hampton 7 - Hamp's Small Combos 1947-1950 (MCA [F] 510.181)
Lionel Hampton - Hamp's Golden Favorites (Decca DL 4296, DL 74296)
Wes Montgomery – Complete Recordings with Lionel Hampton (Definitive Records DRCD 11241)

Lionel Hampton And His Orchestra

Benny Bailey, Wendell Culley, Duke Garrette, Leo Shepherd, Walter Williams (tp) Lester Bass, Al Grey, Benny Powell, Jimmy Wormick (tb) Johnny Board, Bobby Plater (as) Gene Morris, John Sparrow, Billy Williams (ts) Ben Kynard (bars) Lionel Hampton (vib, p, vo) Albert Ammons (p) Wes Montgomery (g) Roy Johnson (b) Earl Walker (d) Sonny Parker (vo -2)
NYC, January 28, 1949

1.	Hamp's Boogie Woogie, No. 2	MCA [F] 510.181
2.	Hamp's Gumbo	-
3.	Beulah's Sister's Boogie	Coral [G] 6.22421
4.	Wee Albert	-

Issued as;
Lionel Hampton 7 - Hamp's Small Combos 1947-1950 (MCA [F] 510.181)
Lionel Hampton, Vol. 8: 1949-1950 (Coral [G] 6.22421)
Wes Montgomery – Complete Recordings with Lionel Hampton (Definitive Records DRCD 11241)

Lionel Hampton Sextet

Benny Bailey (tp -1) Lionel Hampton (vib) Samuel B. Price (p -1,2) Wes Montgomery (g) Roy Johnson (b) Earl Walker (d) Sonny Parker (vo -1,2)
NYC, April 26, 1949

1.	What's Happening Baby	Coral [G] 6.22421
2.	Drinking Wine / Spo-Dee-O-Dee / Drinking Wine	-
3.	Moonglow	-

Issued as:
Lionel Hampton, Vol. 8: 1949-1950 (Coral [G] 6.22421)
Wes Montgomery – Complete Recordings with Lionel Hampton (Definitive Records DRCD 11241)

Lionel Hampton And His Orchestra

Wendell Culley (tp) Benny Bailey, Ed Mullens, Leo Shepherd, Walter Williams (tp -1,2) Lester Bass, Al Grey, Chippy Outcalt, Jimmy Wormick (tb -1,2) Johnny Board, Bobby Plater (as -1,2) Gene Morris (ts) John Sparrow, Billy Williams (ts -1,2) Ben Kynard (bars) Lionel Hampton (vib) France Gadison (p -1,2) Doug Duke (org -3) Wes Montgomery (g) Roy Johnson (b) Earl Walker (d) Betty Carter (vo -1) The Hamp-Tones (vo -2) Sonny Parker (vo -3)
NYC, May 10, 1949

1.	The Hucklebuck	Coral [G] 6.22421
2.	Baby, You're Great	-
3.	Lavender Coffin	-

Issued as;
Lionel Hampton, Vol. 8: 1949-1950 (Coral [G] 6.22421)
Wes Montgomery – Complete Recordings with Lionel Hampton (Definitive Records DRCD 11241)

Lionel Hampton And His Orchestra

Hampton plays (vib, d). Duke Garrette (tp) Benny Powell (tb) Albert Ammons (p) replaces Mullens, Outcalt, Gadison, Duke, Carter, The Hamp-Tones, Parker
TV broadcast, 'Adventures In Jazz', CBS-TV, NYC, May 13, 1949

Hampology	Alto AL 708; Jazz-Club LP 121
Flying Home, Pt. 1	-
Flying Home, Pt. 2	-

Issued as:
Lionel Hampton - Colossal Vibes And Sticks (Alto AL 708)
Lionel Hampton And His Orchestra 1944-1950 (Jazz-Club LP 121)
Wes Montgomery – Complete Recordings with Lionel Hampton (Definitive Records DRCD 11241)

Sonny Parker And His All Stars

Walter Williams (tp) Al Grey (tb) Johnny Board (as) Gene Morris (ts) Floyd Dixon (p) Wes Montgomery (g) Roy Johnson (b) Ellis Bartee (d) Sonny Parker (vo)
Radio Recorders, Hollywood, CA, September 7, 1949

1.	Hamp's Gumbo	Blue Moon [Sp] **BMCD 6003**
2.	Pretty Baby	Riverboat [F] 900 263
3.	Sonny's Blues	unissued
4.	Sad Feelin'	Riverboat [F] 900 263
5.	I Want A Little Girl	-

Various Artists - The Best Of Blues Shouters (Riverboat [F] 900 263)
Sonny Parker The Complete 1948-1953 (Blue Moon [Sp] BMCD 6003)
Wes Montgomery – Complete Recordings with Lionel Hampton (Definitive Records DRCD 11241)

Lionel Hampton And His Orchestra

Benny Bailey, Wendell Culley, Duke Garrette, Leo Shepherd, Walter Williams (tp) Lester Bass, Al Grey, Benny Powell, Jimmy Wormick (tb) Johnny Board, Bobby Plater (as) Gene Morris, John Sparrow, Billy Williams (ts) Ben Kynard (bars) Lionel Hampton (vib, d) Albert Ammons (p) Wes Montgomery (g) Roy Johnson (b) Earl Walker (d -1,2) Curley Hamner (d -3)
NYC, autumn 1949

1.	Beulah's Boogie, Pt. 1	Jazz-Club LP 121
2.	Beulah's Boogie, Pt. 2	-
3.	Drumology	-

Issued as:
Lionel Hampton And His Orchestra 1944-1950 (Jazz-Club LP 121)

Lionel Hampton And His Orchestra

Benny Bailey, Duke Garrette, Ed Mullens, Leo Shepherd, Walter Williams (tp) Al Grey, Paul Lee Higaki, Benny Powell, Jimmy Wormick (tb) Bobby Plater, Jerome Richardson (as) Johnny Board, Curtis Lowe, Billy Williams (ts) Lonnie Shaw (bars) Lionel Hampton (vib) Doug Duke (p, org) Wes Montgomery (g) Roy Johnson (b) Ellis Bartee (d) Sonny Parker (vo -2)
NYC, December 29, 1949

1.	Rag Mop	Coral [G] 6.22421
2.	For You My Love	-
3.	Sky Blue	-
4.	Mary Had A Little Lamb	Alto AL 708

Issued as:
Lionel Hampton, Vol. 8: 1949-1950 (Coral [G] 6.22421)
Lionel Hampton - Colossal Vibes And Sticks (Alto AL 708)
Wes Montgomery – Complete Recordings with Lionel Hampton (Definitive Records DRCD 11241)

1950

Lionel Hampton And His Orchestra

Benny Bailey, Duke Garrette, Ed Mullens, Leo Shepherd, Walter Williams (tp) Al Grey, Paul Lee Higaki, Benny Powell, Jimmy Wormick (tb) Bobby Plater, Jerome Richardson (as) Johnny Board, Curtis Lowe, Billy Williams (ts) Lonnie Shaw (bars) Lionel Hampton (vib) Doug Duke (p, org) Wes Montgomery (g) Roy Johnson (b) Ellis Bartee (d)
radio broadcast, "Apollo Theater", NYC, January 4, 1950

1.	Symphony In Jazz	Alto AL 708
2.	Bopology	-
3.	Hamp's Basement	-

Issued as:
Lionel Hampton - Colossal Vibes And Sticks (Alto AL 708)

Lionel Hampton And His Orchestra

Benny Bailey, Duke Garrette, Ed Mullens, Leo Shepherd, Walter Williams (tp) Al Grey, Paul Lee Higaki, Benny Powell, Jimmy Wormick (tb) Bobby Plater, Jerome Richardson (as) Johnny Board, Curtis Lowe, Billy Williams (ts) Lonnie Shaw (bars) Lionel Hampton (vib) Doug Duke (p, org) Wes Montgomery (g) Roy Johnson (b) Ellis Bartee (d) Jimmy Scott (vo -1) Sonny Parker (vo -2,3)
NYC, January 5, 1950

1.	I've Been A Fool	Coral [G] 6.22421
2.	How You Sound	-
3.	I Almost Lost My Mind	-

Issued as:
Lionel Hampton, Vol. 8: 1949-1950 (Coral [G] 6.22421)
Wes Montgomery – Complete Recordings with Lionel Hampton (Definitive Records DRCD 11241)

Lionel Hampton And His Orchestra

Benny Bailey, Duke Garrette, Ed Mullens, Leo Shepherd, Walter Williams (tp) Al Grey, Paul Lee Higaki, Benny Powell, Jimmy Wormick (tb) Bobby Plater, Jerome Richardson (as) Johnny Board, Curtis Lowe, Billy Williams (ts) Lonnie Shaw (bars) Lionel Hampton (vib) Doug Duke (p, org) Wes Montgomery (g) Roy Johnson (b) Ellis Bartee (d) Irma Curry (vo -1,2) Sonny Parker (vo -3,4) Jimmy Scott (vo -5,6)
NYC, January 25, 1950

1.	Everybody's Somebody's Fool	Decca DL 4296
2.	I'll Never Be Free	Coral [G] 6.22421
3.	Sad Feelin'	Coral [G] 6.22422
4.	Hamp's Gumbo	-
5.	Please Give Me A Chance	-
6.	I Wish I Knew	-

Issued as:
Lionel Hampton - Hamp's Golden Favorites (Decca DL 4296, DL 74296)
Lionel Hampton, Vol. 8: 1949-1950 (Coral [G] 6.22421)
Lionel Hampton, Vol. 9: 1950 (Coral [G] 6.22422)
Wes Montgomery – Complete Recordings with Lionel Hampton (Definitive Records DRCD 11241)

Lionel Hampton Sextet

Jerome Richardson (fl -2) Lionel Hampton (vib) Doug Duke (org) Wes Montgomery (g) Roy Johnson (b) Earl Walker (d)
NYC, January 26, 1950

1.	75754	Where Or When	Decca DL 8230
2.	75755	There Will Never Be Another You	-

Issued as:
Lionel Hampton - Moonglow (Decca DL 8230)
Wes Montgomery – Complete Recordings with Lionel Hampton (Definitive Records DRCD 11241)

Gene Morris Quintet

Gene Morris (ts) Douglas Duke (p) Wes Montgomery (g) probably Roy Johnson (b) Ellis Bartee (d -1,2) Earl Walker (d -3,4) Sonny Parker (vo -2,3)

Fresno, CA, 1950

1.	King Trotter	Spire 11-003
2.	Rocking With G.H.	Spire 11-003; Riverboat [F] 900 263
3.	Carlena's Blues	Spire 11-004; **Blue Moon [Sp] BMCD 6003**
4.	Smooth Evening	Spire 11-004

Issued as:
Various Artists - The Best Of Blus Shouters (Riverboat [F] 900 263)
Gene Morris - King Trotter c/w Rocking With G.H. (Spire 11-003)
Gene Morris - Carlena's Blues c/w Smooth Evening (Spire 11-004)
Sonny Parker The Complete 1948-1953 (Blue Moon [Sp] BMCD 6003)

1955

Robert Johnson Quintet

Alonzo Johnson (ts) Buddy Montgomery (p) Wes Montgomery (g) Monk Montgomery (b) Robert Johnson (d)
NYC, June 15, 1955

1.	Love For Sale	Columbia FC 38509

Issued as:
Various Artists - Almost Forgotten: Various-Instrumentalists (Columbia FC 38509)

1957

The Montgomery Brothers And Five Others

Freddie Hubbard (tp -2,4,5,7) Waymon Atkinson, Alonzo Johnson (ts -2,4,5,7) Buddy Montgomery (vib -2/7) Joe Bradley (p -1/5,7) Wes Montgomery (g) Monk Montgomery (b) Paul Parker (d)
Indianapolis, IN, December 30, 1957

1.	Finger Pickin'	Pacific Jazz 651, X-301, PJ 1240; World Pacific JWC 509; Blue Note BN-LA 531-H2; **Pacific Jazz CDP7243 8379 2 8**
2.	Sound Carrier	Pacific Jazz PJ 1240, PJ 17; **Pacific Jazz CDP7243 8379 2 8**
3.	Lois Ann	Pacific Jazz PJ 1240 ; **Pacific Jazz CDP7243 8379 2 8**
4.	Bud's Beaux Arts	-
5.	Bock To Bock	Pacific Jazz PJ 1240, PJ 17; Blue Note BN-LA 531-H2; **Pacific Jazz CDP7243 8379 2 8**
6.	All The Things You Are	Pacific Jazz PJ1240; **Pacific Jazz CDP7243 83792 8**
7.	Billie's Bounce	Pacific Jazz PJ 1240; Blue Note BN-LA 531-H2; **Pacific Jazz CDP7243 8379 2 8**

Issued as:
The Montgomery Brothers And Five Others (Pacific Jazz PJ 1240, WP 1240)
Various Artists - The Blues, Vol. 2: Have Blues, Will Travel (World Pacific JWC 509)
Wes Montgomery - Beginnings (Blue Note BN-LA 531-H2)

The Montgomery Brothers - Wes, Buddy And Monk Montgomery (Pacific Jazz PJ 17)
Bud Shank - A Tribute To An African Pennywhistle c/w Wes Montgomery - Finger Pickin' (Pacific Jazz 651)
The Montgomery Story, tracks 2 & 5 (Fontana 688 113 ZL)
Wes Montgomery - Finger Pickin' c/w Summertime (Pacific Jazz X-301)
Wes Montgomery – Finger Pickin' (Pacific Jazz CDP7243 37987 2 8)

1958

The Montgomery Brothers

Harold Land (ts) Buddy Montgomery (p) Wes Montgomery (g) Monk Montgomery (b) Tony Bazley (d)
Los Angeles, CA, April 18, 1958

1.	Far Wes	Pacific Jazz PJ 5; Blue Note BN-LA 531-H2; **Pacific Jazz CDP 94475 2**
2.	Leila	-
3.	Old Folks	-
4.	Wes' Tune	-
5.	Hymn For Carl	Pacific Jazz PJ 17; World Pacific JWC 513; Blue Note BN-LA 531-H2; **Pacific Jazz CDP 94475 2**
6.	Montgomeryland Funk (Montgomery Funk)	Pacific Jazz PJ 17; World Pacific JWC 512; **Pacific Jazz CDP 94475 2**
7.	Stompin' At The Savoy	Pacific Jazz PJ 17; **Pacific Jazz CDP 94475 2**

Issued as:
Wes Montgomery - Montgomeryland (Pacific Jazz PJ 5, ST 5, LLJ 80062-Jap)
Wes Montgomery - Beginnings (Blue Note BN-LA 531-H2)
The Montgomery Brothers - Wes, Buddy And Monk Montgomery (Pacific Jazz PJ 17)
Various Artists - The Blues In Stereo (World Pacific JWC 513, ST 1021)
Various Artists - The Blues, Vol. 3: Blowin' The Blues (World Pacific JWC 512, ST 1029)
The Montgomery Story, tracks 5, 6 & 7 only (Fontana 688 113 ZL)
Wes Montgomery – Far Wes (Pacific Jazz CDP 94475 2)

The Mastersounds With Wes Montgomery

Buddy Montgomery (vib) Richie Crabtree (p) Wes Montgomery (g) Monk Montgomery (el.b) Benny Barth (d)
Forum Theatre, Los Angeles, CA, April 22, 1958

1.	Overture: Not Since Nineveh	World Pacific WP 1243; **Lonehill Jazz LHJ 10133**
2.	Overture: Olive Tree	-
3.	Overture: Stranger In Paradise	-
4.	Overture: And This Is My Beloved	-
5.	Overture: Night Of My Nights	-
6.	Overture: Sands Of Time	-
7.	Olive Tree	-
8.	Not Since Nineveh	- ; **Blue Note CDP 7243 8 37987 2 8**
9.	Baubles, Bangles And Beads	World Pacific WP 1243; Pacific Jazz PJ 17; Blue Note BN-LA 531-H2; **Lonehill Jazz LHJ 10133; Blue Note CDP 7243 8 37987 2 8**
10.	Fate	World Pacific WP 1243; **Lonehill Jazz LHJ 10133**
11.	And This Is My Beloved	-
12.	Stranger In Paradise	World Pacific EP 4-79, WP 1243, JWC 510; Blue Note BN-LA 531-H2 ; **Lonehill Jazz LHJ 10133; Blue Note CDP 7243 8 37987 2 8**

Issued as:
The Mastersounds - Kismet (World Pacific WP 1243, ST 1243, ST 1010)
The Mastersounds With Wes Montgomery - Kismet (Pacific Jazz PJ 10130, ST 20130)
The Montgomery Brothers - Wes, Buddy And Monk Montgomery (Pacific Jazz PJ 17)
Wes Montgomery - Beginnings (Blue Note BN-LA 531-H2)
Various Artists - Jazz West Coast, Vol. 4 (World Pacific JWC 510, ST 1009)
The Mastersounds With Wes Montgomery (no details) (World Pacific EP 4-79)
The Montgomery Story, track 9 (Fontana 688 113 ZL)
Wes Montgomery All-Stars/ A Good Git-Together (Lonehill Jazz LHJ10133)
Finger Pickin' (Blue Note CDP 7243 8 37987 2 8)

The Mastersounds With Wes Montgomery plus Roy Harte And Milt Holland

Buddy Montgomery (vib) Richie Crabtree (p) Wes Montgomery (g) Monk Montgomery (el.b) Benny Barth (d) overdubs: Roy Harte, overdubs: Milt Holland (per)
Forum Theatre, Los Angeles, CA, April 22, 1958

    Not Since Nineveh   World Pacific WP 1405

Issued as:
The 44 Instruments Of Roy Harte And Milt Holland - Perfect Percussion (World Pacific WP 1405, ST 1405)

1959

The Montgomery Brothers

Pony Poindexter (as -2/4) Buddy Montgomery (p) Wes Montgomery (g) Monk Montgomery (b) Louis Hayes (d)
Los Angeles, CA, October 1, 1959

1.	Summertime	Pacific Jazz X-301, PJ 5; Blue Note BN-LA 531-H2; **Pacific Jazz CDP 94475-2**
2.	Monk's Shop	Pacific Jazz PJ 5; Blue Note BN-LA 531-H2; **Pacific Jazz CDP 94475-2**
3.	Falling In Love With Love	-
4.	Renie	-

Issued as:
Wes Montgomery - Montgomeryland (Pacific Jazz PJ 5, ST 5)
Wes Montgomery - Beginnings (Blue Note BN-LA 531-H2)
Wes Montgomery - Finger Pickin' c/w Summertime (Pacific Jazz X-301)
Wes Montgomery – Far Wes (Pacific Jazz CDP 94475-2)

Wes Montgomery Trio

Mel Rhyne (org) Wes Montgomery (g) Paul Parker (d)
Reeves Sound Studios, NYC, October 5, 1959

1.	'Round About Midnight	Riverside R 45431, RLP 12-310
2.	Satin Doll (take 5)	**Fantasy OJCCD 034-2**
3.	Satin Doll (take 7)	Riverside RLP 12-310
4.	Missile Blues (take 5)	**Fantasy OJCCD 034-2**
5.	Missile Blues (take 6)	Riverside RLP 12-310, RLP 494

Issued as:
The Wes Montgomery Trio (Riverside RLP 12-310, RLP 1156; Fantasy OJC 034, **OJCCD 034-2**)
Wes Montgomery - 'Round Midnight (Riverside RS 3014)
Wes Montgomery - Guitar On The Go (Riverside RLP 494; Fantasy OJC 489, **OJCCD 489-2**)
Wes Montgomery - 'Round Midnight c/w Yesterdays (Riverside R 45431)

Wes Montgomery Trio

same personnel
Reeves Sound Studios, NYC, October 6, 1959

1.	Yesterdays	Riverside R 45431, RLP 12-310
2.	The End Of A Love Affair	Riverside RLP 12-310
3.	Whisper Not	-
4.	Ecaroh (Ecorah)	-
5.	Too Late Now	-
6.	Jingles	-

Issued as:
The Wes Montgomery Trio (Riverside RLP 12-310, RLP 1156; Fantasy OJC 034, **OJCCD 034-2**; SMJ 6080 Jap.)
Wes Montgomery - 'Round Midnight (Riverside RS 3014)
Wes Montgomery - 'Round Midnight c/w Yesterdays (Riverside R 45431)

Jon Hendricks

Pony Poindexter (as, vo) Gildo Mahones (p) Wes Montgomery (g) Monk Montgomery (b) Walter Bolden (d) Jon Hendricks (vo)
"Fugazi Hall", San Francisco, CA, October, 1959

1.	Everything Started In The House Of The Lord	World Pacific 819, WP 1283; **Lonehill Jazz LHJ10133**
2.	Feed Me	World Pacific WP 1283, WP 1289; **Lonehill Jazz LHJ10133**
3.	A Good Git-Together	World Pacific 819, WP 1283

Issued as:
Jon Hendricks - A Good Git-Together (World Pacific WP 1283, ST 1283; **Pacific Jazz 09463 6981222**)
Various Artists - Swingin' Like Sixty, Vol. 1: The Singers/The Swingers (World Pacific WP 1289)
Jon Hendricks - A Good Git-Together c/w Everything Started In The House Of The Lord (World Pacific 819)
Wes Montgomery All-Stars (Lonehill Jazz LHJ 10133)

Jon Hendricks

Nat Adderley (cor) Cannonball Adderley (as) Gildo Mahones (p) Wes Montgomery (g) Ike Isaacs (b) Jimmy Wormsworth (d) Jon Hendricks (vo)
"Fugazi Hall", San Francisco, CA, October, 1959

1.	Music In The Air	World Pacific WP 1283; **Lonehill Jazz LHJ10133**
2.	Pretty Strange	-
3,	The Shouter	-
4.	Social Call	-
5.	Out Of The Past	-

Issued as:
Jon Hendricks - A Good Git-Together (World Pacific WP 1283, ST 1283, **Pacific Jazz 0946 3 6981 12 2 2)**
Wes Montgomery All-Stars (Lonehill Jazz LHJ 10133)

Jon Hendricks

Pony Poindexter (as, vo) Buddy Montgomery (vib) Gildo Mahones (p) Wes Montgomery (g) Ike Isaacs (b) Jimmy Wormsworth (d) Jon Hendricks (vo)
"Fugazi Hall", San Francisco, CA, October, 1959

1.	I'll Die Happy	World Pacific WP 1283; **Lonehill Jazz LHJ10133**
2.	Minor Catastrophe	-
3.	Everything Started In The House Of The Lord, Pt. 2 (I'm Gonna Shout)	World Pacific 819, WP 1283

Issued as:
Jon Hendricks - A Good Git-Together (World Pacific WP 1283, ST 1283, 0946 3 6981 12 2 2)
Jon Hendricks - A Good Git-Together c/w Everything Started In The House Of The Lord (World Pacific 819)
Wes Montgomery All-Stars (**Lonehill Jazz LHJ 10133**)

1960

Nat Adderley Sextet

Nat Adderley (cor) Bobby Timmons (p -1,2) Wes Montgomery (g) Sam Jones (cello, b -1/3) Keter Betts (b) Louis Hayes (d)
Reeves Sound Studios, NYC, January 25, 1960

1.	Pretty Memory	Riverside RLP 12-318; **Fantasy OJCCD 363-2**
2.	Fallout	-
3.	My Heart Stood Still	-
4.	Mean To Me	-

Issued as:
Nat Adderley - Work Song (Riverside RLP 12-318, RLP 1167; Fantasy OJC 363, **OJCCD 363-2**)

Wes Montgomery Quartet

Tommy Flanagan (p) Wes Montgomery (g) Percy Heath (b) Albert "Tootie" Heath (d)
Reeves Sound Studios, NYC, January 26, 1960

1.	Airegin	Riverside R 45441, RLP 12-320; **Fantasy OJCCD 363-2**
2.	D-Natural Blues	Riverside RLP 12-320
3.	Four On Six	-
4.	West Coast Blues	-
5.	In Your Own Sweet Way	-

Issued as:
The Incredible Jazz Guitar Of Wes Montgomery (Riverside RLP 12-320, RLP 1169; Fantasy OJC 036, **OJCCD 036-2**)
Wes Montgomery - Airegin c/w Mr. Walker (Riverside R 45441, SMJ-6046 Jap.)
The Genius of Wes Montgomery (109561/3) 3 LP box set also includes RLP 434 RLP 362
Vibratin' (Riverside (Orpheum) 499)

Nat Adderley Sextet

Nat Adderley (cor) Bobby Timmons (p -1/3) Wes Montgomery (g) Sam Jones (cello, b) Percy Heath (b -1/3) Louis Hayes (d -1/3)
Reeves Sound Studios, NYC, January 27, 1960

1.	Work Song	Riverside RLP 12-318; **Fantasy OJCCD 363-2**
2.	Sack O' Woe	-
3.	Scrambled Eggs	-
4.	I've Got A Crush On You	-
5.	Violets For Your Furs	-

Issued as:
Nat Adderley - Work Song (Riverside RLP 12-318, RLP 1167; Fantasy OJC 363, **OJCCD 363-2**)

Wes Montgomery Quartet

Tommy Flanagan (p) Wes Montgomery (g) Percy Heath (b) Albert "Tootie" Heath (d)
Reeves Sound Studios, NYC, January 28, 1960

1.	Polka Dots And Moonbeams	Riverside RLP 12-320; **Fantasy OJCCD 036-2**
2.	Mr. Walker	Riverside R 45441, RLP 12-320
3.	Gone With The Wind	Riverside RLP 12-320

Issued as:
The Incredible Jazz Guitar Of Wes Montgomery (Riverside RLP 12-320, RLP 1169; Fantasy OJC 036, **OJCCD 036-2**, SMJ-6046 Jap.)
Wes Montgomery - Airegin c/w Mr. Walker (Riverside R 45441)
The Genius of Wes Montgomery (109561/3) 3 LP box set also includes RLP 434 RLP 362

Harold Land Sextet

Joe Gordon (tp) Harold Land (ts) Barry Harris (p) Wes Montgomery (g) Sam Jones (b) Louis Hayes (d)
"Fugazi Hall", San Francisco, CA, May 17, 1960

1.	Terrain	Jazzland JLP 20;Fantasy **OJCCD 146-2**
2.	Compulsion	-

Issued as:
Harold Land - West Coast Blues! (Jazzland JLP 20; Fantasy OJC 146, **OJCCD 146-2)**

Harold Land Sextet

same personnel
"Fugazi Hall", San Francisco, CA, May 18, 1960

1.	Ursula	Jazzland JLP 20; **Fantasy OJCCD 146-2**
2.	Klactoveedsedstene	-
3.	Don't Explain	-
4.	West Coast Blues	Jazzland JLP 20, JLP 1001

Issued as:
Harold Land - West Coast Blues! (Jazzland JLP 20; Fantasy OJC 146, **OJCCD 146-2**)
Various Artists - The Stars Of Jazz 1961 (Jazzland JLP 1001)

Cannonball Adderley Quintet

Cannonball Adderley (as) Victor Feldman (p, vib) Wes Montgomery (g) Ray Brown (b) Louis Hayes (d)
"Fugazi Hall", San Francisco, CA, May 21, 1960

1.	The Chant	Riverside R 45465, RLP 355; **Landmark LCD 1304-2**
2.	Lolita	-
3.	Azule Serape	Riverside RLP 355

Issued as:
Cannonball Adderley And The Poll-Winners (Riverside RLP 355, **Capitol Jazz 7243 5 20086 2 9**)
The Cannonball Adderley Collection, Vol. 4 - Cannonball Adderley And The Poll-Winners (Landmark LLP 1304, **LCD 1304-2**)
Cannonball Adderley - The Chant c/w Lolita (Riverside R 45465)
Cannonball Adderley and Friends (Capitol SVBB 11233)

Cannonball Adderley Quintet

same personnel
Los Angeles, CA, June 5, 1960

1.	Au Privave (take 1)	Landmark LLP 1304, **LCD 1304-2**
2.	Au Privave (take 2)	Riverside RLP 355
3.	Yours Is My Heart Alone	-
4.	Never Will I Marry	-

Issued as:Cannonball Adderley And The Poll-Winners (Riverside RLP 355; **Capitol Jazz 7243 5 20086 2 9**)
The Cannonball Adderley Collection, Vol. 4 - Cannonball Adderley And The Poll-Winners (Landmark LLP 1304, **LCD 1304-2**)
Cannonball Adderley and Friends (Capitol SVBB 11233)

The Montgomery Brothers

Buddy Montgomery (p) Wes Montgomery (g) Monk Montgomery (b) Lawrence Marable (d)
San Francisco, CA, July, 1960

1.	Lover Man	Fantasy LP 3308; **Milestone MCD-47076-2**)
2.	Jingles	-
3.	D-Natural Blues (Monterey Blues)	-
4.	June In January	-
5.	Bud's Tune	-

Issued as:
The Montgomery Brothers (Fantasy LP 3308)
Wes Montgomery- Groove Brothers (Milestone MCD-47076-2)

Wes Montgomery Quintet

James Clay (ts, fl -1/6,8/13) Victor Feldman (p) Wes Montgomery (g, bag) Sam Jones (b) Louis Hayes (d)
United Recording Studios, Los Angeles, CA, October 12, 1960

1.	Movin' Along (take 1)	Milestone M 47065, **MCD 47065-2**
2.	Movin' Along (take 4)	Milestone M 47040, M 9110
3.	Movin' Along (take 5)	Riverside R 45459, RLP 342
4.	Movin' Along (take 5) (ed.)	**Riverside 12RCD 4408-2**
5.	Tune-Up (take 4)	Riverside R 45459, RLP 342
6.	Tune-Up (take 9)	Milestone M 47065, **MCD 47065-2**; **Fantasy OJCCD 089-2**
7.	(I Don't Stand A) Ghost Of A Chance (With You)	Riverside RLP 342
8.	Sandu	-
9.	Body And Soul (take 2)	Milestone M 47065, **MCD 47065-2**; **Fantasy OJCCD 089-2**
10.	Body And Soul (take 4/6)	Milestone M 9110
11.	Body And Soul (take 7)	Riverside RLP 342
12.	So Do It! (take 1)	**Riverside 12RCD 4408-2**
13.	So Do It! (take 6)	Riverside RLP 342
14.	Says You	-

Issued as:
The Alternative Wes Montgomery (Milestone M 47065)
Wes Montgomery - Encores (Milestone M 9110)
Wes Montgomery - Movin' Along (Riverside RLP 342; Milestone M 47040;
Wes Montgomery - Movin' Along c/w Tune-Up (Riverside R 45459)
Wes Montgomery – So Do It (Riverside Standard 2360 003)
Wes Montgomery – Go (Fontana FJL 109, UK issue)
Fantasy OJC 089, **OJCCD 089-2, SMJ-6199 Jap.)**
The Alternative Wes Montgomery (Milestone MCD 47065-2)
Wes Montgomery - The Complete Riverside Recordings (Riverside 12RCD 4408-2)

1961

The Montgomery Brothers

Buddy Montgomery (vib, p) Wes Montgomery (g) Monk Montgomery (b) Bobby Thomas (d)
Plaza Sound Studios, NYC, January 3, 1961

1.	Bock To Bock (take 1)	Milestone M 47065, **MCD 47065-2**
2.	Bock To Bock (take 3)	Riverside RLP 362
3.	Groove Yard	-
4.	If I Should Lose You (take 2)	Milestone M 9110, **MCD 9298-2**
5.	If I Should Lose You (take 4)	Riverside RLP 362; **Milestone MCD 9298-2**
6.	Delirium	Riverside RLP 362
7.	Just For Now	-
8.	Doujie (take 6)	-
9.	Doujie (take 7)	Milestone M 47065
10.	Doujie (take 8)	**Riverside 12RCD 4408-2**
11.	Heart Strings	Riverside RLP 362
12.	Remember	-

Issued as:
The Alternative Wes Montgomery (Milestone M 47065)
The Montgomery Brothers - Groove Yard (Riverside RLP 362; Fantasy OJC 139, **OJCCD 139-2, VICJ-23655 (Jap.)**)
The Genius of Wes Montgomery (109561/3) 3 LP box set also includes RLP 434 RLP 362
Wes Montgomery - Encores (Milestone M 9110)
The Alternative Wes Montgomery (Milestone MCD 47065-2)
Wes Montgomery - Dangerous (Milestone MCD 9298-2)
Wes Montgomery - The Complete Riverside Recordings (Riverside 12RCD 4408-2)

Wes Montgomery Quintet

Hank Jones (p) Wes Montgomery (g) Ron Carter (b) Les Humphries (d) Ray Barretto (cga -1/3,5,6)
Plaza Sound Studios, NYC, August 4, 1961

1.	Twisted Blues	Riverside RLP 382; Fantasy OJC 233 and **OJCCD 233-2)**
2.	Cotton Tail	-
3.	I Wish I Knew	-
4.	I'm Just A Lucky So And So	-
5.	Repetition	-
6.	Somethin' Like Bags	-
7.	While We're Young	-
8.	One For My Baby (And One More For The Road)	-

Issued as:
Wes Montgomery - So Much Guitar! (Riverside RLP 382; Fantasy OJC 233, **OJCCD 233-2**, SMJ-6100 Jap.)

The Montgomery Brothers

Buddy Montgomery (vib, p) Wes Montgomery (g) Monk Montgomery (b) Billy Hart (d)
"Jorgie's Jazz Club", St. Louis, MO, August 19, 1961

1.	All Of You	VGM 0001, **VGM-SOU CD1**
2.	Heart Strings	-
3.	Summertime	-
4.	Back To Bach To Bock	-
5.	Stella By Starlight (Starlight)	VGM 0008
6.	'Round About Midnight	-

Issued as:
Wes Montgomery Live At Jorgies Jazz Club (VGM 0001, **VGM-SOU CD Vol.1, DR CD 1147, MRCD 124)**
Wes Montgomery Live At Jorgies And More (VGM 0008, **DRCD 11247, MRCD 124)**
Wes Montgomery Complete Live at Jorgies (DRCD 11247, MRCD 124)
Wes Montgomery Live `61 (MRCD 124)

The Montgomery Brothers

Buddy Montgomery (vib -1/8) Wes Montgomery (g) Monk Montgomery (b) Paul Humphries (d)
"The Cellar", Vancouver B.C., Canada, September 16, 1961

1.	Jeannine (Jeanie)	Fantasy LP 3323; **Milestone MCD-47076-2**
2.	Snowfall	-
3.	Barbados	-
4.	You Don't Know What Love Is	-
5.	On Green Dolphin Street	-
6.	On Green Dolphin Street (take 2)	**Milestone MCD 9298-2**
7.	Stella By Starlight (take 1)	-
8.	Stella By Starlight (take 2)	-
9.	Angel Eyes	Fantasy LP 3323
10.	Bud's Beaux Arts (Beaux Arts)	-

Issued as:
The Montgomery Brothers In Canada (Fantasy LP 3323, LP 8066, OJC 283)
Wes Montgomery - Dangerous (Milestone MCD 9298-2)
Wes Montgomery – Groove Brothers (Milestone MCD-47076-2)

George Shearing And The Montgomery Brothers

Buddy Montgomery (vib) George Shearing (p) Wes Montgomery (g) Monk Montgomery (b) Walter Perkins (d -1,2,5/9,11/14) Armando Peraza (cga, bgo -3,4,10) Ricardo Chimelis (tim, cga -3,4,10)
United Recording Studios, Los Angeles, CA, October 9 & 10, 1961

1.	Love Walked In (take 1)	**Fantasy OJCCD 040-2**
2.	Love Walked In (take 2)	Jazzland J 45710, JLP 55
3.	Mambo In Chimes (take 1)	**Fantasy OJCCD 040-2**
4.	Mambo In Chimes (take 2)	Jazzland J 45710, JLP 55
5.	Love For Sale	Jazzland J 45711, JLP 55
6.	Double Deal	-
7.	No Hard Feelings	Jazzland J 45712, JLP 55

8.	Darn That Dream (take 1)	**Fantasy OJCCD 040-2**
9.	Darn That Dream (take 8)	Jazzland J 45712, JLP 55
10.	The Lamp Is Low	Jazzland J 45713, JLP 55
11.	And Then I Wrote	-
12.	Stranger In Paradise	Jazzland J 45714, JLP 55
13.	Lois Ann	-
14.	Enchanted	Jazzland JLP 55

Issued as:
George Shearing And The Montgomery Brothers (Jazzland JLP 55; Fantasy OJC 040, **OJCCD 040-2, SMJ 6087 Jap.**)
George Shearing/Wes Montgomery - Love Walked In c/w Mambo In Chimes (Jazzland J 45710)
George Shearing/Wes Montgomery - Love For Sale c/w Double Deal (Jazzland J 45711)
George Shearing/Wes Montgomery - No Hard Feelings c/w Darn That Dream (Jazzland J 45712)
George Shearing/Wes Montgomery - The Lamp Is Low c/w And Then I Wrote (Jazzland J 45713)
George Shearing/Wes Montgomery - Stranger In Paradise c/w Lois Ann (Jazzland J 45714)

Milt Jackson - Wes Montgomery Quintet

Milt Jackson (vib) Wynton Kelly (p) Wes Montgomery (g) Sam Jones (b) Philly Joe Jones (d)
Plaza Sound Studios, NYC, December 18, 1961

1.	Stablemates (take 2)	**Riverside 12RCD 4408-2**
2.	Stablemates (take 4)	Riverside RLP 407
3.	Stairway To The Stars (take 2)	Milestone M 47013, M 47065, **MCD 47065-2; Fantasy OJCCD 234-2**
4.	Stairway To The Stars (take 6)	Riverside R 45472, RLP 407
5.	Blue Roz (take 3)	Milestone M 47013, M 9110
6.	Blue Roz (take 4)	Riverside RLP 407
7.	Jingles (take 8)	Milestone M 47013, M 47065, **MCD 47065-2; Fantasy OJCCD 234-2**
8.	Jingles (take 9)	Riverside RLP 407

Issued as:
Milt Jackson/Wes Montgomery - Bags Meets Wes! (Riverside RLP 407; Fantasy OJC 234, **OJCCD 234-2, SMJ-6068 Jap.**)
Wes Montgomery/Milt Jackson/George Shearing - Wes And Friends (Milestone M 47013)
The Alternative Wes Montgomery (Milestone M 47065)
Wes Montgomery - Encores (Milestone M 9110)
Milt Jackson/Wes Montgomery - Stairway To The Stars c/w S.K.J. (Riverside R 45472)
Wes Montgomery - The Complete Riverside Recordings (Riverside 12RCD 4408-2)
The Alternative Wes Montgomery (Milestone MCD 47065-2)

Milt Jackson - Wes Montgomery Quintet

same personnel
Plaza Sound Studios, NYC, December 19, 1961

1.	S.K.J. (take 4)	**Riverside 12RCD 4408-2**
2.	S.K.J. (take 7)	Riverside R 45472, RLP 407
3.	Sam Sack (take 2)	**Riverside 12RCD 4408-2**
4.	Sam Sack (take 3)	Riverside RLP 407
5.	Delilah (take 3)	Milestone M47013, M 9110; **Fantasy OJCCD 234-2**
6.	Delilah (take 4)	Riverside RLP 407

Issued as:
Milt Jackson/Wes Montgomery - Bags Meets Wes! (Riverside RLP 407; Fantasy OJC 234, **OJCCD 234- 2**, SMJ-6058 Jap.)
Wes Montgomery/Milt Jackson/George Shearing - Wes And Friends (Milestone M 47013)
Wes Montgomery - Encores (Milestone M 9110)
Milt Jackson/Wes Montgomery - Stairway To The Stars c/w S.K.J. (Riverside R 45472)
Wes Montgomery - The Complete Riverside Recordings (Riverside 12RCD 4408-2)

1962

Wes Montgomery Quintet

Johnny Griffin (ts -1,3/11) Wynton Kelly (p -1,3/13) Wes Montgomery (g) Paul Chambers (b) Jimmy Cobb (d)
"Tsubo", Berkeley, CA, June 25, 1962

1.	Full House	Riverside RLP 434
2.	I've Grown Accustomed To Her Face	-
3.	Blue 'N' Boogie (take 1)	**Riverside 12RCD 4408-2**
4.	Blue 'N' Boogie (take 2)	Riverside RLP 434
5.	Blue 'N' Boogie (take 2) (ed.)	**Riverside 12RCD 4408-2**
6.	Cariba (take 1)	-
		Riverside RLP 434
7.	Cariba (take 2)	
8.	Come Rain Or Come Shine (take 1)	Milestone M 47065, **MCD 47065-2**; Fantasy **OJCCD 106-2**
9.	Come Rain Or Come Shine (take 2)	Riverside RLP 434
10.	S.O.S. (take 2)	Milestone M 47065, **MCD 9298-2**; Fantasy **OJCCD 106-2**
11.	S.O.S. (take 3)	Riverside RLP 434; **Milestone MCD 9298-2**
12.	Born To Be Blue! (take 1)	**Riverside 12RCD 4408-2**
13.	Born To Be Blue! (take 2)	Milestone M 47065, **MCD 47065-2**; Fantasy **OJCCD 106-2**

Issued as:
Wes Montgomery - Full House (Riverside RLP 434; Fantasy OJC 106, **OJCCD 106-2**, SMJ-6069 Jap.)
The Alternative Wes Montgomery (Milestone M 47065)
The Genius of Wes Montgomery (109561/3) 3 LP box set also includes RLP 434 RLP 362
Wes Montgomery - The Complete Riverside Recordings (Riverside 12RCD 4408-2)
The Alternative Wes Montgomery (Milestone MCD 47065-2)
Wes Montgomery - Dangerous (Milestone MCD 9298-2)

1963

Wes Montgomery With Jimmy Jones Orchestra

Phil Bodner (woodwinds) Mac Ceppos, Winston Collymore, Arnold Eidus, Leo Kruczek, Harry Lookofsky, David Nadien, Gene Orloff, Raoul Poliakin, Isadore Zir (vln) Alfred Brown, Burt Fisch (vla) Charles McCracken, George Ricci (vlc) Gloria Agostini (harp) Hank Jones (p, cel) Kenny Burrell, Wes Montgomery (g) Milt Hinton (b) Osie Johnson (d) Jimmy Jones (arr, cond)
Plaza Sound Studios, NYC, April 18, 1963

1.	All The Way	Riverside RLP 472
2.	Prelude To A Kiss (take 2)	**Riverside 12RCD 4408-2**
3.	Prelude To A Kiss (take 3)	Riverside RLP 472
4.	My Romance	-
5.	God Bless' The Child (take 2)	Milestone M 47030
6.	God Bless' The Child (take 4)	Riverside RLP 472

Issued as;
Wes Montgomery - Fusion!*(Riverside RLP 472; Fantasy OJC 368, **OJCCD 368-2**)
Wes Montgomery - In The Wee, Small Hours (Riverside RS 3002)
Wes Montgomery - Pretty Blue (Milestone M 47030)
Wes Montgomery - The Complete Riverside Recordings (Riverside 12RCD 4408-2)
* also called Dark Velvet (UK issue)

Wes Montgomery With Jimmy Jones Orchestra

Dick Hyman (p) replaces Hank Jones
Plaza Sound Studios, NYC, April 18, 1963

1.	Pretty Blue (take 1)	**Fantasy OJCCD 368-2**
2.	Pretty Blue (take 1) (ed.)	**Riverside 12RCD 4408-2**
3.	Pretty Blue (take 2)	Riverside RLP 472
4.	In The Wee, Small Hours Of The Morning	-
5.	The Girl Next Door (take 1)	**Riverside 12RCD 4408-2**
6.	The Girl Next Door (take 2)	Riverside RLP 472

Issued as:
Wes Montgomery - Fusion!* (Riverside RLP 472; Fantasy OJC 368, **OJCCD 368-2**, SMJ-6210 Jap.)
Wes Montgomery - In The Wee, Small Hours (Riverside RS 3002)
Wes Montgomery - The Complete Riverside Recordings (Riverside 12RCD 4408-2)
* also called Dark Velvet (UK issue)

Wes Montgomery With Jimmy Jones Orchestra

Sam Rand, Sylvan Shulman, Paul Winter (vln) Ralph Hersh (vla) Kermit Moore, Lucient Schmit (vlc) Margaret Rose (harp) replaces Eidus, Kruczek, Poliakin, Brown, McCracken, Ricci, Agostini
Plaza Sound Studios, NYC, April 19, 1963

1.	Tune-Up (take 1)	**Riverside 12RCD 4408-2**
2.	Tune-Up (take 2&3)	Milestone M 47065, **MCD 47065-2; Fantasy OJCCD 368-2**
3.	Tune-Up (take 4)	Milestone M 47030, M9110; **Fantasy OJCCD 368-2**
4.	Tune-Up (take 5)	Riverside RLP 472

5.	Tune-Up (take 5) (ed.)	**Riverside 12RCD 4408-2**
6.	Somewhere	Riverside RLP 472
7.	Baubles, Bangles And Beads (take 3)	**Riverside 12RCD 4408-2**
8.	Baubles, Bangles And Beads (take 4)	Riverside RLP 472

Issued as:
The Alternative Wes Montgomery (Milestone M 47065)
Wes Montgomery - Pretty Blue (Milestone M 47030)
Wes Montgomery - Encores (Milestone M 9110)
Wes Montgomery - Fusion! * (Riverside RLP 472; Fantasy OJC 368, **OJCCD 368-2**, SMJ-6210 Jap.)
Wes Montgomery - In The Wee, Small Hours (Riverside RS 3002)
Wes Montgomery - The Complete Riverside Recordings (Riverside 12RCD 4408-2)
The Alternative Wes Montgomery (Milestone MCD 47065-2)
* also called Dark Velvet (UK issue)

Wes Montgomery Trio

Mel Rhyne (org) Wes Montgomery (g) Jimmy Cobb (d)
Plaza Sound Studios, NYC, April 22, 1963

1.	Besame Mucho (take 2)	Milestone M 47065, **MCD 47065-2**; **Fantasy OJCCD 261-2**
2.	Besame Mucho (take 3)	Riverside RLP 459
3.	Dearly Beloved	-
4.	Days Of Wine And Roses	Riverside RLP 459; Milestone M 47030
5.	The Trick Bag (take 2/5)	Riverside RLP 459
6.	The Trick Bag (take 6)	Milestone M 9110
7.	Canadian Sunset	Riverside RLP 459
8.	Fried Pies (take 1)	Milestone M 47065, **MCD 47065-2**; **Fantasy OJCCD 261-2**
9.	Fried Pies (take 2)	Riverside RLP 459, RLP 494
10.	Fried Pies (take 2) (ed.)	**Riverside 12RCD 4408-2**
11.	The Breeze And I	Riverside RLP 459
12.	For Heaven's Sake	-

Issued as:
The Alternative Wes Montgomery (Milestone M 47065)
Wes Montgomery - Boss Guitar (Riverside RLP 459; Fantasy OJC 261, SMJ 611 Jap.,**OJCCD 261-2**)
This is Wes Montgomery (Riverside RS 3012)
Wes Montgomery - Yesterdays (Milestone M 47057)
Wes Montgomery - Pretty Blue (Milestone M 47030)
Wes Montgomery - Encores (Milestone M 9110)
Wes Montgomery - Guitar On The Go (Riverside RLP 494; Fantasy OJC 489, SMJ-6168 Jap., **OJCCD 489-2**)
The Alternative Wes Montgomery (Milestone MCD 47065-2)
Wes Montgomery - The Complete Riverside Recordings (Riverside 12RCD 4408-2)
Note: Riverside RLP 459 also issued in Japan as: Besame Mucho VIJ 4029

Wes Montgomery Trio

Mel Rhyne (org -1/6) Wes Montgomery (g) George Brown (d -1/6)
Plaza Sound Studios, NYC, October 10, 1963

1.	Freddie Freeloader	Riverside RLP 492
2.	Blues Riff (Movin' Along)	-
3.	Blues Riff (Movin' Along) (alt. take)	**Riverside 12RCD 4408-2**

4.	Moanin' (take 7)	Riverside RLP 492
5.	Moanin' (take 7) (ed.)	Milestone M 47057; **Fantasy OJCCD 144-2**
6.	**Dreamsville**	**Riverside RLP 494; Milestone M 47030**
7.	**Mi Cosa (take 1)**	**Fantasy OJCCD 489-2**

Issued as:
Wes Montgomery - Portrait Of Wes (Riverside RLP 492; Fantasy OJC 144, SMJ-6202, **OJCCD 144-2**)
Wes Montgomery - Yesterdays (Milestone M 47057)
Wes Montgomery - Guitar On The Go (Riverside RLP 494; Fantasy OJC 489, SMJ-6168 Jap., **OJCCD 489-2**)
Wes Montgomery - Pretty Blue (Milestone M 47030)
Wes Montgomery - The Complete Riverside Recordings (Riverside 12RCD 4408-2)
Note Riverside RLP 492 also issued in Japan as: Wes Montgomery-Moanin` VIJ 4028

Wes Montgomery Trio

Same personnel
Plaza Sound Studios, NYC, November 27, 1963

1.	Lolita	Riverside RLP 492
2.	Lolita (alt. take)	**Riverside 12RCD 4408-2**
3.	Dangerous	Riverside RLP 492
4.	Dangerous (alt. take)	**Riverside 12RCD 4408-2; Milestone MCD 9298-2**
5.	Yesterday's Child	Riverside RLP 492
6.	Yesterday's Child (alt. take)	**Riverside 12RCD 4408-2; Milestone MCD 9298-2**
7.	The Way You Look Tonight (take 1)	Riverside RLP 494
8.	The Way You Look Tonight (take 2)	Milestone M 47065, **MCD 47065-2; Fantasy OJCCD 489-2**
9.	Geno	Riverside RLP 494
10.	For All We Know	Riverside RLP 494; Milestone M 47030
11	Moanin' (take 10)	Milestone M 47057, M 9110
12.	Blues Riff (take 7)	Milestone M 47057, **MCD 9298-2**
13	Blues Riff (take 8)	Milestone M 47057; **Fantasy OJCCD 144-2**

Issued as:
Wes Montgomery - Portrait Of Wes (Riverside RLP 492; Fantasy OJC 144, **OJCCD 144-2**; SMJ- 6202   Jap.)
Wes Montgomery - Guitar On The Go (Riverside RLP 494; Fantasy OJC 489, **OJCCD 489-2**; SMJ- 6168 Jap.)
The Alternative Wes Montgomery (Milestone M 47065)
Wes Montgomery - Pretty Blue (Milestone M 47030)
Wes Montgomery - Yesterdays (Milestone M 47057)
Wes Montgomery - Encores (Milestone M 9110)
Wes Montgomery - The Complete Riverside Recordings (Riverside 12RCD 4408-2)
Wes Montgomery - Dangerous (Milestone MCD 9298-2)
The Alternative Wes Montgomery (Milestone MCD 47065-2)
Note - Riverside RLP 492 also issued in Japan as: Wes Montgomery-Moanin` VIJ 4028

1964

Joe Williams With Billy Taylor Quartet

Billy Taylor (p) Wes Montgomery (g) Ben Tucker (b) Grady Tate (d) Joe Williams (vo -1/8)
radio broadcast, 'The Navy Swings', NYC, spring 1964

1.	A Beautiful Thing	Program 49GH; VGM 0001; **LHJ 10211**
2.	More Than Likely	-
3.	Have A Good Time	Program 50GH; **Norma [J] NOCD 5645**; **LHJ 10211**
4.	Until I' Met You	-
5.	I Won't Cry Anymore	Program 51GH; **Norma [J] NOCD 5645**; **LHJ 10211**
6.	S'posin'	-
7.	All My Life	Program 52GH; **Norma [J] NOCD 5645**; **LHJ 10211**
8.	Alone Together	-
9.	There Will Never Be Another You	Program 49GH; VGM 0001, **LHJ 10211**
10.	The More I See You	-
11.	A Grand Night For Swingin'	Program 50GH; **Norma [J] NOCD 5645**; **LHJ 10211**
12.	Afterthoughts	-
13.	Capricious	Program 51GH; **Norma [J] NOCD 5645**; **LHJ 10211**
14.	Body And Soul	-
15.	Paraphrase	Program 52GH; **Norma [J] NOCD 5645**; **LHJ 10211**

Issued as:
Various Artists - The Navy Swings (Program 49GH)
Wes Montgomery Live At Jorgies Jazz Club (VGM 0001, **VGM-SOU CD1**)
Various Artists - The Navy Swings (Program 50GH)
Various Artists - The Navy Swings (Program 51GH)
Various Artists - The Navy Swings (Program 52GH)
Wes Montgomery - Billy And Wes (Norma [J] NOCD 5645)
Wes Montgomery and the Billy Taylor Trio (LHJ 10211)

Wes Montgomery With Johnny Pate Orchestra

Ernie Royal, Clark Terry, Snooky Young (tp) Jimmy Cleveland, Urbie Green, Quentin Jackson, Chauncey Welsch (tb) Don Butterfield or Harvey Phillips (tu) Jerome Richardson (fl, ss, ts) Bobby Scott (p) Wes Montgomery (g) Bob Cranshaw (b) Grady Tate (d) Willie Bobo (per -4) Johnny Pate (arr, cond)
A&R Studios, NYC, November 11, 1964

1.	Matchmaker (aka Matchmaker, Matchmaker)	Verve V/V6 8610, V6 8796
2.	People	Verve V/V6 8610
3.	Senza Fine (aka The Phoenix Love Theme)	Verve VK 10443, V/V6 8610
4.	Moca Flor	Verve V/V6 8610, V6 8796
5.	Theodora	-

Issued as:
Wes Montgomery - Movin' Wes (Verve V/V6 8610, SMJ-6069 Jap, **Verve 521 433-2, 810 045-2**)
Wes Montgomery - Eulogy (Verve V6 8796)
Wes Montgomery - Senza Fine c/w Caravan (Verve VK 10443)

Wes Montgomery With Johnny Pate Orchestra

Ernie Royal, Clark Terry, Snooky Young (tp) Jimmy Cleveland, Urbie Green, Quentin Jackson, Chauncey Welsch (tb) Don Butterfield or Harvey Phillips (tu) Jerome Richardson (fl, ss, ts) Bobby Scott (p) Wes Montgomery (g) Bob Cranshaw (b) Grady Tate (d) Willie Bobo (per -3/5) Johnny Pate (arr, cond)
A&R Studios, NYC, November 16, 1964

1.	Movin' Wes, Pt. 1	Verve VK 143, V/V6 8610, V/V6 8714
2.	Movin' Wes, Pt. 2	Verve VK 143, V/V6 8610
3.	West Coast Blues	Verve V/V6 8610, V3HB 8839, **Verve 521 690-2**
4.	In And Out	Verve V/V6 8610
5.	Caravan	Verve VK 10443, V/V6 8610, V/V6 8714, 2V6S 8818, **Verve 521 690-2**
6.	Born To Be Blue	Verve V/V6 8610

Issued as:
Wes Montgomery - Movin' Wes (Verve V/V6 8610, SMJ 6069 Jap, **Verve 521 433-2, 810 045-2**)
The Best Of Wes Montgomery (Verve V/V6 8714)
Wes Montgomery - Return Engagement (Verve V3HB 8839)
Various Artists - We Love You Madly - A Tribute To Duke Ellington (Verve 2V6S 8818)
Wes Montgomery - Movin' Wes, Pt. 1&2 (Verve VK 143)
Wes Montgomery - Senza Fine c/w Caravan (Verve VK 10443)
Wes Montgomery – Impressions – The Verve Jazz Sides (Verve 521 690-2)

1965

Wes Montgomery Quartet

Harold Mabern (p) Wes Montgomery (g) Arthur Harper (b) Jimmy Lovelace (d)
radio broadcast, WABC-FM, "Half Note", NYC, February 12, 1965

1.	Caravan	Beppo [E] BE KOG 14800, **definitive Records DRCD 11224**
2.	'Round About Midnight	-
3.	Four On Six	-
4.	Here's That Rainy Day	no label or number given on LP
5.	West Coast Blues	Unissued

Issued as;
Wes Montgomery - Kings Of The Guitar (Beppo [E] BE KOG 14800)
Wes Montgomery - Stretching Out Live In '65 (no label no number) omit track 5.
Wes Montgomery – Private Recordings and Rarities (Suisa JZCD 378) omit track 5.
The Incredible Jazz Guitar of Wes Montgomery – ultra-rare American Club Performance (definitive Records DRCD 11224

Wes Montgomery With Don Sebesky Orchestra

Arnold Eidus, Lewis Eley, Paul Gershman, Louis Haber, Julius Held, Harry Lookofsky, Jos Malignaggi, Gene Orloff, Sol Shapiro (vln) Harold Coletta, Dave Schwartz (vla) Charles McCracken, George Ricci (vlc) Margaret Ross (harp) Roger Kellaway (p) Wes Montgomery (g) Bob Cranshaw (b) Grady Tate (d) Candido Camero (bgo, cga) Don Sebesky (arr, cond)
Rudy Van Gelder Studio, Englewood Cliffs, NJ, March 16, 1965

1.	Musty	Verve V/V6 8625, 2V6S 8813, V3HB 8839, **Verve 539 062-2**
2.	Just Walkin'	Verve V6 8804, 314 539 062-2, **Verve 539 062-2**
3.	Just Walkin' (alt. take)	Verve 314 539 062-2, **Verve 539 062-2**

| 4. | Here's That Rainy Day | Verve V/V6 8625, 2V6S 8813, V3HB 8839, **Verve 539 062-2** |

Issued as:
Wes Montgomery - Bumpin' (Verve V/V6 8625, 314 539 062-2, **Verve 539 062-2 (CD incl. track 3, 821 985-2)**.
The History Of Wes Montgomery (Verve 2V6S 8813)
Wes Montgomery - Return Engagement (Verve V3HB 8839)
Wes Montgomery - Just Walkin' (Verve V6 8804)

Wes Montgomery Quartet

Harold Mabern (p) Wes Montgomery (g) Arthur Harper (b) Jimmy Lovelace (d)
TV broadcast, 'Jazz 625', BBC-TV Centre, London, England, March 25, 1965

	West Coast Blues (edited intro)	**Gambit Records 69225**
	Yesterdays	-
	Jingles	-
	'Round About Midnight	-
	Twisted Blues	-
	Full House	-
	West Coast Blues (edited outro)	-

Issued as:
Wes Montgomery Quartet, Live in Belgium 1965 (Gambit Records 69225)
See also Appendix 2 – Film Footage.

Wes Montgomery Quartet

Harold Mabern (p) Wes Montgomery (g) Arthur Harper (b) Jimmy Lovelace (d)
TB Broadcast `Jazz Prisma`, Universal Studio, Brussels, Belgium, March 1965

1.	Impressions	**Gambit Records 69225**
2.	Twisted Blues	-
3.	Here's That Rainy Day	-
4.	Jingles	-
5.	The Girl Next Door	-

Issued as:
Wes Montgomery Quartet, Live in Belgium 1965 (Gambit Records 69225)
See also Appendix 2 – Film Footage.

Wes Montgomery Quintet

Johnny Griffin (ts -8/11) Harold Mabern (p) Wes Montgomery (g) Arthur Harper (b) Jimmy Lovelace (d)
"Theatre Des Champs-Elysees", Paris, France, March 27, 1965

1.	Four On Six	BYG [J] YX 4016/17; Affinity [E] AFF 13
2.	Twisted Blues (Wes' Rhythm)	-
3.	Impressions	-
4.	To Wane (To When)	-
5.	Jingles (Mr. Walker)	BYG [J] YX 4016/17; Affinity [E] AFF 18

6.	The Girl Next Door (To Django)	-
7.	Here's That Rainy Day	-
8.	'Round About Midnight	-
9.	Full House	Esoldun [F] FC 108
10.	Blue 'N' Boogie	-
11.	West Coast Blues	-

Issued as:
Wes Montgomery - Solitude (BYG [J] YX 4016/17)
Wes Montgomery - Impressions (Affinity [E] AFF 13)
Wes Montgomery - Solitude (Affinity [E] AFF 18)
Wes Montgomery Live In Paris 1965 (Esoldun [F] FC 108)
Wes Montgomery – 'Round Midnight (tracks 1,3,6,7& 8) Affinity/Charly CD 13, Charly LE Jazz CD 34)

Wes Montgomery Quintet

Clark Terry (tp, flh) Pim Jacobs (p) Wes Montgomery (g) Ruud Jacobs (b) Han Bennink (d)
Radio broadcast, Vara Radio Studio 7, Hilversum, Holland, April 2, 1965

1.	Opus Caprice (Rhythm-A-Ning)	Vara Jazz [H] 8219; **Jazz Door 1227**
2.	Just Friends	-
3.	In A Mellowtone	-
4.	Straight, No Chaser	-
5.	The Theme	-

Issued as:
Wes Montgomery And Clark Terry (Vara Jazz [H] 8219, Jazz Door 1227, **Bandstand BDCD 1504 Jap**.)
Wes Montgomery and the Billy Taylor Trio (Lonehill Jazz JHJ 102110 – omit The Theme.
Wes Montgomery/Clark Terry – Straight, No Chaser (Jazz Door 1227)
*The Bandstand and Jazz Door issues list the rhythm section as Mabern (p), Harper (b) & Lovelace (d).

Wes Montgomery Quartet

Stan Tracey (p) Wes Montgomery (g) Rick Laird (b) Ronnie Stephenson (d)
Ronnie Scott's Club, London, England, April 5, 1965

1.	Sonny Boy	(**JHAS 604**)
2.	D-Natural Blues (Wes' Easy Blues)	

Issued as:
Wes Montgomery - Body And Soul (JHAS 604)

Wes Montgomery Quartet

Stan Tracey (p -1/8) Wes Montgomery (g) Rick Laird (b -1/8) Ronnie Stephenson (d -1/8)
Ronnie Scott's Club, London, England, April 9, 1965

3.	Mi Cosa (Solo Ballad In A Major)	**RSJH Music [E] JHAS 604**

Issued as:
Wes Montgomery - Body And Soul (JHAS 604)

Wes Montgomery Octet

Hans Koller (as -1/5) Ronnie Scott (ts -1/5) Johnny Griffin (ts -1/5,10,11) Ronnie Ross (bars -1/5) Martial Solal (p) Wes Montgomery (g) Michel Gaudry (b) Ronnie Stephenson (d)
NDR Studio 10, Hamburg, West Germany, April 30, 1965

1.	Blue Grass	**Philology [It] W 97-2**
2.	Last Of The Wine (Glass Of Cool Wine)	-
3.	The Leopard Walks	-
4.	West Coast Blues	-
5.	West Coast Blues (theme)	unissued
6.	Here's That Rainy Day	**Philology [It] W 97-2**
7.	Four On Six	-
8.	Twisted Blues	-
9.	West Coast Blues	unissued
10.	Blue Monk	**Philology [It] W 97-2**
11.	unknown title (2nd opening theme)	unissued

Issued as:
Wes Montgomery Live In Europe (Philology [It] W 97-2)
Wes Montgomery – Private Recordings and Rarities (Suisa JZCD 378)

Wes Montgomery Octet

Hans Koller (as) Johnny Griffin, Ronnie Scott (ts) Ronnie Ross (bars) Martial Solal (p) Wes Montgomery (g) Michel Gaudry (b) Ronnie Stephenson (d)
TV broadcast, Hamburg, West Germany, April, 1965

1.	West Coast Blues	Green Line [It] VID JAZZ 39, **Philology W97-2, Suisa JZCD 378**

Issued as:
Wes Montgomery Live In Europe (Philology [It] W 97-2)
Wes Montgomery – Private Recordings and Rarities (Suisa JZCD 378)
See also Appendix 2 – Film Footage

Wes Montgomery With Don Sebesky Orchestra

Arnold Eidus, Lewis Eley, Paul Gershman, Louis Haber, Julius Held, Harry Lookofsky, Jos Malignaggi, Gene Orloff, Sol Shapiro (vln -2) Harold Coletta, Dave Schwartz (vla -2) Charles McCracken, George Ricci (vlc -2) Margaret Ross (harp -2) Roger Kellaway (p) Wes Montgomery (g) Bob Cranshaw (b) Grady Tate (d) Candido Camero (bgo, cga -2) Don Sebesky (arr, cond -2)
Rudy Van Gelder Studio, Englewood Cliffs, NJ, May 18, 1965

1.	Tear It Down	Verve V/V6 8625, V6 8796, **Verve 539 062-2**
2.	The Shadow Of Your Smile	Verve VK 10373, VK 10444, V/V6 8625, V/V6 8714, 2V6S 8813, **Verve 539 062-2**

Issued as:
Wes Montgomery - Bumpin' (Verve V/V6 8625, 314 539 062-2, **539 062-2, 821 985-2**)
Wes Montgomery - Eulogy (Verve V6 8796)
The Best Of Wes Montgomery (Verve V/V6 8714)
The History Of Wes Montgomery (Verve 2V6S 8813)

Wes Montgomery - The Shadow Of Your Smile c/w Bumpin', Pt. 2 (Verve VK 10373)
Wes Montgomery - The Shadow Of Your Smile c/w A Quiet Thing (Verve VK 10444)

Wes Montgomery With Don Sebesky Orchestra

Helcio Millito (d) replaces Tate, Camero
Rudy Van Gelder Studio, Englewood Cliffs, NJ, May 19, 1965

1.	Con Alma	Verve V/V6 8625, V/V6 8714, V3HB 8839, **Verve 539 062-2**
2.	A Quiet Thing	Verve VK 10444, V/V6 8625, **Verve 539 062-2**

Issued as:
Wes Montgomery - Bumpin' (Verve V/V6 8625, 314 539 062-2, **Verve 539 062-2, 821 985-2**)
The Best Of Wes Montgomery (Verve V/V6 8714)
Wes Montgomery - Return Engagement (Verve V3HB 8839)
Wes Montgomery - The Shadow Of Your Smile c/w A Quiet Thing (Verve VK 10444)

Wes Montgomery With Don Sebesky Orchestra

Arnold Eidus, Lewis Eley, Paul Gershman, Louis Haber, Julius Held, Harry Lookofsky, Jos Malignaggi, Gene Orloff, Sol Shapiro (vln) Harold Coletta, Dave Schwartz (vla) Charles McCracken, George Ricci (vlc) Margaret Ross (harp) Roger Kellaway (p -2/4) Wes Montgomery (g) Bob Cranshaw (b) Grady Tate (d -2/4) Candido Camero (bgo, cga -2,3) Don Sebesky (arr, cond)
Rudy Van Gelder Studio, Englewood Cliffs, NJ, May 20, 1965

1.	Mi Cosa (aka My Thing)	Verve V/V6 8625, V6 8796, **Verve 539 062-2**
2.	Bumpin', Pt. 1	Verve VK 10441, V/V6 8625, V6 8757, V3HB 8839, **Verve 539 062-2**
3.	Bumpin', Pt. 2	Verve VK 10373, VK 10441, V/V6 8625, V6 8757, 2V6S 8813, V3HB 8839, **Verve 539 062-2**
4.	My One And Only Love	Verve V6 8804, 314 539 062-2, **Verve 539 062-2**

Issued as:
Wes Montgomery - Bumpin' (Verve V/V6 8625, 314 539 062-2, **Verve 539 062-2, 821 985-2**)
Wes Montgomery - Eulogy (Verve V6 8796)
The Best Of Wes Montgomery, Vol. 2 (Verve V6 8757)
Wes Montgomery - Return Engagement (Verve V3HB 8839)
The History Of Wes Montgomery (Verve 2V6S 8813)
Wes Montgomery - Just Walkin' (Verve V6 8804)
Wes Montgomery - Bumpin', Pt. 1&2 (Verve VK 10441)
Wes Montgomery - The Shadow Of Your Smile c/w Bumpin', Pt. 2 (Verve VK 10373)

Wynton Kelly Trio With Wes Montgomery

Wynton Kelly (p) Wes Montgomery (g) Paul Chambers (b) Jimmy Cobb (d)
"Half Note", NYC, June 24, 1965

1.	No Blues	Verve V/V6 8633, VE2 2513, [J] J28J 25117, **Verve 539 062-2, LHJ 10181 2**
2.	If You Could See Me Now	-

Issued as:
Wynton Kelly/Wes Montgomery - Smokin' At The Half Note (Verve V/V6 8633, **Verve 829 578-2**)
Wes Montgomery - The Small Group Recordings (Verve VE2 2513)
Wynton Kelly/Wes Montgomery - Smokin' At The Half Note, Vol. 2 (Verve [J] J28J 25117, **Verve POCJ-1902 Jap. CD**)
Wynton Kelly/Wes Montgomery – Complete Live At The Half Note (Lonehill LHJ 10181 2)

Wynton Kelly Trio With Wes Montgomery

same personnel
"Half Note", NYC, June 25, 1965

1.	The Surrey With The Fringe On Top	Verve V6 8765, [J] J28J 25117, Verve 539 062-2, **LHJ 10181 2**
2.	Willow Weep For Me	Verve VE2 2513, [J] J28J 25117, Verve 539 062-2, **LHJ 10181 2**
3.	Portrait Of Jennie	-

Issued as:
Wes Montgomery - Willow Weep For Me (Verve V6 8765, MV-1077 Jap., Verve SVLP 9238, Verve Select 2317 023, **Universal 314 589 486-2**)
Wes Montgomery - The Small Group Recordings (Verve VE2 2513)
Wynton Kelly/Wes Montgomery - Smokin' At The Half Note, Vol. 2 (Verve [J] J28J 25117, **Verve POCJ-1902 Jap. CD**)
Wynton Kelly/Wes Montgomery – Complete Live At The Half Note (Lonehill LHJ 10181 2)
Wes Montgomery – Impressions – The Verve Jazz Sides (Verve 539 062-2)

Wynton Kelly Trio With Wes Montgomery plus Claus Ogerman Orchestra

Wynton Kelly (p) Wes Montgomery (g) Paul Chambers (b) Jimmy Cobb (d) Claus Ogerman (arr, cond) unidentified brass and woodwinds
"Half Note", NYC, June 25, 1965, October 8, 1968

1.	Willow Weep For Me (overdubbed ver.)	Verve V6 8765, V3HB 8839
2.	Portrait Of Jennie (overdubbed ver.)	Verve V6 8765

Issued as:
Wes Montgomery - Willow Weep For Me (Verve V6 8765, MV-2077 Jap., Verve SVLP 9238, Verve Select 2317 023, **Universal 314 589 486-2**)
Wes Montgomery - Return Engagement (Verve V3HB 8839)

Wynton Kelly Trio With Wes Montgomery

Wynton Kelly (p) Wes Montgomery (g) Paul Chambers (b) Jimmy Cobb (d)
"Half Note", NYC, August 13, 1965

1.	Four On Six	Verve V6 8765, [J] J28J 25117, **Verve 539 062-2, LHJ 10181 2**
2.	Oh, You Crazy Moon	Verve [J] J28J 25117, **Verve 539 062-2, LHJ 10181 2**

Issued as:
Wes Montgomery - Willow Weep For Me (Verve V6 8765, MV-2077 Jap., Verve SVLP 9238, Verve Select 2317 023, **Universal 314 589 486-2**)
Wynton Kelly/Wes Montgomery - Smokin' At The Half Note, Vol. 2 (Verve [J] J28J 25117, **Verve POCJ-1902 Jap. CD**)
Wynton Kelly/Wes Montgomery – Complete Live At The Half Note (Lonehill LHJ 10181 2)
Wes Montgomery – Impressions – The Verve Jazz Sides (Verve 539 062-2)

Wynton Kelly Trio With Wes Montgomery plus Claus Ogerman Orchestra

Wynton Kelly (p) Wes Montgomery (g) Paul Chambers (b) Jimmy Cobb (d) Claus Ogerman (arr, cond) unidentified brass and woodwinds
"Half Note", NYC, August 13, 1965, October 8, 1968

| 1. | Oh, You Crazy Moon (overdubbed version) | Verve V6 8765 |

Issued as:
Wes Montgomery - Willow Weep For Me (Verve V6 8765, MV-2077 Jap., Verve SVLP 9238, Verve Select 2317 023, **Universal 314 589 486-2**)
Wynton Kelly/Wes Montgomery – Complete Live At The Half Note (Lonehill LHJ 10181 2)

Wynton Kelly Trio With Wes Montgomery

Wynton Kelly (p) Wes Montgomery (g) Paul Chambers (b) Jimmy Cobb (d)
"Half Note", NYC, September 17, 1965

| 1. | Impressions | Verve V6 8765, V3HB 8839, VE2 2513, [J] J28J 25117, **Verve 521 690-2, LHJ 10181 2** |
| 2. | Misty | Verve VE2 2513, [J] J28J 25117, **Verve 521 690-2, LHJ 10181 2** |

Issued as:
Wes Montgomery - Willow Weep For Me (Verve V6 8765, MV-2077 Jap., Verve SVLP 9238, Verve Select 2317 023, **Universal 314 589 486-2**)
Wes Montgomery - Return Engagement (Verve V3HB 8839)
Wes Montgomery - The Small Group Recordings (Verve VE2 2513)
Wynton Kelly/Wes Montgomery - Smokin' At The Half Note, Vol. 2 (Verve [J] J28J 25117, **Verve POCJ-1902 Jap. CD**)
Wynton Kelly/Wes Montgomery – Complete Live At The Half Note (Lonehill LHJ 10181 2)
Wes Montgomery – Impressions – The Verve Jazz Sides (Verve 539 062-2)

Wynton Kelly Trio With Wes Montgomery plus Claus Ogerman Orchestra

Wynton Kelly (p) Wes Montgomery (g) Paul Chambers (b) Jimmy Cobb (d) Claus Ogerman (arr, cond) unidentified brass and woodwinds
"Half Note", NYC, September 17, 1965, (October 8, 1968)

| 1. | Misty (overdubbed ver.) | Verve V6 8765 |

Issued as:
Wes Montgomery - Willow Weep For Me (Verve V6 8765, MV-2077 Jap., Verve SVLP 9238, Verve Select 2317 023, **Universal 314 589 486-2**)

Wynton Kelly Trio With Wes Montgomery

Wynton Kelly (p) Wes Montgomery (g) Paul Chambers (b) Jimmy Cobb (d)
Rudy Van Gelder Studio, Englewood Cliffs, NJ, September 22, 1965

1.	Unit Seven	Verve V/V6 8633, VE2 2513, **Verve 521 690-2**
2.	Four On Six	-
3.	What's New?	-

Issued as:
Wynton Kelly/Wes Montgomery - Smokin' At The Half Note (Verve V/V6 8633, Verve 829 578-2)
Wes Montgomery - The Small Group Recordings (Verve VE2 2513)
Wes Montgomery – Impressions – The Verve Jazz Sides (Verve 539 062-2)

Wynton Kelly Trio With Wes Montgomery

Wynton Kelly (p) Wes Montgomery (g) Paul Chambers (b) Jimmy Cobb (d) Alan Grant (ann)
Radio broadcast, WABC-FM, "Half Note", NYC, September 24, 1965

1.	Laura	Toko [J] WM94 12; All Blues [J] ABR-010
2.	Cariba	-
3.	A Little Blues (The Theme)	All Blues [J] ABR-010

Issued as:
Wes Montgomery - Smokin' Guitar (Toko [J] WM94 12)
Wes Montgomery - Other Sessions At The Half Note 1965 (All Blues [J] ABR-010)

Wynton Kelly Trio With Wes Montgomery

Wynton Kelly (p) Wes Montgomery (g) Ron Carter (b) Jimmy Cobb (d) Alan Grant (ann)
Radio broadcast, WABC-FM, "Half Note", NYC, November 5, 1965

1.	Impressions	All Blues [J] ABR-010
2.	Mi Cosa	-
3.	No Blues	-

Issued as:
Wes Montgomery - Other Sessions At The Half Note 1965 (All Blues [J] ABR-010)

Wynton Kelly Trio With Wes Montgomery

Wynton Kelly (p) Wes Montgomery (g) Larry Ridley (b) Jimmy Cobb (d) Alan Grant (ann)
Radio broadcast, WABC-FM, "Half Note", NYC, November 12, 1965

1.	Birks' Works	Toko [J] WM94 12; All Blues [J] ABR-010
2.	Four On Six	-
3.	The Theme (aka Alan Grant talks)	All Blues [J] ABR-010

Issued as:
Wes Montgomery - Smokin' Guitar (Toko [J] WM94 12)
Wes Montgomery - Other Sessions At The Half Note 1965 (All Blues [J] ABR-010)

Wynton Kelly Trio With Wes Montgomery

Wynton Kelly (p) Wes Montgomery (g) Herman Wright (b) Jimmy Cobb (d) Alan Grant (ann)
Radio broadcast, WABC-FM, "Half Note", NYC, November 19, 1965

1.	All The Things You Are	Toko [J] WM94 12; All Blues [J] ABR-010
2.	I Remember You	-
3.	No Blues (inc.)	All Blues [J] ABR-010

Issued as:
Wes Montgomery - Smokin' Guitar (Toko [J] WM94 12)
Wes Montgomery - Other Sessions At The Half Note 1965 (All Blues [J] ABR-010)

Wes Montgomery With Oliver Nelson Orchestra

Donald Byrd, Joe Newman, Ernie Royal (tp) Wayne Andre, Jimmy Cleveland, Quentin Jackson, Donny Moore, Tony Studd (tb) Phil Woods (as, cl) Jerry Dodgion (as, cl, fl, picc) Romeo Penque (ts, cl, fl, picc, ob, ehr) Danny Bank (bars, fl, afl, bcl) Bob Ashton (sax, cl, fl) Herbie Hancock or Roger Kellaway (p) Wes Montgomery (g) George Duvivier (b) Grady Tate or Sol Gubin (d) Candido Camero (cga) Oliver Nelson (arr, cond)
Rudy Van Gelder Studio, Englewood Cliffs, NJ, November 20, 1965

1.	Goin' Out Of My Head	Verve VK 10384, VK 10440, V/V6 8642, V/V6 8714, 2V6S 8813, V3HB 8839, V6 654-2, **Verve 825 676-2**
2.	Boss City	Verve VK 10384, V/V6 8642, V6 8796, 2V6S 8813, V3HB 8839, **Verve 825 676-2**

Issued as:
Wes Montgomery - Goin' Out Of My Head (Verve V/V6 8642, **825 676-2**)
The Best Of Wes Montgomery (Verve V/V6 8714)
The History Of Wes Montgomery (Verve 2V6S 8813)
Wes Montgomery - Return Engagement (Verve V3HB 8839)
Various Artists - 24 Karat Gold For Groovin' (Verve V6 654-2)
Wes Montgomery - Eulogy (Verve V6 8796)
Wes Montgomery - Goin' Out Of My Head c/w Boss City (Verve VK 10384)
Wes Montgomery - Goin' Out Of My Head c/w Tequila (Verve VK 10440, VK 137)

Wes Montgomery With Oliver Nelson Orchestra

same personnel
Rudy Van Gelder Studio, Englewood Cliffs, NJ, December 22, 1965

1.	Naptown Blues	Verve V/V6 8642, V/V6 8714, V3HB 8839, **Verve 521 690-2, Verve 825 676-2**
2.	The End Of A Love Affair	Verve V/V6 8642, V/V6 8714, **Verve 825 676-2**
3.	Twisted Blues	Verve V/V6 8642, V6 8757, 2V6S 8813, **Verve 521 690-2, Verve 825 676-2**
4.	Golden Earrings	Verve V/V6 8642, V6 8796, **Verve 521 690-2, Verve 825 676-2**
5.	Chim Chim Cheree	Verve V/V6 8642, **Verve 825 676-2**
6.	O Morro (aka Once I Loved)	Verve V/V6 8642, V6 8757, 2V6S 8813, **Verve 825 676-2**
7.	It Was A Very Good Year	Verve V/V6 8642, **Verve 825 676-2**

Issued as:
Wes Montgomery - Goin' Out Of My Head (Verve V/V6 8642, **Verve 825 676-2**)
The Best Of Wes Montgomery (Verve V/V6 8714)
Wes Montgomery - Return Engagement (Verve V3HB 8839)
The Best Of Wes Montgomery, Vol. 2 (Verve V6 8757)
The History Of Wes Montgomery (Verve 2V6S 8813)
Wes Montgomery - Eulogy (Verve V6 8796)
Wes Montgomery – Impressions – The Verve Jazz Sides (Verve 539 062-2)

1967

Wes Montgomery Quartet With Claus Ogerman Orchestra

Bernard Eichen, Arnold Eidus, Paul Gershman, Emanuel Green, Julius Held, Harry Lookofsky, Joe Malin, Gene Orloff (vln -1/3,5/9) Abe Kessler, Charles McCracken, George Ricci, Harvey Shapiro (vlc -1/3,5/9) George Devens (vib -2,4,5,8,9) Wes Montgomery (g) Ron Carter (b) Grady Tate (d -1/5,7/9) Ray Barretto (cga -1,3,6,7) Claus Ogerman (arr, cond -1/3,5/9)
Rudy Van Gelder Studio, Englewood Cliffs, NJ, March 17, 1966

1.	Wives And Lovers	Verve V6 8804, 2V6S 8813
2.	Midnight Mood	Verve V/V6 8653, V6 8757, V3HB 8839, **Verve 547-769-2**
3.	Bumpin' On Sunset	Verve VK 10432, VK 10442, V/V6 8653, V/V6 8714, V3HB 8839, **Verve 547-769-2**
4.	What The World Needs Now Is Love	Verve V/V6 8653, V6 8757, V3HB 8839, **Verve 547-769-2**
5.	Little Child (aka Daddy Dear)	Verve V/V6 8653, V6 8796, **Verve 547-769-2**
6.	How Insensitive (aka Insensatez)	Verve VK 145, V/V6 8653, V6 8757, V/V6 8714, 2V6S 8813, **Verve 547-769-2**
7.	Bumpin' On Sunset (alt. take)	Verve V6 8804, 2V6S 8813, **Verve 547-769-2**
8.	The Big Hurt	Verve V/V6 8653, V6 8757, **Verve 547-769-2**
9.	The Big Hurt (alt. take)	Verve V6 8804, 2V6S 8813, **Verve 547-769-2**

Issued as:
Wes Montgomery - Just Walkin' (Verve V6 8804)
The History Of Wes Montgomery (Verve 2V6S 8813)
Wes Montgomery - Tequila (Verve V/V6 8653, **Verve 547-769-2 CD – including tracks 7 & 9, 831 671-2**)
The Best Of Wes Montgomery, Vol. 2 (Verve V6 8757)
Wes Montgomery - Return Engagement (Verve V3HB 8839)
The Best Of Wes Montgomery (Verve V/V6 8714)
Wes Montgomery - Eulogy (Verve V6 8796)
Wes Montgomery - Bumpin' On Sunset c/w Tequila (Verve VK 10432)
Wes Montgomery - Bumpin' On Sunset c/w ??? (Verve VK 10442)
Wes Montgomery - California Dreaming c/w How Insensitive (Verve VK 145)

Wes Montgomery Quartet

Wes Montgomery (g) Ron Carter (b) Grady Tate (d) Ray Barretto (cga)
Rudy Van Gelder Studio, Englewood Cliffs, NJ, March 21, 1966

1.	The Thumb	Verve V/V6 8653, 2V6S 8813, V3HB 8839, **Verve 547-769-2**
2.	Tequila	Verve VK 10432, VK 10440, V/V6 8653, V/V6 8714, V3HB 8839, V6 654-2, **Verve 547-769-2**
3.	Tequila (alt. take)	Verve V6 8804, 2V6S 8813, **Verve 547-769-2**

Issued as:
Wes Montgomery - Tequila (Verve V/V6 8653), **Verve 547-769-2 CD, 831 671-2**)
The History Of Wes Montgomery (Verve 2V6S 8813)
Wes Montgomery - Return Engagement (Verve V3HB 8839)
The Best Of Wes Montgomery (Verve V/V6 8714)
Various Artists - 24 Karat Gold For Groovin' (Verve V6 654-2)
Wes Montgomery - Just Walkin' (Verve V6 8804)
Wes Montgomery - Bumpin' On Sunset c/w Tequila (Verve VK 10432)
Wes Montgomery - Goin' Out Of My Head c/w Tequila (Verve VK 10440, VK 137)

Wes Montgomery With Don Sebesky Orchestra

Mel Davis, Bernie Glow, Jimmy Nottingham (tp) Wayne Andre, John Messner, Bill Watrous (tb) James Buffington (frh) Don Butterfield (tu) Walter Kane (cl, basn, ts) Ray Beckenstein (as, fl, picc) Stan Webb (as, bars, ehr, cl) Jack Jennings (vib, cast, scra) Herbie Hancock (p) Al Casamenti, Wes Montgomery, Bucky Pizzarelli (g) Richard Davis (b) Grady Tate (d) Ray Barretto (cga) Don Sebesky (arr, cond)
Rudy Van Gelder Studio, Englewood Cliffs, NJ, September 14, 1966

| 1. | California Dreaming | Verve VK 10489, VK 145, V/V6 8672, V6 8757, 2V6S 8813, V3HB 8839, V6 654-2, **Verve 827 842-2** |

Issued as:
Wes Montgomery - California Dreaming (Verve V/V6 8672, **Verve 827 842-2**)
The Best Of Wes Montgomery, Vol. 2 (Verve V6 8757)
The History Of Wes Montgomery (Verve 2V6S 8813)
Wes Montgomery - Return Engagement (Verve V3HB 8839)
Various Artists - 24 Karat Gold For Groovin' (Verve V6 654-2)
Wes Montgomery - California Dreaming c/w Mr. Walker (Verve VK 10489)
Wes Montgomery - California Dreaming c/w How Insensitive (Verve VK 145)

Wes Montgomery With Don Sebesky Orchestra

same personnel
Rudy Van Gelder Studio, Englewood Cliffs, NJ, September 15, 1966

| 1 | Green Peppers | Verve V/V6 8672, **Verve 827 842-2** |
| 2 | South Of The Border | - |

Issued as:
Wes Montgomery - California Dreaming (Verve V/V6 8672, **Verve 827 842-2**)

Wes Montgomery Quintet With Don Sebesky Orchestra

Mel Davis, Bernie Glow, Jimmy Nottingham (tp -1/6) Wayne Andre, John Messner, Bill Watrous (tb -1/6) James Buffington (frh -1/6) Don Butterfield (tu -1/6) Walter Kane (cl, basn, ts -1/6) Ray Beckenstein (as, fl, picc -1/6) Stan Webb (as, bars, ehr, cl -1/6) Jack Jennings (vib, cast, scra -1/6, vib -7/9) Herbie Hancock (p -1/6) Wes Montgomery (g) Al Casamenti, Bucky Pizzarelli (g -1/6) Richard Davis (b) Grady Tate (d) Ray Barretto (cga) Don Sebesky (arr, cond -1/6)
Rudy Van Gelder Studio, Englewood Cliffs, NJ, September 16, 1966

1.	Oh, You Crazy Moon	Verve V/V6 8672, **Verve 827 842-2**
2.	More, More, Amor	-
3.	Winds Of Barcelona	Verve V/V6 8672, V6 8757, **Verve 827 842-2**
4.	Sun Down	Verve V/V6 8672, V6 8796, **Verve 827 842-2**
5.	Sun Down (alt. take)	Metro [F] 2355008
6.	Mr. Walker	Verve VK 10489, V/V6 8672, 2V6S 8813, **Verve 827 842-2**
7.	Sunny	Verve V/V6 8672, **Verve 827 842-2**
8.	Sunny (alt. take)	Verve V6 8804, **Verve 827 842-2**
9.	Without You	Verve V/V6 8672, **Verve 827 842-2**

Issued as:
Wes Montgomery - California Dreaming (Verve V/V6 8672, **Verve 827 842-2, CD version includes track. 8**)
The Best Of Wes Montgomery, Vol. 2 (Verve V6 8757)
Wes Montgomery - Eulogy (Verve V6 8796)

Wes Montgomery - Jazz Spectrum, Vol. 8 (Metro [F] 2355008)
The History Of Wes Montgomery (Verve 2V6S 8813)
Wes Montgomery - Just Walkin' (Verve V6 8804)
Wes Montgomery - California Dreaming c/w Mr. Walker (Verve VK 10489)
Wes Montgomery – Impressions – The Verve Jazz Sides (Verve 521 690-2)

Jimmy Smith - Wes Montgomery With Oliver Nelson Orchestra

Jimmy Maxwell, Joe Newman, Ernie Royal (tp) Clark Terry (tp, flh) Jimmy Cleveland, Quentin Jackson, Melba Liston (tb) Dick Hixson (btb) Jerome Richardson (fl, cl) Phil Woods (as, cl) Jerry Dodgion (as, cl, fl) Bob Ashton (ts, cl, fl) Danny Bank (bars, bcl) Jimmy Smith (org) Wes Montgomery (g) Richard Davis (b) Grady Tate (d) Ray Barretto (cga) Oliver Nelson (arr, cond)
Rudy Van Gelder Studio, Englewood Cliffs, NJ, September 21, 1966

1.	13 (Death March)	Verve V/V6 8678
2.	Milestone	Verve V6 8766, **Verve 521 690-2, Verve 314-519802-2**

Issued as:
Jimmy Smith/Wes Montgomery - The Dynamic Duo: Jimmy And Wes (Verve V/V6 8678, 314 521 445-2, MV-2062 Jap., **Verve 521 445-2, Verve CD 8271 577-2**)
Further Adventures Of Jimmy Smith And Wes Montgomery (Verve V6 8766, **Verve 314-519802-2**)
Wes Montgomery – Impressions – The Verve Jazz Sides (Verve 521 690-2)

Jimmy Smith - Wes Montgomery With Oliver Nelson Orchestra

Tony Studd (btb) replaces Hixson, Barretto
Rudy Van Gelder Studio, Englewood Cliffs, NJ, September 23, 1966

1.	Down By The Riverside	Verve V/V6 8678
2.	Happy-Go-Lucky Local (aka Night Train)	-

Issued as:
Jimmy Smith/Wes Montgomery - The Dynamic Duo: Jimmy And Wes (Verve V/V6 8678, 314 521 445-2, MV-2062 Jap., **Verve 521 445-2, Verve CD 8271 577-2**)

Jimmy Smith - Wes Montgomery Duo

Jimmy Smith (org) Wes Montgomery (g)
Rudy Van Gelder Studio, Englewood Cliffs, NJ, September 23, 1966

1.	'Round About Midnight	Verve V6 8804, V3HB 8839, **Verve 521 690-2, Verve 314-519802-2**

Issued as:
Wes Montgomery - Just Walkin' (Verve V6 8804)
Wes Montgomery - Return Engagement (Verve V3HB 8839)
Wes Montgomery – Impressions – The Verve Jazz Sides (Verve 521 690-2)

Jimmy Smith - Wes Montgomery Quartet

Jimmy Smith (org) Wes Montgomery (g) Grady Tate (d) Ray Barretto (cga)
Rudy Van Gelder Studio, Englewood Cliffs, NJ, September 28, 1966

1.	O.G.D. (aka Road Song)	Verve V/V6 8677, V6 8766, **Verve 521 690-2, Verve 314-519802-2**
2.	O.G.D. (aka Road Song) (alt. take)	Verve 314 521 445-2

3.	Call Me	Verve V6 8766
4.	Baby, It's Cold Outside	Verve V/V6 8678
5.	Maybe September	Verve V6 8766
6.	Mellow Mood	Verve V6 8766, VE2 2513, **Verve 521 690-2, Verve 314-519802-2**
7.	James And Wes	Verve V/V6 8678, VE2 2513, **Verve 521 690-2**
8.	King Of The Road	Verve V6 8766, **Verve 314-519802-2**

Issued as:
Leonard Feather - Encyclopedia Of Jazz, Vol. 1 (Verve V/V6 8677)
Further Adventures Of Jimmy Smith And Wes Montgomery (Verve V6 8766, MV-2090 Jap, **Verve 314-519802-2**.)
Jimmy Smith/Wes Montgomery - The Dynamic Duo: Jimmy And Wes (Verve V/V6 8678, 314 521 445-2, **Verve 521 445-2, Verve CD 8271 577-2**)
Wes Montgomery - The Small Group Recordings (Verve VE2 2513)
Wes Montgomery – Impressions – The Verve Jazz Sides (Verve 521 690-2)

1967

Wes Montgomery With Don Sebesky Orchestra

Ray Alonge (frh) George Marge, Romeo Penque, Joe Soldo (bfl) Stan Webb (bfl, woodwinds) Phil Bodner (woodwinds) Julius Brand, Peter Buonconsiglio, Mac Ceppos, Lewis Eley, Harry Glickman, Harry Katzman, Leo Kruczek, Gene Orloff, Tosha Samaroff, Sylvan Shulman, Harry Urbont, Jack Zayde (vln) Harold Coletta, Emanuel Vardi (vla) Charles McCracken, Alan Shulman (vlc) Margaret Ross (harp) Herbie Hancock (p) Wes Montgomery (g) Ron Carter (b) Grady Tate (d) Ray Barretto (cga) Jack Jennings, Joe Wohletz (per) Don Sebesky (arr, cond)
Rudy Van Gelder Studio, Englewood Cliffs, NJ, June 6, 1967

1.	A Day In The Life	A&M LP 2001
2.	California Nights	-

Issued as:
Wes Montgomery - A Day In The Life (A&M LP 2001, SP 3001, SP 9 3001, AML-301 Jap, **A&M CD 0816, BGO CD718 coupled with Down Here On The Ground.**)

Wes Montgomery Quintet With Don Sebesky Orchestra

Ray Alonge (frh -2,3,5/9) George Marge, Romeo Penque, Joe Soldo (bfl -2,3,5/9) Stan Webb (bfl, woodwinds -2,3,5/9) Phil Bodner (woodwinds -2,3,5/9) Julius Brand, Peter Buonconsiglio, Mac Ceppos, Lewis Eley, Harry Glickman, Harry Katzman, Leo Kruczek, Gene Orloff, Tosha Samaroff, Sylvan Shulman, Harry Urbont, Jack Zayde (vln -2,3,5/9) Harold Coletta, Emanuel Vardi (vla -2,3,5/9) Charles McCracken, Alan Shulman (vlc -2,3,5/9) Margaret Ross (harp -2,3,5/9) Herbie Hancock (p) Wes Montgomery (g) Ron Carter (b) Grady Tate (d) Ray Barretto (cga -1/3,5/9) Jack Jennings, Joe Wohletz (per -2,3,5/9) Don Sebesky (arr, cond -2,3,5/9)
Rudy Van Gelder Studio, Englewood Cliffs, NJ, June 7, 1967

1. tk.22	Angel (Switchin')	**A&M CD 2520**
2. tk.24	The Joker	A&M LP 2001
3. tk.29	Eleanor Rigby	-
4. tk.33	Hello, Young Lovers	**A&M CD 2520**
5. tk.35	When A Man Loves A Woman?	A&M LP 2001
6. tk.41	Windy	-
7. tk.47	Watch What Happens	-
8. tk.52	Never On Sunday	unissued
9. tk.58	Angel	A&M LP 2001

Issued as:
Wes Montgomery - A Day In The Life (A&M LP 2001, SP 3001, SP 9 3001, AML-301 Jap, **A&M CD 0816, BGO CD718 coupled with Down Here On The Ground**.)
Wes Montgomery - Classics, Vol. 22 (A&M CD 2520)
Wes Montgomery - Greatest Hits (A&M 314 540 519-2)

Wes Montgomery With Don Sebesky Orchestra

same personnel
Rudy Van Gelder Studio, Englewood Cliffs, NJ, June 26, 1967

1.	Trust In Me	A&M LP 2001
2.	Willow Weep For Me	-

Issued as:
Wes Montgomery - A Day In The Life (A&M LP 2001, SP 3001, SP 9 3001, AML-301 Jap, **A&M CD 0816, BGO CD718 coupled with Down Here On The Ground**)

Wes Montgomery With Don Sebesky Orchestra

Hubert Laws, George Marge, Romeo Penque (fl, ob) Gene Orloff, Raoul Poliakin (vln) Emanuel Vardi (vla) George Ricci (vlc) Mike Mainieri (vib) Herbie Hancock (p) Wes Montgomery (g) Ron Carter (b) Grady Tate (d) Ray Barretto (cga) Bobby Rosengarden (per) Don Sebesky (arr, cond)
Rudy Van Gelder Studio, Englewood Cliffs, NJ, December 20, 1967

1. tk.10	I Say A Little Prayer For You	A&M SP 3006
2. tk.15	Goin' On To Detroit	-

Issued as:
Wes Montgomery - Down Here On The Ground (A&M SP 3006, SP 9 3006, AML-352 Jap, **A&M CD 0802, BGO CD718 coupled with A Day In The Life**)

Wes Montgomery Quintet With Don Sebesky Orchestra

Hubert Laws, George Marge, Romeo Penque (fl, ob -1,2,4/6) Gene Orloff, Raoul Poliakin (vln -1,2,4/6) Emanuel Vardi (vla -1,2,4/6) George Ricci (vlc -1,2,4/6) Mike Mainieri (vib -1,2,4/6) Herbie Hancock (p) Wes Montgomery (g) Ron Carter (b) Grady Tate (d) Ray Barretto (cga -1,2,4/6) Bobby Rosengarden (per -1,2,4/6) Don Sebesky (arr, cond -1,2,4/6)
Rudy Van Gelder Studio, Englewood Cliffs, NJ, December 21, 1967

1. tk.32	Up And At It	A&M SP 3006
2. tk.39	Know It All	-
3. tk.42	Pata Pata	**A&M CD 2520**
4. tk.46	Down Here On The Ground	A&M SP 3006
5. tk.49	The Fox	-
6. tk.53	Hearts Beat	unissued
7. tk.58	Butterfly	**A&M CD 2520**

Issued as:
Wes Montgomery - Down Here On The Ground (A&M SP 3006, SP 9 3006, AML-352 Jap, **A&M CD 0802, BGO CD718 coupled with A Day In The Lif**e)
Wes Montgomery - Classics, Vol. 22 (A&M CD 2520)
Wes Montgomery - Greatest Hits (A&M 314 540 519-2)

1968

Wes Montgomery With Don Sebesky Orchestra

Hubert Laws, George Marge, Romeo Penque (fl, ob) Gene Orloff, Raoul Poliakin (vln) Emanuel Vardi (vla) George Ricci (vlc) Mike Mainieri (vib) Herbie Hancock (p) Wes Montgomery (g) Ron Carter (b) Grady Tate (d) Ray Barretto (cga) Bobby Rosengarden (per) Don Sebesky (arr, cond)
Rudy Van Gelder Studio, Englewood Cliffs, NJ, January 22 & 26, 1968

1.	tk.84	The Other Man's Is Always Greener	A&M SP 3006
2.	tk.86	Georgia On My Mind	-
3.	tk.93	Wind Song	-
4.	tk.110	Down Here On The Ground	
5.		When I Look In Your Eyes	A&M SP 3006
6.		The Other Man's Is Always Greener (alt. take)	unissued
7.		Goin' On To Detroit (alt. take)	-

Issued as:
Wes Montgomery - Down Here On The Ground (A&M SP 3006, SP 9 3006, **A&M CD 0802, BGO CD718 coupled with A Day In The Life**)

Wes Montgomery With Don Sebesky Orchestra

Marvin Stamm (tp) Harvey Estrin, Don Hammond (fl, reco) Berrard Krainis (reco) Don Ashworth (ob, reco) Walter Kane (basn) Bernard Eichen, Charles Libove (vln) Emanuel Vardi (vla) George Ricci (vlc) Hank Jones (p, hpsc) Wes Montgomery (g) Richard Davis (b) Grady Tate (d) Don Sebesky (arr, cond)
Rudy Van Gelder Studio, Englewood Cliffs, NJ, May 7, 1968

1.	tk.4	Yesterday	A&M SP 3012
2.	tk.11/12	Scarborough Fair	-
3.	tk.27/29	I'll Be Back	-
4.	tk.32	Fly Me To The Moon	-

Issued as:
Wes Montgomery - Road Song (A&M SP 3012, SP 9 3012, **A&M CD 0822**)

Wes Montgomery Quartet With Don Sebesky Orchestra

Bernie Glow, Marvin Stamm (tp -2/5) Wayne Andre, Paul Faulise (tb -2/5) James Buffington (frh -2/5) George Marge (fl -2/5) Harvey Estrin, Don Hammond (fl, reco -2/5) Shelley Grushkin, Berrard Krainis, Eric Leber (reco -2/5) Morris Newman (reco, basn -2/5) Don Ashworth (ob, reco -2/5) Stan Webb (ob, reco, cl -2/5) Bernard Eichen, Charles Libove, Marvin Morganstern, Tosha Samaroff (vln -2/5) Emanuel Vardi (vla -2/5) Charles McCracken, George Ricci, Alan Shulman (vlc -2/5) Sivert Johnson Jr. (hpsc -2/5) Herbie Hancock (p) Wes Montgomery (g) Richard Davis (b) Ed Shaughnessy (d) Ray Barretto (cga -2/5) Jack Jennings (per -2/5) Don Sebesky (arr, cond -2/5)
Rudy Van Gelder Studio, Englewood Cliffs, NJ, May 8, 1968

1.	tk.39	My Favorite Things	**A&M CD 2520**
2.	tk.43	Where Have All The Flowers Gone?	A&M SP 3012
3.	tk.53	Green Leaves Of Summer	-

4. tk.67		Greensleeves	-
5. tk.68		Road Song	-

Issued as:
Wes Montgomery - Road Song (A&M SP 3012, SP 9 3012, **A&M CD 0822**)
Wes Montgomery - Greatest Hits (A&M 314 540 519-2)
Wes Montgomery – Classics, Vol. 22 (A & M CD 2520)

Wes Montgomery With Don Sebesky Orchestra

Marvin Stamm (tp) George Marge, Stan Webb (fl, ob, cl) Don Ashworth (fl, ob, cl, ehr) Morris Newman (reco, basn) Bernard Eichen, Charles Libove (vln) Emanuel Vardi (vla) George Ricci (vlc) Eric Leber (hpsc, reco) Wes Montgomery (g) Don Sebesky (arr, cond)
Rudy Van Gelder Studio, Englewood Cliffs, NJ, May 9, 1968

1.   Serene   A&M SP 3012

Issued as:
Wes Montgomery - Road Song (A&M SP 3012, SP 9 3012, **A&M CD 0822**)

The Montgomery Brothers

Buddy Montgomery (vib, p) Wes Montgomery (g) Monk Montgomery (b) Billy Hart (d) Elvin Bunn (cga)
TV broadcast, Detroit, MI, 1968
1.   Windy   VGM 0008
2.   California Nights   -

Issued as:
Wes Montgomery Live At Jorgies And More (VGM 0008)

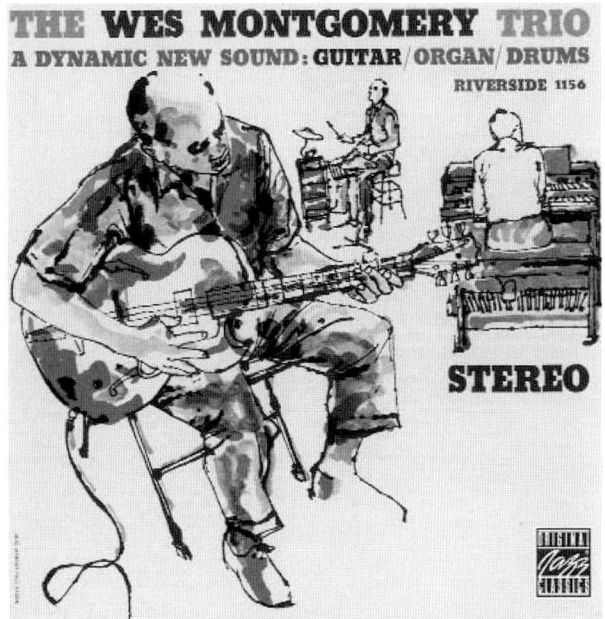

APPENDIX 2
FILM FOOTAGE

FILM FOOTAGE

Only footage that has been issued commercially has been included.

1949

The Lionel Hampton Sextet

Ed Mullens (tp). Al Grey, Jimmy Wormick (tb), Bobby Plater (as), Lionel Hampton (vib), Wes Montgomery (g), Carley Hamner (tap dance – track2), Sonny Parker (v- track 3), Betty Carter (v-track 3)

1. Air Mail Special	Milan Jazz Video 791 285
2. Curley's Dance	-
3. Hamp's Gumbo	-
4. Jay Bird	-
5. Introducing Flying Home	-

Issued as:
This Hot Club of France (HCF) production for Milan Jazz was first issued in 1992 reference number: Home Video 791 285. It was also issued in Italy as: Milan Jazz MV 015.

1965

The Wes Montgomery Quartet

Wes Montgomery (g), Harold Mabern (p), Arthur Harper (b), Jimmy Lovelace (d)

1. Yesterdays
2. Jingles
3. 'Round Midnight
4. Twisted Blues
5. Full House
6. West Coast Blues (short, edited outro)

Issued as:
Wes Montgomery, Live in '65 (Jazz Icons, Reelin' In The Years production, Naxos 2.119003)
Wes Montgomery in Europe 1965, * omit track 6 above (Impro-Jazz IJ 504)
Wes Montgomery: Twisted Blues, * omit track 6 above (Salt-Peanuts 44611)

Wes Montgomery, Belgium 1965

Wes Montgomery Quartet, same personnel.

1. Impressions
2. Twisted Blues
3. Here's That Rainy Day
4. Jingles
5. The Girl Next Door

Issued as:
Wes Montgomery, Live in '65 (Jazz Icons, Reelin' In The Years production, Naxos 2.119003)
Wes Montgomery in Europe 1965, (Impro-Jazz IJ 504)
Wes Montgomery: Twisted Blues, * omit track 4 above (Salt-Peanuts 44611)
Wes Montgomery Belgium 1965 (Vestapol OV11479VHS and Vestapol 13084DVD)

The Wes Montgomery Quartet

Wes Montgomery (g), Stan Tracey (p), Rick Laird(b), Jackie Dougan (d)

1. Four on Six
2. Full House
3. Here's That Rainy Day
4. Twisted Blues
5. West Coast Blues

Issued as:
Wes Montgomery, Live in '65 (Jazz Icons, Reelin' In The Years production, Naxos 2.119003)

Wes Montgomery Octet

Hans Koller (a.s.), Johnny Griffin, Ronnie Scott (t.s.), Ronnie Ross (bar.s.), Martial Solal (p), Michel Gaudry (b), Ronnie Stephenson (d).

1. West Coast Blues

Issued as:
Americans in Europe Vol. 2 (Vidjazz 39, Green Line Video)

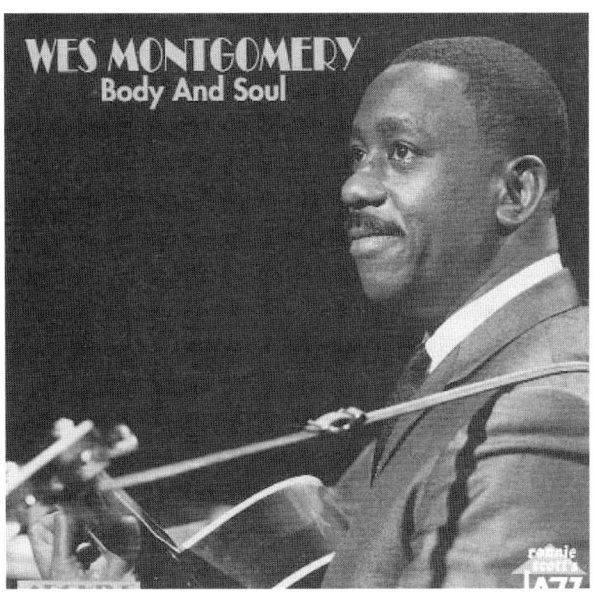
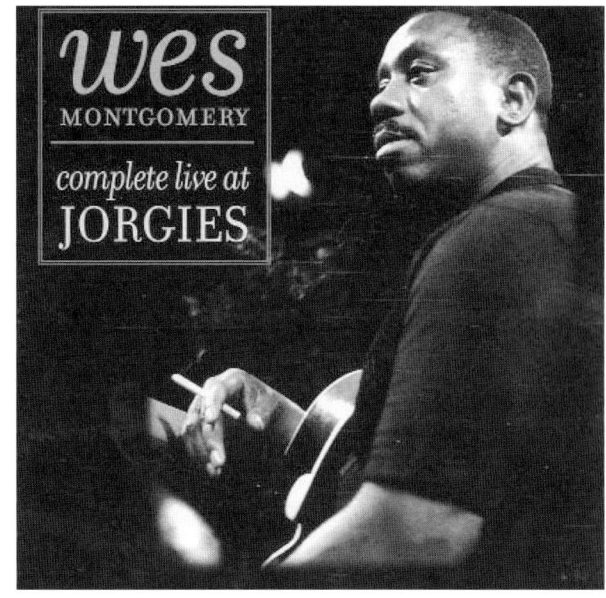

APPENDIX 3
TRANSCRIPTIONS & METHODS

The following publications are legitimate commercially available issues, listed by the chronological date of first publication.

1968

Wes Montgomery Jazz Guitar Method

Pub. by: Robbins Music Corporation, NY, USA Issue number B3-R4774.

This method, written by Lee Garson and Jimmy Stewart, includes the following complete transcriptions:

Stairway to the Stars	Bags Meets Wes!	Riverside RLP 407
The Shadow of Your Smile	Bumpin'	Verve V/V6 8625
If You Could See Me Now	Smokin' at Half Note	Verve V/V6 8633
Tear It Down	Bumpin'	Verve V/V6 8625
Bumpin' On Sunset	Tequila	Verve V/V6 8653
Windy	A Day In The Life	A+M SP3001 & LP2001
Bumpin'	Bumpin'	Verve V/V6 8625
Tequila	Tequila	Verve V/V6 8653
Boss City	Goin' Out Of My Head	Verve V/V6 8642

1975

Wes Montgomery – Jazz Improvisation Volumes 1 & 2.

Pub. by Nichion Publications Inc, Japan.

These two volumes of transcriptions by Sadanori Nakamure contain 29 transcriptions, 14 in Volume 1 and 15 in Volume 2, which are supported by an examination of Wes's octave technique. However, all the text is in Japanese.

Volume 1

Airegin	The Incredible Jazz Guitar	Riverside RLP12 320
SKJ	Bags Meets Wes!	Riverside RLP 407
Blue 'N' Boogie	Full House	Riverside RLP12 434
Come Rain or Come Shine	Full House	Riverside RLP12 434
People	Movin' Wes	Verve V/V6 8610
Movin' Wes Parts 1 & 2	Movin' Wes	Verve V/V6 8610
Unit 7	Smokin' At The Half Note	Verve V/V6 8633
Portrait Of Jennie	Willow Weep For Me	Verve V/V6 8765
Misty	Willow Weep For Me	Verve V/V6 8765
Night Train	The Dynamic Duo	Verve V/V6 8678
Baby Its Cold Outside	The Dynamic Duo	Verve V/V6 8678
O G D (Road Song)	Further Adventures Of….	Verve V/V6 8677
Call Me	Further Adventures Of….	Verve V/V6 8677

Volume 2

West Coast Blues	The Incredible Jazz Guitar	Riverside RLP12 320
June In January	The Montgomery Brothers	Fantasy LP 3308
Twisted Blues	So Much Guitar	Riverside RLP 382

I Wish I Knew	So Much Guitar	Riverside RLP 382
Something Like Blues	So Much Guitar	Riverside RLP 382
Besame Mucho	Boss Guitar	Riverside RLP 459
Days Of Wine & Roses	Boss Guitar	Riverside RLP 459
Fried Pies	Boss Guitar	Riverside RLP 459
For Heaven's Sake	Boss Guitar	Riverside RLP 459
Watch What Happens	A Day In The Life	A+M SP3001 & LP2001
Wind Song	Down Here On The Ground	A+M SP 3006
Georgia On My Mind	Down Here On The Ground	A+M SP 3006
The Other Man's Grass Is Always Greener	Down Here On The Ground	A+M SP 3006

1976

Wes Montgomery Jazz Guitar Solos

Pub.by ALMO Publications, Hollywood, CA, USA.

This book contains 22 transcriptions by Fred Sokolow:

Angel	A Day In The Life	A+M SP3001 & LP2001
Bumpin'	Bumpin'	Verve V/V6 8625
Bumpin' On Sunset	Tequila	Verve V/V6 8653
Far Wes	Montgomeryland	Pacific Jazz PJ-5
Ghost Of A Chance	Movin' Along	Riverside RLP 342
Goin' To Detroit	Down Here On The Ground	A+M SP3006
Goin' Out Of My Head	Goin' Out Of My Head	Verve V/V6 8642
Green Peppers	California Dreamin'	Verve V/V6 8672
More And More Amor	California Dreamin'	Verve V/V6 8672
Mr Walker	California Dreamin'	Verve V/V6 8672
Polka Dots and Moonbeams	Wes Montgomery Qt..	Riverside RLP.12-320
Road Song	Road Song	A+M SP3012
Round Midnight	Just Walkin'	Verve V6 8804
Tear It Down	Bumpin'	Verve V/V6 8625
Watch What Happens	A Day In The Life	A+M SP3001 & LP2001
West Coast Blues	Movin' Wes	Verve V/V6 8610
Willow Weep For Me	A Day In The Life	A+M SP3001 & LP2001
Winds Of Barcelona	California Dreamin'	Verve V/V6 8672
Wind Song	Down Here On The Ground	A+M SP3006
Windy	A Day In The Life	A+M SP3001 & LP2001
Without You	California Dreamin'	Verve V/V6 8672
Yesterdays	Wes Montgomery Trio	Riverside RLP12-310

1978

The Wes Montgomery Guitar Folio - Improvisations and Interpretations

Pub.by Gopam Enterprises Inc., New York, USA

This folio contains 17 transcriptions supported by the author Steve Khan's commentary and suggestions.
Transcriptions include:

Angel Eyes	The Montgomery Brothers in Canada	Fantasy LP 3323

Bud's Beaux Arts	The Montgomery Brothers	World Pacific PJ1240
Canadian Sunset	Boss Guitar	Riverside RLP 459
Cariba	Full House	Riverside RLP12 434
Four On Six	Incredible Jazz Guitar	Riverside RLP 12-320
Fried Pies	Boss Guitar	Riverside RLP 459
I've Grown Accustomed To Her Face	Full House	Riverside RLP12 434
Midnight Mood	Tequila	Verve MGV 8653
Movin' Along	Movin' Along	Riverside RLP12 342
Mr Walker	Incredible Jazz Guitar	Riverside RLP 12-320
Road Song (or O.G.D.)	Further Adventure of Jimmy Smith and Wes Montgomery	Verve V/V6 8677
Pretty Blue	Fusion	Riverside RLP 422
Sundown	California Dreaming	Verve V/V6 8672
The Thumb	Tequila	Verve MGV 8653
The Trick Bag	Boss Guitar	Riverside RLP 459
Twisted Blues	Goin' Out Of My Head	Verve MGV 8642
West Coast Blues	Incredible Jazz Guitar	Riverside RLP 12-320

1988

Wes Montgomery – Artist Transcriptions for Guitar

Pub. by Hal Leonard Publishing Corporation, USA - #HL00675536

Nine of these transcriptions by Fred Sokolow (asterisked) were published in his 1976 ALMO publication: Wes Montgomery Jazz Guitar Solos. This new music book includes five different transcriptions whilst excluding twelve from the previous work.

*Angel	A Day In The Life	A+M SP3001 & LP2001
Boss City	Goin' Out Of My Head	Verve V/V6 8642
*Bumpin'	Bumpin'	Verve V/V6 8625
*Bumpin' On Sunset	Tequila	Verve V/V6 8653
*Far Wes	Montgomeryland	Pacific Jazz PJ-5
Four On Six	The Incredible Jazz Guitar	Riverside RLP12 320
*Goin' To Detroit	Down Here On The Ground	A+M SP3006
Movin' We – Parts 1 & 2	Movin' Wes	Verve V/V6 8610
*Mr Walker	California Dreamin'	Verve V/V6 8672
Naptown Blues	Goin' Out Of My Head	Verve V/V6 8642
*Road Song	Road Song	A+M SP3012
Serene	Road Song	A+M SP3012
*Tear It Down	Bumpin'	Verve V/V6 8625
*West Coast Blues	Movin' Wes	Verve V/V6 8610

1994

Wes Montgomery – For All Instruments

Pub. by Jamey Aebersold Jazz Inc, Volume 62, play-a-long book and CD set.

Cariba	Full House	Riverside RLP 12 434
Four On Six	The Incredible Jazz Guitar	Riverside RLP 12 320
Road Song (O.G.D.)	Road Song	A+M SP 3012
Jingles	Bags Meets Wes	Riverside RLP 407
West Coast Blues	The Incredible Jazz Guitar	Riverside RLP 12 320

Far Wes	The Montgomery Brothers	Pacific Jazz PJ 5
Leila	The Montgomery Brothers	Pacific Jazz PJ 5
Angel	A Day In The Life	A+M SP3001 & LP2001
D Natural Blues	The Incredible Jazz Guitar	Riverside RLP12 320
Doujie	Grooveyard	Riverside RLP 362
Full House	Full House	Riverside RLP 12 434

1995

Mel Bay Presents: Wes Montgomery Jazz Guitar Artistry

Pub. by Mel Bay Publications, St Louis, USA. Ref: MB95314.

This book contains 14 transcriptions by Zafar Saood presented in both standard notation and tablature. There are useful performance notes and a short biography. Transcriptions include;

Full House	Full House	Riverside RLP 12 434
Doujie	Grooveyard	Riverside RLP 362
Missile Blues	Wes Montgomery Trio	Riverside RLP12 310
Mi Cosa	Guitar On The Go	Riverside RLP 494
Work Song	Nat Adderley/ Work Song	Riverside RLP 494
Double Deal	George Shearing/Wes Montgomery	Jazzland J45710
Jingles	Wes Montgomery Trio	Riverside RLP12 310
So Do It	Movin' Along	Riverside RLP12 318
Sack o' Woe	Nat Adderley/ Work Song	Riverside RLP 494
Fallout	Nat Adderley/ Work Song	Riverside RLP 494
Unit 7	Smokin'At The Half Note	Verve V/V6 8633
Jeannine	The Montgomery Brothers in Canada	Fantasy LP 3323
Blue Roz	Bags Meets Wes	Riverside RLP 407
Something Like Bags	So Much Guitar	Riverside RLP 382

The Boss Guitar of Wes Montgomery

Pub. by H.P. Houston Pub. Inc, distributed by Hal Leonard Corp., Milwaukee, USA.Ref.HL00690120

This collection of 10 transcriptions by Jim Bastian, edited by John Alexander, also includes a transcription by transcription analysis of each solo. Titles include:

Dangerous	Portrait Of Wes	Riverside RLP 9942
Yesterdays	The Wes Montgomery Trio	Riverside RLP12 310
No Blues	Smokin'At The Half Note	Verve V/V6 8633
If I Should Lose You	Grooveyard	Riverside RLP362
Doujie	Grooveyard	Riverside RLP362
Besame Mucho	Boss Guitar	Riverside OJCD 261 2
Fried Pies	Boss Guitar	Riverside OJCD 261 2
Fried Pies (Take 1)	Boss Guitar	Riverside OJCD 261 2
James and Wes	The Dynamic Duo	VerveV/V6 8678
Freddie The Freeloader	Portrait Of Wes	Riverside RLP 9459 and OJCCD 144 2

Wes Montgomery: The Early Years

Pub. by Mel Bay Publications Inc, St Louis, USA. Ref: MB95315BCD

This collection of nine transcriptions by Dan Bowden has a play-a-long CD and includes a short paragraph about each title. Titles include:

Scrambled Eggs	Work Song	RiversideRLP12 318
Compulsion	West Coast Blues	Jazzland JLP20
Terrain	West Coast Blues	Jazzland JLP20
Lolita	Cannonball Adderly and the Poll Winners	Riverside RLP 355
Tune Up	Movin' Along	Riverside RLP 342
Says You	Movin' Along	Riverside RLP 342
Delirium	Grooveyard	Riverside RLP362
No Hard Feelings	George Shearing and the Montgomery Brothers	Jazzland JLP 55
Ursula	West Coast Blues	Jazzland JLP20

1997

Wes Montgomery – Two Unaccompanied Guitar Solos

Pub. by Advance Music , Germany. Ref: #10003

These two chord melody transcriptions have been transcribed and fingered by Michael Jeup. He also gives performance notes The titles are:

While We're Young	So Much Guitar	Riverside RLP-9382
Mi Cosa	Guitar On The Go	Riverside RLP-9494

2000

The Boss Guitar of Wes Montgomery – Vols 1 & 2

Pub. by Coastal Publishing and Educational Resources, Charleston, South Carolina

This two volume collection of transcriptions includes 10 previously published (asterisked) in Bastion and Alexander's 1995 Houston Publishing collection (see page 118).

Volume 1

*Besame Mucho	Boss Guitar	Riverside OJCD 261 2
*Dangerous	Portrait Of Wes	Riverside RLP 9942
*Yesterdays	The Wes Montgomery Trio	Riverside RLP12 310
*No Blues	Smokin' At The Half Note	Verve V/V6 8633
*James and Wes	The Dynamic Duo	VerveV/V6 8678
*Fried Pies	Boss Guitar	Riverside OJCD 261 2
*If I Should Lose You	Grooveyard	Riverside RLP362

Volume 2

Billie's Bounce	The Montgomery Brothers + Five Others	Pacific Jazz 1240
Bock to Bock	The Montgomery Brothers + Five Others	Pacific Jazz 1240
Lolita	Portrait Of Wes	Riverside RLP 9459

D Natural Blues (Monterey Blues)	The Montgomery Brothers	Fantasy LP 3308
Willow Weep For Me	Willow Weep For Me	Verve V/V6 8765
*Fried Pies (Take 1)	Boss Guitar	Riverside OJCD 261 2
*Freddie The Freeloader	Portrait Of Wes	Riverside RLP 9459 & OJCCD 144 2
*Doujie	Grooveyard	Riverside RLP362

2001

Best of Wes Montgomery

Pub. by Hal Leonard Inc, Milwaukee, USA. Ref.: HL00695387

This book and CD set by Wolf Marshall includes 12 transcriptions, each accompanied by an analysis of Wes Montgomery's approach. Titles include:

Missile Blues	The Wes Montgomery Trio	Riverside RLP 12 310
Yesterdays	The Wes Montgomery Trio	Riverside RLP 12 310
West Coast Blues	The Incredible Jazz Guitar	Riverside RLP12 320
Cariba	Full House	Riverside RLP 12 434
I've Grown Accustomed To Her Face	Full House	Riverside RLP 12 434
Besame Mucho	Boss Guitar	Riverside OJCD 261 2
Fried Pies	Boss Guitar	Riverside OJCD 261 2
Mi Cosa	Guitar On The Go	Riverside RLP 494
Four On Six	Smokin' At The Half Note	Verve V/V6 8633
Misty	Willow Weep For Me	Verve V/V6 8765
Sundown	California Dreaming	Verve V/V6 8672
O.G.D. (Road Song)	California Dreaming	Verve V/V6 8672

Essential Jazz Lines, In The Style of Wes Montgomery

Pub. by Mel Bay Publications Inc. Ref: MB99905BCD

This book and CD set by Corey Christiansen contains no Wes Montgomery material whatsoever. Its aim is to analyse Wes Montgomery's approach to improvisation through reference to common be-bop improvisational concepts. There are many useful examples, together with the play-a-long CD. However its link to Wes Montgomery material is tenuous and this is perhaps best illustrated by the book' initial disclaimer: "This book of original studies and analysis by Corey Christiansen is designed to help you develop your own personal improvising style."

2005

The Guitar Style of Wes Montgomery

Pub. by Stefan Grossman's Guitar Workshop Ref: GW 958 (DVD) and OV11488 (VHS)

This DVD and 32-page booklet includes in depth examination of Road Song, Cariba, West Coast Blues and 4 on 6. There are also lessons on the Wes Montgomery style plus film footage of Montgomery in concert from 1965.

2007

Wes Montgomery – Best of Boss Guitar

Pub. by Mel Bay Publications Inc, St Louis, USA. Ref:MB20792

This collection, transcribed by Peter Gaarn Jylor and edited by Henry Johnson, includes six tunes from the Riverside 'organ-trio' recording: Boss Guitar.

Dearly Beloved	Boss Guitar	Riverside RLP 459
Days of Wine and Roses	Boss Guitar	Riverside RLP 459
The Trick Bag	Boss Guitar	Riverside RLP 459
Canadian Sunset	Boss Guitar	Riverside RLP 459
Fried Pies	Boss Guitar	Riverside RLP 459
For Heaven's Sake	Boss Guitar	Riverside RLP 459

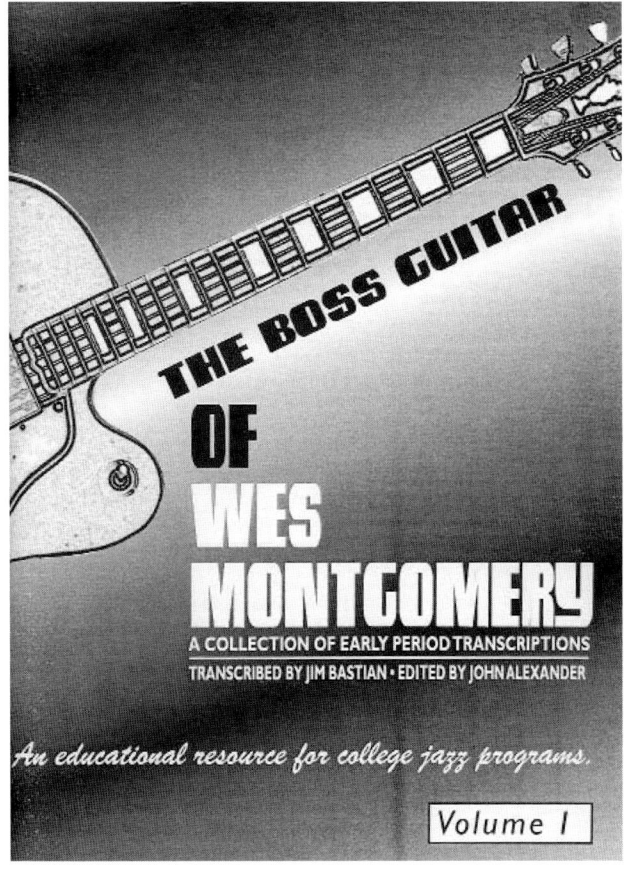

APPENDIX 4
COMPOSITIONS

Gibson, the workingman's guitar.

Wes Montgomery & Gibson at work for MGM/Verve records.

Gibson Guitars advertisement 1967.

COMPOSITIONS

COMPOSITIONS

1. Angel – A Day in the Life, AMLS 2001.
2. Blue 'n' Boogie – Full House, Riverside RLP 434.
3. Blue Roz – Bags Meets Wes, Riverside RLP 407.
4. Boss City – Going Out of My Head, Verve 8642.
5. Bumpin' – Bumpin', Verve 8625.
6. Bumpin' On Sunset – Tequila, Verve 8653.
7. Cariba – Full House, Riversie RLP 434.
8. D-Natural Blues – The Incredible Jazz Guitar of Wes Montgomery, Riverside RLP 12-329 (see also number 25).
9. Double Deal – Love Walked In, Jazzland JLP 55.
10. Doujie – Grooveyard, Riverside RLP 362.
11. Far Wes – Montgomeryland, Pacific Jazz PJ5.
12. Fingerpickin'.
13. Four on Six – The Incredible Jazz Guitar of Wes Montgomery, Riverside RLP 12-329. Smokin' – At Half Note, Verve VLP 9118. Willow Weep for Me, Verve 6-8765.
14. Fried Pies – Boss Guitar, Riverside RLP 459. Guitar On the Go, Riverside 494.
15. Full House – Full House, Riverside RLP 434.
16. Geno – Guitar On the Go, Riverside RLP 494.
17. Goin' To Detroit – Down Here on the Ground, AMLS 3006.
18. In and Out – Movin' Wes, Verve 8610.
19. Jingles – The Montgomery Brothers, Fantasy 8052. Bags Meets Wes, Riverside RLP 407. The Wes Montgomery Trio, Riverside RLP 1156.
20. Leila – Montgomeryland, Pacific Jazz PJ5.
21. Mi Cosa – Bumpin', Verve 8652.
22. Missile Blues – The Wes Montgomery Trio, Riverside RLP 1156. Guitar On the Go, Riverside RLP 494.
23. Mr Walker – The Incredible Jazz Guitar of Wes Montgomery, Riverside RLP 12-329. California Dreaming, Verve 8672.
24. Monk's Shop – Montgomeryland, Pacific Jazz PJ5.
25. Montgomery Blues (D-Natural Blues) – The Montgomery Brothers, Fantasy 8052 (see also number 8).
26. Montgomeryland Funk – The Montgomery Brothers, Pacific Jazz PJ-17.
27. Moving Along – Moving Along, Riverside RLP 342. A Portrait of Wes, Riverside 492.
28. Movin' Wes – Movin' Wes, Verve 8610.
29. Naptown Blues – Going Out of My Head, Verve 8642.
30. O G D (The Road Song) – Further adventures of Jimmy and Wes, Verve V6 8766 (see also number 33).
31. Pretty Blue – Fusion, Riverside RLP 472.
32. Renie – Montgomeryland, Pacific Jazz PJ5.
33. Road Song – Road Song, AMLS 927 (see also number 30).
34. Serene – Road Song, AMLS 927.
35. So Do It – Moving Along, Riverside RLP 342.
36. Something Like Bags – So Much Guitar, Riverside RLP 1382.
37. S O S – Full House, Riverside RLP 432.
38. Sundown – California Dreaming, Verve 8672.
39. Tear It Down – Tequila, Verve 8653.
40. The Thumb – Tequila, Verve 8653.
41. The Trick Bag – Boss Guitar, Riverside RLP 459.
42. Twisted Blues – Going Out of My Head, Verve 8642.
43. Up and At It – Down Here on the Ground, AMLS 3006.
44. West Coast Blues – West Coast Blues, Riverside 920. The Incredible Jazz Guitar of Wes Montgomery, Riverside RLP 12-329. Movin' Wes, Verve 8610.
45. Wes' Tune – Montgomeryland, Pacific Jazz PJ5.

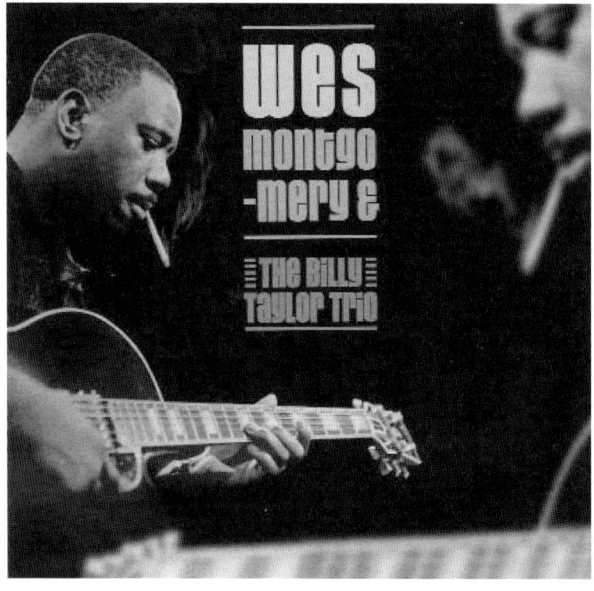

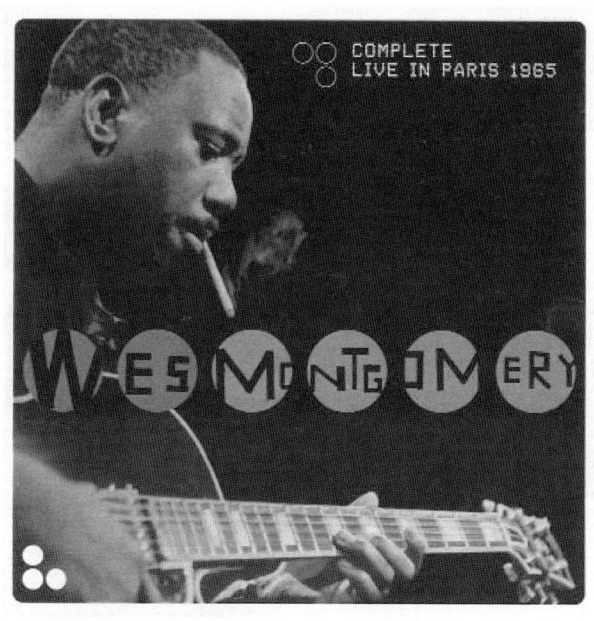

APPENDIX 5
CHORD SHAPES

Wes Montgomery.

CHORD SHAPES

Key: o Root
    x Root (omitted)

Major Seventh Chord Family

Maj 7th	Maj 9th	Maj 7th	Maj 7th 6/9	Maj 7th
	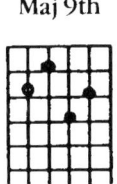	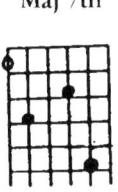	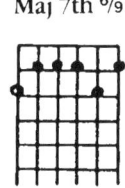	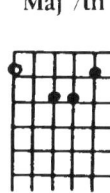

6/9	Maj 9th	Maj 6th	Maj 7th and ♭5
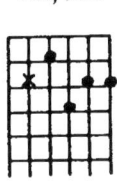		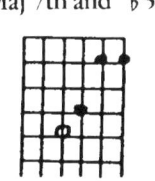	

Dominant Seventh Chord Family

7th	7th (sus 4)	7th	13th	13th	13th
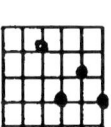	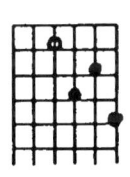				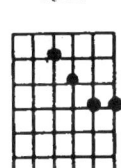

9th	9th	13th	13th	7th ♯5 ♯9	7th ♯9
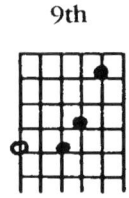		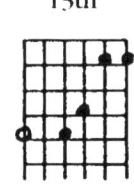			

Minor Chord Family

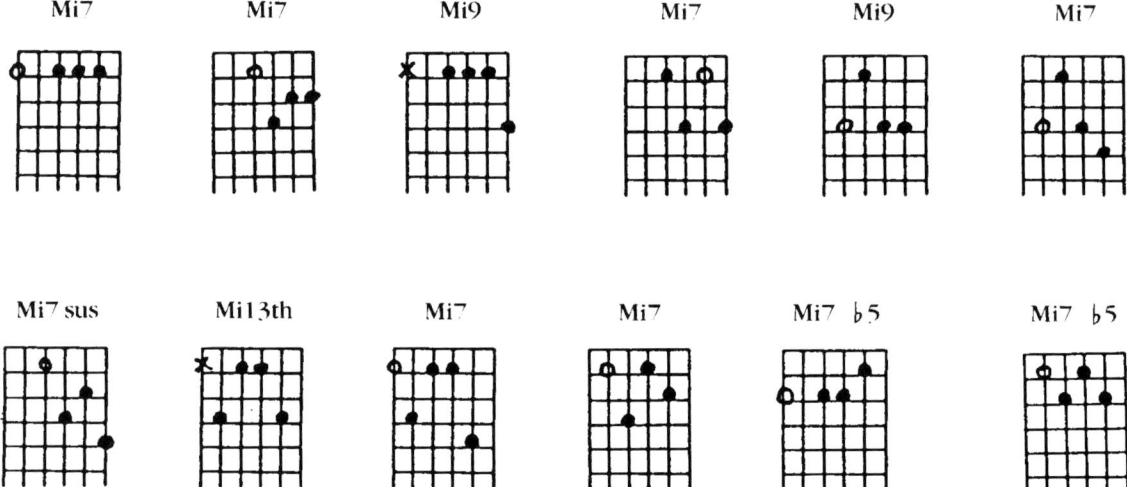

As this publication is primarily of a biographical nature, it is impractical to go further into the technicalities of Wes' chord playing.

For those wishing to know more about his chord vocabulary I would recommend the following publications:
1. The Wes Montgomery Guitar Folio – Steve Khan, Gopam Enterprises.
2. Wes Montgomery Guitar Solos – Fred Sokolow, Almo Publications.
3. Wes Montgomery Jazz Guitar Method – Robbins Music Corporation, New York.

APPENDIX 6
OCTAVE TECHNIQUE

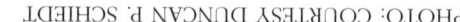

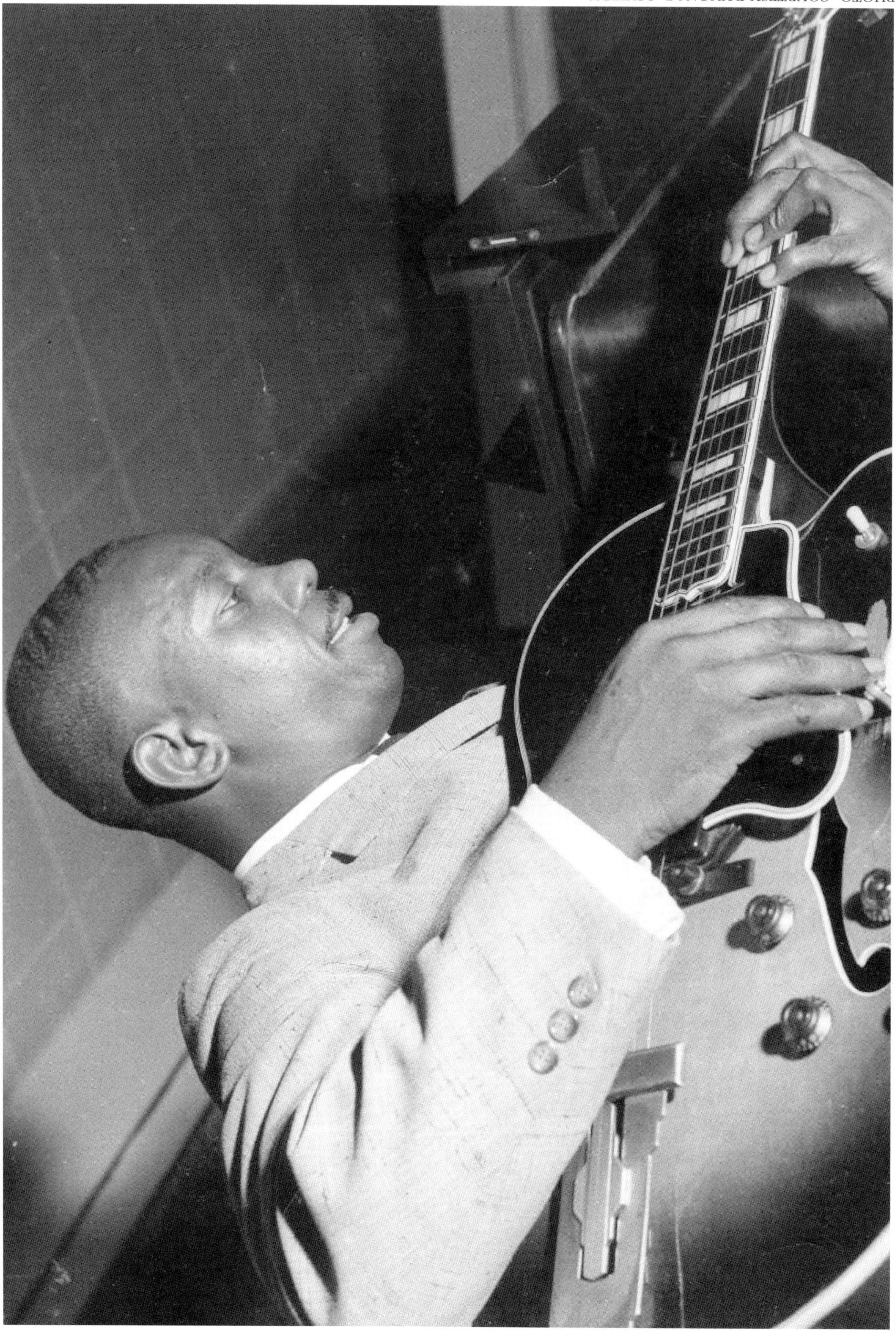

PHOTO: COURTESY DUNCAN P. SCHIEDT

Wes Montgomery 1959.

WES' OCTAVE TECHNIQUE

There are several ways to finger octaves with the left hand. The octave shapes used by Wes are probably the most common and certainly the most logical as they only require the damping of one string.

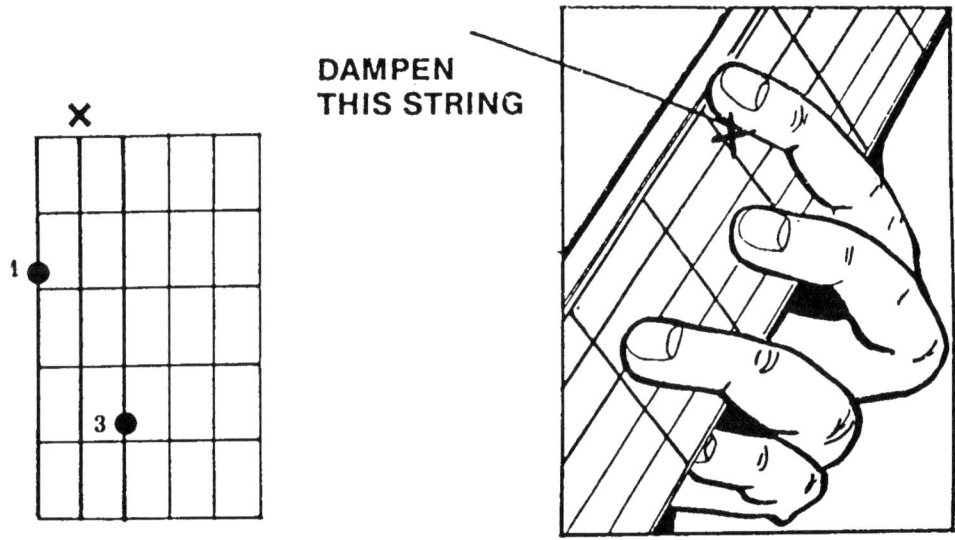

This six string octave shape can be transferred over to the 5th string to form an octave between strings 5 and 3.

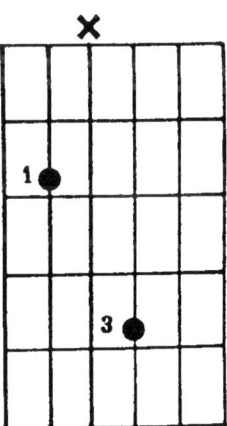

The 4th and 3rd string octave shape requires a different fingering to accommodate the standard guitar tuning (E A D G B E). This shape also necessitates the damping of only one string.

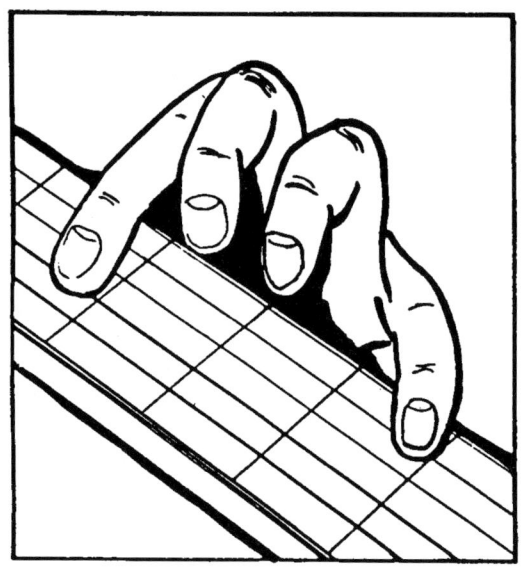 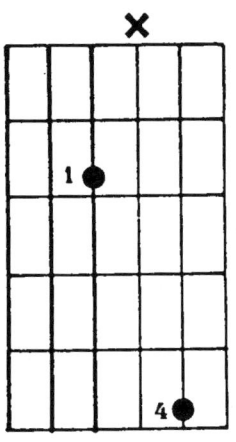

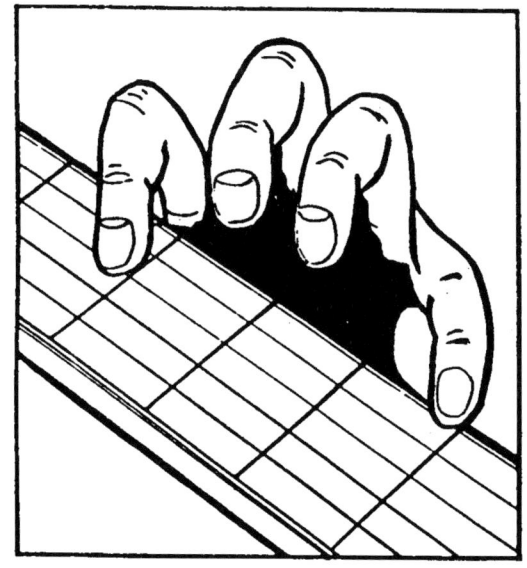 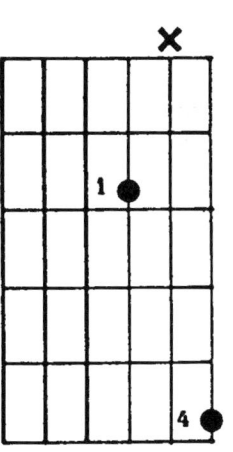

BIBLIOGRAPHY

BOOKS

Dictionary of Jazz	Panassie and Gautier	Cassell (UK) 1956
Indiana, a Century of Negro Progress		1963
The Encyclopaedia of Jazz	Leonard Feather	Quartet ISBN 0 7043 2173 4
The Encyclopaedia of Jazz in the1960s	Leonard Feather	Quartet ISBN 0 7043 2174 2
The Encyclopaedia of Jazz in the 1970s	Leonard Feather	Quartet ISBN 0 7043 2175 0
The Guitar Its History/Music/Players	Kozinn/Welding/Forte	Columbus ISBN 0 86287 0534
The Guitar Player Book		Grove Press ISBN 394 17045 8
The Guitar Players	James Sallis	Morrow ISBN 0688 01375 9
Great Black Hoosier Americans	Luther	Hicks (1977)
The History of the Guitar in Jazz	Norman Mongan	Oak (USA)ISBN 08256 0255 6
Jazz at Ronnie Scott's	Kitty Grime	Hale ISBN 0791 69078
The Jazz Guitar – Its Evolution & Players	Maurice J. Summerfield	Ashley Mark ISBN 09506244 0 0
The Jazz Guitarists	Stan Britt	Blandford ISBN 07137 1511 1
Jazz Guitars (an Anthology)	James Sallis	Quill ISBN 0688 206427
Jazz on Record	McCarthy/Morgan/Oliver/Harrison	Hanover
Modern Jazz Guitar Technique	Adrian Ingram	Hampton ISBN 0 95069 49 0 8
Modern Jazz - The Essential Records		Aquarius ISBN 0 9046 19 0 1
Jazz Records 1942-62 Vol. 5M-N	Jorget Grunnet Jepson	Copylit (Denmark)
Jazz Styles	Mark Grindley	Prentice Hall ISBN 0 13 5098778
My Fifty Fretting Years	Ivor Mairants	Ashley Mark ISBN 0950 622435
Riding on a Blue Note	Gary Giddins	OUP (NY) ISBN 019 502 835 X

PERIODICALS

BANJO, MANDOLIN & GUITAR (B.M.G.)

Wes Montgomery.	April 1962	John W. Duarte
Wes Montgomery.	June 1962	John W. Duarte
Wes Montgomery.	July 1962	John W. Duarte
Wes Montgomery.	August 1962	John W. Duarte
Wes Montgomery.	September 1962	John W. Duarte
Wes Montgomery,	October 1962	John W. Duarte
Wes Montgomery.	January 1963	John W. Duarte
Wes Montgomery,	May 1963	John W. Duarte
Wes Montgomery.	June 1963	John W. Duarte
Wes Montgomery.	July 1963	John W. Duarte
Wes Montgomery.	August 1963	John W. Duarte
Wes Montgomery. Natural Genius	August 1968	John W. Duarte
Wes Montgomery's Recordings.	September 1968	John W. Duarte
Wes Montgomery.	May 1965	Ivor Mairants

CODA Magazine.   April/May 1965 p.26

CRESCENDO INTERNATIONAL

Wes Montgomery.	May 1963	Cedric West
Montgomery the Magnificent.	May 1965	Reviews
Last Words of a Great Jazzman.	July 1968	Les Tomkins
Record Review - Tequila	January 1967	
Can the Quickness of the Hand Deceive the Ear?	May 1967	John Hynam
Record Review - California Dreaming	June 1967	
In Memoriam,	January 1969	Alan Stevens
Record Review - A Portrait of Wes Montgomery.	March 1969	

DOWNBEAT

Report on break-up of Mastersounds		February 1960
Record Review - Harold Land, West Coast Blues Jazzland. JLP 920		November 1960
Monterey Jazz Festival	J. Tynan	November 1960
Blindfold Test, Barney Kessel,	Leonard Feather	July 1961
5th Annual Guitar Issue. R. I. Gleason		July 1961
Record Review - Movin' Along, Riv. 342		July 1961
Monterey Jazz Festival 1961	D. Demichael	November 1961
Record Review - Montgomery Brothers in Canada, Fantasy 3323		May 1962
Record Review - Jackson 'Montgomery. Bags Meets Wes, Riv 407		June 1962
Blindfold Test with Herb Ellis, L. Feather		July 1962
Record Review - Full House, Riv 434		February 1963
Record Review - Boss Guitar, Riv 59		September 1963
Caught in the Act - Montgomery Trio at Showboat Lounge, Washington		January 1964
Record Review - Fusion, Riv4-2		June 1964
Organic Problems and Satisfactions. Ira Gisler		July 196-1
Record Review - Bumpin', Verve 8625		December 1965
Record Review - Tequila, Verve 8653		November 1966
Old Wine, New Bottles.	D. Morgenstern	December 1966
Record Review - Guitar on the Go, Riv -464		February 1967
Record Review - California Dreaming, Verve 86-2		May 1967
Blindfold Test	Leonard Feather	June 1967
Howard Robert's Binary Bag		June 1967
Record Review - Smith/Montgomery, Dynamic Duo, Verve 8678		December 1967
32nd Annual Reader's Poll, First Place		December 1967
Record Review - Wes' Best Fantasy 3376-83-'6, The Best of Verve 8114		March 1968
Caught in the Act 'Los Angeles Music Centre with Stan Kenton and Cannonball Adderley		April 1968
The Thumb's Up or What the View is Like from the Top, B. Quinn		June 1968
2nd Annual Jazz Festival, University of California, Berkeley – Report of Wes Montgomery set		June 1968
Record Review - Down Here on the Ground, A + M 3006		June 1968
Reader's Letters Forum, Three letters about Wes		June 1968
Final Bar - Obituary		July 1968
Record Review - Eulogy, Verve V6088796		
Record Review - Greatest Hits, A + M SP 424		June 1970

GUITAR PLAYER

The Memorable Montgomery, Obituary	October 1968
Review - Wes Montgomery Guitar Method	April 1969
Howard Roberts - Profile of a Pro	April 1970
Record Review - Wes Montgomery Greatest Hits, A+M SP4247	August 1970
Jimmy Stewart by Bill Lee	December 1970
Jazz Roundtable - Barney Kessel, Herb Ellis, Joe Pass, Howard Roberts	September 1972
Wes Montgomery 1925-1968 R. J. Gleason	July/Aug 1973
The Eleventh House, Larry Coryell (talks about Wes and West Coast Blues)	December 1974
Record Review - Pretty Blue, Milestone M47030	May 1976
Record Review - Beginnings, Blue Note BN IA 531 H2	June 1976
A Tribute to Wes Montgomery, Jimmy Stewart	April 1977
Analysis of Movin' Along by Larry Coryell	February 1979
Record Review - Yesterdays, Milestone M47057	October 1981
Record Review - Encores, Milestone M91 10	August 1983

GUITAR MAGAZINE

The World of Jazz Guitar - Wes Montgomery, Maurice J. Summerfield	September 1973
Record Review - While We're Young, Milestone 47003	
Review - Wes Montgomery Jazz Guitar Solos (Fred Sokolow, Almo Pub.)	May 1977
Electric Guitar Greats, No.4	October 1981

GUITAR WORLD

Wax Museum, Wes Montgomery Everybody's Teacher, Pete Welding	January 1984
Wax Museum, Part 2, Discography	February 1984
50 Landmark Recordings. Groove Brothers (Double)	July 1980
La Guide de la Guitare tour sur le Monde, La Guitare – Mon Ami, Wes Montgomery par Johnny Griffen - Tout Sur la Guitare et les Guitarists de Jazz, Wes Montgomery par Christian Excoude	May 1972

JAZZ JOURNAL

Record Review - The Montgomery Brothers and Five Others, Vog. LAE 12137	February 1959
Record Review - Have Blues Will Travel, Wes Montgomery Qtet, Vog. I.AE 121156	March 1959
Record Review - The Mastersounds, Kismet, Vog. LAE 12179	May 1959
Record Review - Jazz West Coast, Vol IV, The Mastersounds, Vog. LAE 12177	August 1959
Monterey Jazz Festival reviews Montgomery Brothers Quartet	November 1960
Record Review - Montgomeryland, Vog. LAE 12246	February 1961
Record Review - Movin' Along, RIB. RLP 342	January 1962
Record Review - G. Shearing – Montgomery Brothers, Jazzland JLP 55	March 1962
Record Review - Montgomery Brothers, Grooveyard, Riv RLP 362	April 1962
Record Review - Wynton Kelly/Wes Montgomery, Smokin' at the Half Note	October 1966
Record Review - Milt Jackson and Wes Montgomery, Bags Meets Wes, Riv RLP 9407	November 1962
Record Review - Giants of Jazz, Jet IA + AB Sampler Double	January 1963
Record Review - Giants of Jazz Collection, EPs various albums, Riv REP 3212	February 1963
Record Review - Montgomery Brothers, Grooveyard, Riv RLP 362	February 1963
Record Review - Movin' Along, RLP 342	May 1963
Record Review - Buddy, Monk and Wes, The Montgomery Story, Fontana 6881 /32L	July 1963
Record Review - Montgomery Brothers in Canada, Vog. LAE 542	September 1963
Record Review - Wes Montgomery Dynamic New Jazz Sound, RLP 1230	December 1963
Record Review - The Montgomery Brothers, Vocation LAE 566	March 1964
Record Review - Full House, RLP 434	April 1964
Record Review - Boss Guitar, RLP 459	October 1964
Record Review - Dark Velvet, RLP 472	February 1965
Record Review - Movin' Wes, Verve VLP 9092	July 1965
Record Review - Bumpin', VLP 9106	December 1965
Record Review - Goin' Out of My Head, V VLP 9126	July 1966
Record Review - Tequila, V VLP 9143	January 1967
Record Review - California Dreaming, V VLP 9126	July 1967
Record Review - J. Smith/Wes Montgomery The Dynamic Duo, V VLP 9160	July 1967
Record Review - The Best of Verve VLP 9191	March 1968
Record Review - A Day in the Life, A + M AML 2001	March 1968
Jazz Basics, Barry McRae No. 20, Wes Montgomery	August 1968
Record Review - A Tribute to Wes Montgomery, VLP 9221	December 1968
Record Review - This is Wes Montgomery, Riv 673001	February 1969
Record Review - Willow Weep for Me, VLP 9238	April 1969
Record Review - Round Midnight, Riv 673009	July 1969
Record Review - Further Adventures of Jimmy and Wes, Verve VLP 9241	August 1969
Record Review - The Genius of Wes Montgomery, Riv 109561 /2/3	February 1970
A Jazz Guitar Pedigree, Don Roberts	May 1970
Record Review - So Do It, Riv 2360 003	November 1970
Record Review - Great Guitars of Jazz, MGM 2315/013	June 1972
Record Review - Cannonball Adderley and Friends, Capitol SUBB 11233	May 1974
Record Review - Pretty Blue, Milestone M47030	March 1976
Interview with Joe Pass and Burnett Jones	May 1976
Joe Pass & Louis Stewart review Wes' performance of 'I've Grown Accustomed'	June 1977
Crossover Crusader `a rare interview with Creed Taylor' by Mike Hennessy	November 1979
Record Review - Smokin' at the Half Note, Verve 2304 480	April 1981
Record Review - Live at Jorgies Jazz Club, VGM 0001	March 1981
Record Review - Movin' Wes, Verve 2304 377	January 1982
Goin' Wes, formation of Wes Montgomery Appreciation Society	November 1982
Record Review - Full House, OJC (RLP 9434)	November 1984

Jazz, Wes Montgomery by Jim Gosa	November 1966
Jazz Beat, articles p. 4 and 5	May 1965
Jazz Beat, Record Review - Smokin' at the Half Note, VLP 9118	November 1966
Jazz and Blues, Wes Montgomery, Ralph Gleason	October 1973
Jazz Hot, Interviews with Johnny Griffin, M. Cullaz	February 1969
Jazz Monthly, Musicians Talking, Valerie Wilmer	May 1965
Jazz Monthly, Record Review - Encyclopedia of Jazz in the 60's	December 1967
Jazz Monthly, Record Review - A Portrait of Wes, Liberty LBS 83178E and Record Review - Round Midnight, Riv. 673 009	July 1969
Jazz and Pop, Wes Montgomery 1925-1968	1968
Jazz Review, Indiana Renaissance, Gunther Schuller	September 1959
Jazz Review, Record Review - Wes Montgomery a Dynamic New Sound, Riv 12 -310	June 1960

NEWSPRINT

Melody Maker (UK)		3 April 1965
The Observer (UK)	Page 24	25 April 1965
The Sunday Times (UK)	Page 27	11 April 1965
Indianapolis News, Home Folks Lost when Wes left		17 March 1966
Indianapolis News, Famous City Man big jazz artist - R. Gleason		27 September 1966
Indianapolis Star, Montgomery, Talented Hoosier		8 May 1968
Time, Westward Ho		17 May 1968
Indianapolis Star, Guitarist Wes Montgomery Dies		16 June 1968
Indianapolis News, Wes Montgomery Rites Tomorrow		17 June 1968
Indianapolis News, Wes leaves legacy and a Legend		18 June 1968
Indianapolis Star, 2400 Pay Last Respects to Wes		19 June 1968
National Observer (USA), I Don't Need It		24 June 1968
Indianapolis News, Wes Had a Way with His Guitar		26 June 1968
Indianapolis News, Scholarships Honor Noted Jazz Star		7 March 1969
Indianapolis Star, Wes among prominent jazz musicians from Indianapolis		7 November 1971
Indianapolis News, Serene on Wes		1 June 1977
Indianapolis Star, Tribute to Wes part of Mayor's Black History Month		14 January 1978
Indianapolis News, Tribute concert at the Expo Centre		4 February 1978
Indianapolis News, Review of Tribute Concert		6 February 1978
Indianapolis Star, Wes Memorial Concert		7 February 1978
Indianapolis Star, 2nd Annual Wes Montgomery Memorial Concert		9 February 1979
Indianapolis News, Fine Tribute to Montgomery, Ervena M Floyd		26 July 1984

THE GIBSON WES MONTGOMERY MODEL GUITAR

In 1993, a specifically designated production-line 'Wes Montgomery' guitar was unveiled by the Gibson Guitar Corporation, which had, by that time, moved its manufacturing plant from Kalamazoo to Nashville. The new model was closely based upon the two single-pickup L5 CES (Cutaway Electric Spanish) that Wes Montgomery had taken delivery of during 1965. The electric cutaway L5 CES was usually manufactured with a twin pickup format. This comprised of the two pickups with four rotary controls; a tone and volume for each pickup, and a three-way selector switch which allowed for the use of either pickup individually or both simultaneously. Since the launch of the original L5 CES in 1951 there had only been a nominal number of single pickup variants. These had been 'one-off' custom orders, as the single pickup version was never officially available as a regular production-line model. Consequently, the 1993 'Wes Montgomery' guitar was not, strictly speaking, a re-issue. Neither was it a faithfully accurate replica of either the 1965 'Wes Montgomery' 'special request' guitars. This is because those models were identified by specifically decorative (and protective) mother-of-pearl plates on the upper, treble (cutaway) bout. Even these differed aesthetically; one was the shape of a diamond whilst the other was a heart, both included the designation 'Wes Montgomery' (engraved on the heart and inlaid around the sides of the diamond). Ostensibly a decorative feature, early pictures of Wes Montgomery with his mid-1950s L5 CES, reveal how his method of supporting his right hand, by spreading the fingers across the pickguard to grip the 'waist' of the guitar, had worn initially through the finish (see front cover photograph) and eventually the wood itself!

In 1997, Gibson decided to launch a special limited edition of 25 instruments with the heart inlay, a move initiated by the discovery of Montgomery's 1965 original guitar. This had previously thought to have been lost, but was discovered, in rather poor shape, after being rescued from a fire. The damaged instrument was returned to Gibson for restoration where Hutch Hutchings (at that time responsible for their Custom Shop and arch top guitars) was able to faithfully replicate the instrument, together with its heart inlay, ready for the limited edition run. Unlike Montgomery's guitars, both of which were sunburst, the 1997 models were also available in blonde (natural) finish.

The regular (non-inlaid) Gibson Wes Montgomery model, introduced in 1993, is currently still available and is offered in two finishes: Sunburst and Wine Red.

Wes Montgomery

TONE, BEAUTY AND PERFORMANCE

Following in tradition, Gibson has again created a guitar with the inherent quality, versatility, and rich impressive appearance that has gained high acclaim from professional musicians everywhere. The Wes Montgomery model guitar, like the legend whose name it wears, is destined for history. Guitarists everywhere are singing the praise of the comfortable neck, the fast easy playing action and quick response. Just like its predecessor the L-5 CES, the Wes Montgomery has a carved spruce top with a highly figured maple back, rims and a five-piece maple neck. This model features only one '57 Classic PAF reissue humbucking pickup, placed in the neck position so that achieving the *Wes tone* is now something that truly anyone can achieve. Available in Ebony, Wine Red, Vintage Sunburst, and Natural.

- Modern cutaway design
- Gibson ABR-1 bridge
- One Gibson '57 Classic PAF reissue humbucking pickup
- Pickup has adjustable pole pieces and separate tone and volume controls which can be preset
- Schaller M-6 machine heads
- Professional 20 fret fingerboard
- Gibson adjustable tuss rod neck construction
- Body size: length 21"; width 17"
- Decorative accents to the beauty of the Wes Montgomery include gold plated metal parts, deluxe pearl inlays and multi black-white-black binding
- Case for above Instruments—193 Faultless

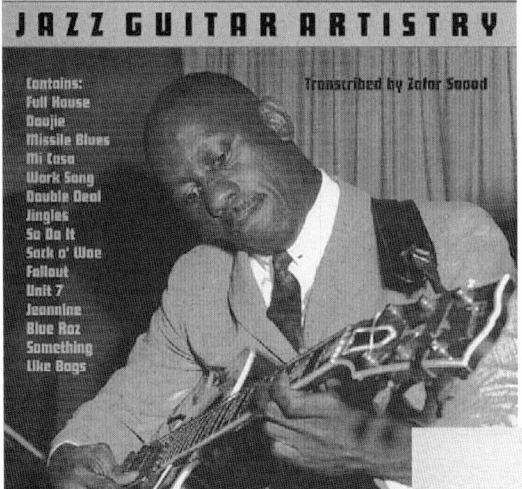

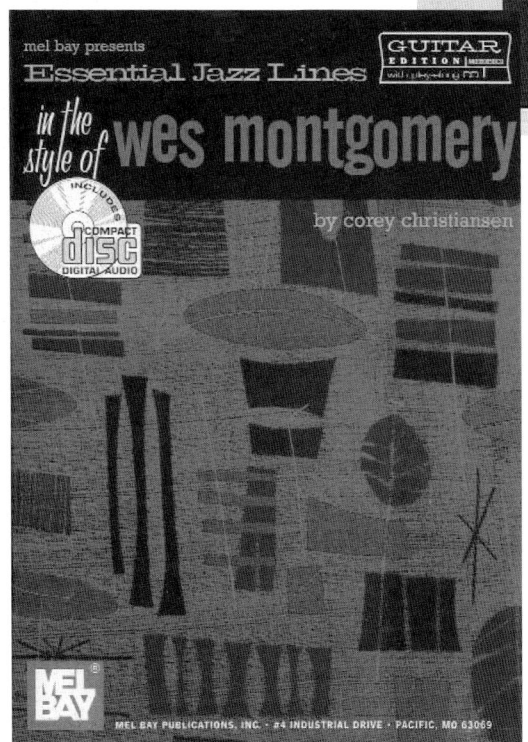